Microcredentials for Excellence: A Practical Guide

Rebecca Ferguson and Denise Whitelock

]u[

ubiquity press
London

Published by
Ubiquity Press Ltd.
6 Osborn Street, Unit 3N
London E1 6TD

www.ubiquitypress.com

Text © Rebecca Ferguson and Denise Whitelock, 2024

First published 2024

Cover design by Tom Grady

Cover image: *Flock of Birds Flying* by Dave Hoefler on Unsplash

Print and digital versions typeset by Siliconchips Services Ltd.

ISBN (Paperback): 978-1-914481-48-2
ISBN (PDF): 978-1-914481-49-9
ISBN (EPUB): 978-1-914481-50-5
ISBN (Mobi): 978-1-914481-51-2

DOI: https://doi.org/10.5334/bcz

This work is licensed under the Creative Commons Attribution-NonCommercial 4.0 International (CC BY-NC 4.0) License (unless stated otherwise within the content of the work). To view a copy of this license, visit https://creativecommons.org/licenses/by-nc/4.0/ or send a letter to Creative Commons, 444 Castro Street, Suite 900, Mountain View, California, 94041, USA. This license allows for copying and distributing the work, providing author attribution is clearly stated and that you are not using the material for commercial purposes.

The full text of this book has been peer-reviewed to ensure high academic standards. For full review policies, see https://www.ubiquitypress.com/

Suggested citation:
Ferguson, R. and Whitelock, D. 2024. *Microcredentials for Excellence: A Practical Guide*. London: Ubiquity Press. DOI: https://doi.org/10.5334/bcz. License: CC BY-NC 4.0

To read the free, open access version of this book online, visit https://doi.org/10.5334/bcz or scan this QR code with your mobile device:

Contents

Chapter 1. Introduction   1
Chapter 2. Pedagogy of microcredentials   19
Chapter 3. Creating microcredentials and supporting learners   51
Chapter 4. Planning your first microcredentials   83
Chapter 5. Learning design and innovation in production   111
Chapter 6. Student wellbeing   141
Chapter 7. Assessing microcredentials   173
Chapter 8. Quality and evaluation   217
Chapter 9. Microcredentials futures   263
Index   297

CHAPTER 1

Introduction

When employers advertise a job at graduate level, they are likely to receive a mass of applications from freshly minted graduates with little to choose between them. How much better would it be if one of the candidates produced evidence that they already had the skills and knowledge required for the job? If they could demonstrate that they had studied with experts around the world, not only within universities but also in industry? If they had credentials that showed they could apply their knowledge, as well as essential workplace skills like teamwork, collaboration and creativity? This is the vision that has prompted the development of microcredentials: short, stackable courses – usually offered online – with an emphasis on the needs of the workplace.

How to cite this book chapter:
Ferguson, R. and Whitelock, D. 2024. Introduction. In: Ferguson, R. and Whitelock, D. *Microcredentials for Excellence: A Practical Guide.* Pp. 1–17. London: Ubiquity Press. DOI: https://doi.org/10.5334/bcz.a. License: CC BY-NC 4.0

The vision has other elements. In the future, learners will be able to access courses whenever they need them. They will not be restricted to degree courses that run for multiple years with annual start dates. They will be able to return to study whenever they want to do so. They will be able to study alongside their work, refreshing and updating their skills. They will be able to access the qualifications that they need to get the jobs they want, retraining and upskilling whenever necessary.

These are exciting possibilities, but are they really feasible? In this book, we look at what is possible. We provide a background to microcredentials, identify what makes them distinctive, and then provide detailed guidance on how to go about producing them and supporting learners. In the process, we identify relevant pedagogies, suggest innovative and successful production processes, introduce ways of assessing and evaluating these courses, and discuss learner wellbeing. Finally, we look at visions of the future – how this field may develop nationally, internationally and within individual institutions.

Each chapter is rooted in experience, research and practice. Both authors work at The Open University (OU) in the UK, the country's biggest university, with extensive expertise in teaching at a distance. Our department, the Institute of Educational Technology (IET), has been producing and researching online courses for more than 25 years. Together, we led the academic development and evaluation of the OU's first microcredentials, working with teams from across the university to identify and solve the problems associated with setting up an extensive new qualification programme. By 2023, the OU's Microcredential Unit had developed 29 microcredentials and registered over 12,000 learners.

Alongside the practical work involved in producing and presenting microcredentials, we also produced annual evaluation reports of the entire programme, investigating the extent to which these new qualifications were working for learners, educators and the institution as a whole (Chandler 2023; Papathoma & Ferguson 2020; Papathoma & Ferguson 2021). Other members of our department carry out research and scholarship on the subject, so we have access to the latest insights on subjects including learner benefits, assessment and stackability of microcredentials (see, for example, Chandler & Perryman 2023; Iniesto et al. 2022; Rienties et al. 2023; Sargent et al. 2023). All this builds on previous work within IET related to the foundations of microcredentials, including work on digital badging (Cross, Whitelock & Galley 2014), learning design (Nguyen, Rienties & Whitelock 2020), assessment and feedback (Whitelock 2018), massive open online courses (Ferguson et al. 2018) and open educational resources (Law 2019). Many of these insights are brought together in the courses that make up the OU's Masters in Online Teaching (MAOT) and, as authors of this book, we acknowledge our debt to the authors of those courses, particularly Dr Leigh-Anne Perryman.

What is a microcredential?

In 2021 the Organisation for Economic Co-operation and Development gathered definitions of the term 'microcredential' from around the world as part of its review of innovation in the area (Golden, Kato & Weko 2021). Elements included in these definitions varied. Of the eight quoted in the report, four referred to skills, two to competencies, one to knowledge and one to learning outcomes. Some focused on the work undertaken and some on the credit gained. All the definitions indicated that the course was short or small-scale. Overall, the report found that:

Most definitions of micro-credentials denote **an organised learning activity with an associated credential** – the credential recognises a skill or competency that has been acquired through an organised learning process and validated through an assessment. Consequently, the term 'micro-credential' is commonly understood to refer to both the credential itself and the education or training programme which leads to the credential award. (Golden, Kato & Weko 2021: 2)

The same report identified issues that limit the development of microcredentials, all of which relate to the lack of agreement about what these credentials are.

- There is a lack of common agreement about the definition of microcredentials.
- 'Microcredentials' is used as an umbrella term that describes a wide variety of programmes.
- It is not clear how microcredentials should be integrated with existing short courses.
- Study load, targeting of learning material and certification process all vary between providers.
- Microcredentials do not have an established relationship to other qualifications.
- Lack of standardised information on how and why microcredentials are used. (Golden, Kato & Weko 2021)

Developing a common definition for microcredentials (also written as micro credentials or micro-credentials) has proved to be a tricky problem. Within Europe, the MICROBOL project focused on ways of linking microcredentials to the vision of education set out in the Bologna key commitments (European Ministers of Education 1999). The basic definition agreed on by the project was short – 'A micro-credential is a certified small volume of learning' (MICROBOL 2022) – but was set in the wider context of their use, constitutive elements and quality assurance processes.

In a parallel project, also funded by Europe's Erasmus programme, the European MOOC Consortium developed the Common Microcredential Framework (Antonaci, Henderikx & Ubachs 2021), setting these qualifications firmly at higher education level and aligning them with both the European/National Qualification Framework (EQF/NQF) and the European Credit Transfer and Accumulation System (ECTS). This had several criteria:

- Workload of 100 to 150 hours (4–6 ECTS).
- Level 6 (bachelor) to 7 (master) of the EQF/NQF, with options for level 5.
- Assessment enabling the award of academic credit, either following successful completion of the course or recognition of prior learning.
- Reliable method of ID verification at the point of assessment.
- Transcript setting out the learning outcomes for a course, hours of study required, EQF level, and number of credit points earned. (Antonaci, Henderikx & Ubachs 2021)

However, this proved to be over-specific and not all microcredentials produced by consortium members met all the criteria. Some courses were much shorter, some were at different levels and others did not award academic credit.

In 2022 the European Union adopted a recommendation on a European approach to microcredentials for lifelong learning and employability:

> 'Micro-credential' means the record of the learning outcomes that a learner has acquired following a small volume of learning. These learning outcomes will have been

assessed against transparent and clearly defined criteria. Learning experiences leading to micro-credentials are designed to provide the learner with specific knowledge, skills and competences that respond to societal, personal, cultural or labour market needs. Micro-credentials are owned by the learner, can be shared and are portable. They may be stand-alone or combined into larger credentials. They are underpinned by quality assurance following agreed standards in the relevant sector or area of activity. (General Secretariat of the Council 2022)

Although this appears definitive, it remains vague. How much learning is a 'small volume'? At what level does that learning take place? In addition, this does not entirely align with other authoritative definitions. For example, the view in New Zealand is that:

Micro-credentials are units of learning designed to allow recognition of a discrete set of skills that meet specific learner, employer, industry, community, and iwi needs. NZQA-approved [New Zealand Qualifications Authority] micro-credentials:

- certify the achievement of a coherent set of skills and knowledge
- meet a specified need
- include an assessment component
- are no more than 40 credits
- can be at any level on the NZQCF [New Zealand Quality and Credentials Framework]. (NZQA 2023)

One of the problems with defining a microcredential is deciding which of its elements should take precedence and in which system these qualifications fit best. Some definitions focus on academic credit, assuming microcredentials to be a new form of higher education course offered by universities. Some focus on the value of these credentials for employers, viewing them as a way of accrediting the training programmes offered by organisations such as Google and Cisco. Others draw attention to the potential of microcredentials to bridge the two approaches by enabling academic and industry credit to be evidenced using the same system. One reason for this tension is that microcredentials emerged at the same time as digital badges and for similar reasons. The development of the two is intertwined.

In her presidential address to the American Educational Research Association (AERA) in 2007, Eva Baker talked about the need to create a system of qualifications that would reflect the needs of the 21st century, a system that could be used not only to report test results but also to validate a range of accomplishments (Baker 2007). She suggested this might involve an approach similar to the award of merit badges.

Around a decade later, digital badges made this idea a reality. A digital badge is an online record of achievements that includes information about the achievement, the community that recognised that achievement and the work that was carried out to achieve it. These badges have two elements: an image file that represents the badge, and an electronic record of the award's criteria and validator (Hauck & MacKinnon 2016).

However, badges by themselves are not an effective credentialing system, in part because their status is not clear. A review of the literature on digital badges notes that, '[a]mong the limited number of studies with employers, hiring managers lacked a strong understanding of the DB [digital badge]' (Cumberland et al. 2023). Like merit badges, digital badges only make sense to someone who is familiar with the system in which they are awarded. It is possible to gain badges that represent accomplishment at playing the piano, sailing a small boat, reaching a particular standard at gymnastics or collecting objects in an online game. However, each of these sets of badges exists within its own ecosystem and there is no centralised agreement about how to collect, compare, display or validate the badges from different ecosystems. They offer flexibility but little or no standardisation.

In 2011, the Mozilla Foundation, an American non-profit organisation, developed a technical standard called Open Badges, which could be used to issue, collect and display digital badges on multiple sites (Surman 2011). Using this open standard, which is now maintained by the IMS Global Learning Consortium, badges 'can represent skills and knowledge gained from open platforms and informal learning experiences, providing details about potential employees such as which specific verified skills the individual has mastered, when and how the skills were attained, and who issued the Badge' (Young, West & Nylin 2019).

Development of the open badge standard was followed by the launch of the Badge Alliance, which brought together more than 650 organisations from around the world (Surman 2011). The foundation also developed a digital 'backpack' that could be used to store and display badges. Other organisations developed similar backpacks and online platforms including Canvas, Desire2Learn and LinkedIn provided options for collecting and displaying badges.

In 2014, IBM piloted the use of digital badges on its online learning platform, Cognitive Class. The aim was to increase engagement and completion rates on its courses. Within weeks of the programme's start, enrolments increased by 129%, and enrolled learners who completed courses increased by 226%. Some of this rise can be attributed to increased emphasis on and publicity for the programme, but subsequent surveys showed that digital badge awards motivated employees and customers to develop current skills, recognised employee achievement, helped to identify and acquire verified talent and led to an increase in sales (Leaser 2019). By 2019, the company had issued more than two million digital badges across 195 countries.

At the same time, universities and other educational institutions were experimenting with the use of digital badges. To give just one example, the OpenLearn website issued 38,000 digital badges in 2022 for completion of its badged open courses (Law & Roberts 2022). These badges, together with statements of participation, can be downloaded from the platform and shared on eportfolio platforms. They provide a way of evidencing engagement with a course without the formality of having to sit an exam. They have also been shown to have a positive impact on the learning journey to formal study (Law 2015).

Digital badges are usually awarded for relatively small pieces of work, such as attendance at a learning event or completion of a short course and so they are frequently referred to as microcredentials. 'Some scholars have used the terms DB, microcredential and open badge almost interchangeably' (Cumberland et al. 2023). However, despite an initial tendency to conflate these terms, 'microcredential' is now more likely to be used in the sphere of formal education to describe quality-assured accreditation and courses lasting several weeks or months, while digital badges tend to be shorter and are more likely to be informal. In some cases, a digital badge is awarded at the end of a microcredential course.

Despite their overlap, digital badges and microcredentials were developed for different reasons. As opportunities for 'informal learning' (where learners are in control of both the process and goals of their learning) increased, demand grew for ways of recognising informal learning achievements. Digital badges provided a way of meeting this need (Law 2015). Microcredentials, on the other hand, were a response to a skills gap between the supply of newly trained graduates and the demands of the job market. As new types of career and new ways of working emerged, employers searched for ways of training people so they would be able to demonstrate necessary skills and capabilities.

In England, the Shadbolt Review considered the employability of computer science graduates, and the Wakeham Review examined the skills requirements of lawyers and how accreditation systems might provide better support for graduates. In a report to Parliament, the Higher Education Funding Council for England summarised these two reports, noting that:

- 'Employers are looking for "work-ready" graduates, who can apply their academic studies and abilities in a commercial or work context. Work experience is invaluable, but not all employers want the same things, or are willing (and sufficiently resourced) to mould and train staff;
- 'Industry is changing at a rapid rate. This presents a dilemma for universities and colleges if they try to keep up with industry demands;
- 'Graduates need to upskill and adapt to a changing jobs market. Their degree will only get them in so far in a career that may span 50 years.' (House of Commons Science and Technology Committee 2016: 20)

Similar observations have been made worldwide. At the same time, '[a]s the digital divide between supply and demand widens and the war for scarce talent intensifies, many global employers do not have time to wait for graduates to complete traditional diplomas and bachelor degrees' (Bowles et al. 2023: 427). This has led to increasing pressure from governments on universities to produce shorter courses, tailored to the needs of industry.

Microcredentials are a way of meeting that challenge, and this book explains how that can be done.

Because microcredentials are a new type of qualification with their own distinctive characteristics, some approaches to teaching and learning are more appropriate than others. Both learners and educators need to acquire and develop new skills to make the most of this broad set of accredited courses. **Chapter 2** identifies the ways in which microcredentials differ from qualifications and other courses at higher education level and the implications of these differences for their production and presentation.

These new qualifications do not fit neatly into the existing systems set up for undergraduate, postgraduate and vocational courses. It takes a team to create and run a microcredential. Differences in scale, funding, learners and presentation are just some of the factors that mean microcredentials are not typical courses. Setting them up and sustaining them effectively requires thought and change in all areas of the institution, as well as new or extended partnerships with employers and professional organisations. **Chapter 3** examines the range of roles that contribute to a successful microcredential, including ways of reconceptualising the role of educator.

Chapter 4 looks at processes and frameworks that have been developed to help with the development of a microcredentials programme. These range from national guidelines to personal experiences, and each of them draws attention to aspects that should be taken into account, beginning with a consideration of the benefits of microcredentials for an educational institution and its learners. The chapter ends with a series of examples from around the world, focusing on the decisions that were made and the processes followed in each case.

For most institutions, production of microcredentials is a new experience that requires a shift in production procedures. This may involve a shift from a single educator producing a course to a team experience of producing an online course. It may involve speeding up production methods to offer the most up-to-date thinking on fast-moving areas such as computer security or artificial intelligence. It may involve partnerships between higher education institutions and professional bodies. If the new microcredentials are to form a qualification, or part of a qualification, then there may be a need to produce multiple courses at speed. Whatever the situation, a shift to microcredentials can be a catalyst for rethinking both learning design and course production. **Chapter 5** outlines the changes implemented at our own institution, the UK's Open University, and methods we have found successful when making the move to microcredentials.

Traditionally, universities provide support and facilities for students in addition to opportunities for learning. Campus-based universities are homes for students, and even institutions that are distributed across sites will offer social and sporting activities as well as opportunities for eating, shopping and finance. Together, these facilities and societies can create a feeling of belonging, which ties students to their course or qualification and may later keep them engaged as alumni. Similarly, extended workplace training is also often accompanied by opportunities to work together, eat together and socialise together. Microcredentials break this pattern. They are relatively short and often studied online. Learners may never meet each other or their educators and, if the microcredential is offered on a generic platform, they may have only a hazy idea of which institution is responsible for their study. Nevertheless, they are likely to encounter some of the same challenges to mental health and wellbeing as full-time students and are likely also to be facing competing demands on their time from family and workplace. **Chapter 6** focuses on wellbeing and mental health, considering the ways in which these affect microcredential learners, and how learners can be supported during their studies.

Assessment is both a defining characteristic of microcredentials and one of the greatest challenges to their success. These are not simply short courses; they are short courses that lead to a credential warranting the holder has certain skills, capacities or knowledge – typically those that employers are looking for. To be able to state authoritatively that this is the case, microcredential providers must assess learners against defined criteria. Doing this in a way that will be accepted as authoritative requires expensive infrastructure. An additional challenge is the expectation that learners will be able to 'stack' microcredentials from different providers to form qualifications. This implies some degree of alignment between those providers, which requires additional infrastructure as well as complex negotiations. **Chapter 7** begins by looking broadly at assessment and why it is used. It then considers different elements of assessment in the digital age, including its use with groups of students. It moves on to examine innovative practices and feedback, before turning to challenges and possible solutions.

Chapter 8 examines the definitions of 'quality' that become operationalised as a suite of standards in both national and international contexts. These standards are a necessary consideration for providers of accredited qualifications and so the chapter explores the question of whether they are sufficient kitemarks for stackable microcredential qualifications, together with their validation through the process known as 'evaluation'.

Chapter 9 concludes the book by looking at what the future may hold for microcredentials. It begins by examining some of their current expected trajectories, looking at the different visions proposed by those developing them or influencing that development. It goes on to examine the different factors that will influence progress towards those visions, identifying some of the challenges that lie ahead. It ends by looking at recent developments in teaching and learning that could, in future, be incorporated within microcredentials.

Acknowledgments

This book draws on the innovative approach and practical work of the Open University Microcredentials Studio set up by Matthew Moran, the extensive experience of IET microcredential authors guided by Leigh-Anne Perryman, and the detailed work on OU microcredential evaluation carried out over several years by Tina Papathoma and Kathy Chandler. Our thanks go to all these people, and also to our peer reviewers Monty King and Kathy Chandler for their time, effort and helpful suggestions.

References

Antonaci, A., Henderikx, P. and Ubachs, G. (2021). The common microcredentials framework for MOOCs and short learning programmes. *Journal of Innovation in Polytechnic Education*, 3(1): 5–9.

Baker, E. L. (2007). 2007 presidential address—the end(s) of testing. *Educational Researcher*, 36(6): 309–317. DOI: https://doi.org/10.3102/0013189X07307970

Bowles, M., Brooks, B., Curnin, S. and Anderson, H. (2023). Application of microcredentials to validate human capabilities in a large telecommunications organisation: Strategic transformation to a future-ready workforce. *International Journal of Information and Learning Technology*, 40(5): 425–438.

Chandler, K. (2023). *Microcredentials evaluation phase 3 final report (internal report)*. Milton Keynes: Open University.

Chandler, K. and Perryman, L.-A. (2023). 'People have started calling me an expert': The impact of Open University microcredential courses. *Journal of Interactive Media in Education*, 2023(1), Article 8. DOI: https://doi.org/10.5334/jime.804

Cross, S., Whitelock, D. and Galley, R. (2014). The use, role and reception of Open Badges as a method for formative and summative reward in two massive open online courses. *International Journal of e-Assessment*, 4(1).

Cumberland, D. M., Deckard, T. G., Kahle-Piasecki, L., Kerrick, S. A. and Ellinger, A. D. (2023). Making sense of the digital badging landscape in education and workplace settings: A scoping review of the empirical literature. *European Journal of Training and Development*, 48(1/2): 253–275

European Ministers of Education. (1999). The Bologna Declaration of 19 June 1999. Available at https://web.archive.org/web/20220331214436/http://www.magna-charta.org/resources/files/BOLOGNA_DECLARATION.pdf

Ferguson, R., Herodotou, C., Coughlan, T., Scanlon, E. and Sharples, M. (2018). MOOC development: Priority areas. In: Luckin, R. *Enhancing learning and teaching with technology: What the research says.* London: Institute of Education Press.

General Secretariat of the Council. (2022). *Proposal for a Council recommendation on a European approach to micro-credentials for lifelong learning and employability (interinstitutional file 2021/0402(NLE))*. Available at https://data.consilium.europa.eu/doc/document/ST-9237-2022-INIT/en/pdf

Golden, G., Kato, S. and Weko, T. (2021). *Micro-credential innovations in higher education: Who, what and why?* Paris: OECD.

Hauck, M. and MacKinnon, T. (2016). A new approach to assessing online intercultural exchanges: Soft certification of participant engagement. In: O'Dowd, R. and Lewis, T. *Online intercultural exchange. Policy, pedagogy, practice.* Abingdon: Routledge. pp. 209–234.

House of Commons Science and Technology Committee. (2016). *Digital skills crisis: Second report of Session 2016–17.* Available at https://www.voced.edu.au/content/ngv:73694#

Iniesto, F., Ferguson, R., Weller, M., Farrow, R. and Pitt, B. (2022). Introducing a reflective framework for the assessment and recognition of microcredentials *OTESSA*, 2(2): 1–24.

Law, P. (2015). Digital badging at the Open University: Recognition for informal learning. *Open Learning: The Journal of Open, Distance and e-Learning*, 30(3): 221–234. Available at http://www.tandfonline.com/doi/full/10.1080/02680513.2015.1104500

Law, P. (2019). Refining open educational resources for both learner and institution. Thesis (PhD). The Open University.

Law, P. and Roberts, J. (2022). *OpenLearn: 2022 in review.* Milton Keynes: The Open University

Leaser, D. (2019). *Do digital badges really provide value to businesses?* (18 June). Available at https://www.d2l.com/wp-content/uploads/2023/05/Do-digital-badges-really-provide-value-to-businesses_-IBM-Training-and-Skills-Blog.pdf

MICROBOL. (2022). Common framework for micro-credentials in the EHEA. Available at https://microcredentials.eu/wp-content/uploads/sites/20/2022/03/Micro-credentials_Framework_final-1.pdf

Nguyen, Q., Rienties, B. and Whitelock, D. (2020). A mixed-method study of how instructors design for learning in online and distance education. *Journal of Learning Analytics*, 7(3): 64–78.

NZQA. (2023). *Guidelines for micro-credential listing, approval and accreditation (interim draft for feedback).* Wellington: New Zealand Qualifications Authority.

Papathoma, T. and Ferguson, R. (2020). *Evaluation of Open University microcredentials: Final report of phase one (internal report).* Milton Keynes: The Open University.

Papathoma, T. and Ferguson, R. (2021). *Evaluation of Open University microcredentials: Final report of phase two (internal report).* Milton Keynes: The Open University.

Rienties, B., Calo, F., Corcoran, S., Chandler, K., FitzGerald, E., Haslam, D., Harris, C. A., Perryman, L.-A, Sargent, J., Suttle, M. D. and Wahga, A. (2023). How and with whom do educators learn in an online professional development microcredential. *Social Sciences & Humanities Open*, 8(1): 100626.

Sargent, J., Rienties, B., Perryman, L.-A. and FitzGerald, E. (2023). Investigating the views and use of stackable microcredentials within a Postgraduate Certificate in Academic Practice. *Journal of Interactive Media in Education*, 2023(1): 1–12. DOI: https://doi.org/10.5334/jime.805

Surman, M. (2011). *Mozilla launches Open Badges project* (15 September). Available at https://blog.mozilla.org/en/mozilla/openbadges/

Whitelock, D. (2018). Advice for action with automatic feedback systems. In: Caballé, S. and Conesa, J. *Software data engineering for network eLearning environments. Lecture notes on data engineering and communications technologies.* Springer. pp. 139–160.

Young, D., West, R. E. and Nylin, T. A. (2019). Value of open microcredentials to earners and issuers: A case study of national instruments open badges. *International Review of Research in Open and Distributed Learning*, 20(5): 104–121.

CHAPTER 2

Pedagogy of microcredentials

Microcredentials are a new type of qualification with their own distinctive characteristics. Because of this, some approaches to teaching and learning, some pedagogies, are more appropriate than others. Both learners and educators need to acquire and develop new skills in order to make the most of this broad set of accredited courses. This chapter identifies the ways in which microcredentials differ from qualifications and other courses at higher education level and the implications of these differences for their production and presentation.

How to cite this book chapter:
Ferguson, R. and Whitelock, D. 2024. Pedagogy of microcredentials. In: Ferguson, R. and Whitelock, D. *Microcredentials for Excellence: A Practical Guide*. Pp. 19–50. London: Ubiquity Press. DOI: https://doi.org/10.5334/bcz.b. License: CC BY-NC 4.0

Microcredentials are different

Education serves many purposes. It prepares learners to take their place in society, developing skills, knowledge and values that align with those of others and teaching them to be responsible citizens, contributors and innovators. More specific forms of education are used to build communities – these may be based on shared interests, on localities or on identification with a particular faith, sexuality or ethnic grouping. At a personal level, education is used to develop individuals, enabling them to reflect on experiences and build coherent learning journeys. The notion of developing a healthy mind in a healthy body (*mens sana in corpore sano* in Latin) has resonated in Europe since Roman times. Education can also be used to develop people as learners, exposing them to the diversity of knowledge, encouraging them to reflect on their assumptions, and motivating them to care about truth and knowledge.

Although microcredentials may do all these things to some extent, their main focus is on training people for employment and enabling the transition from learner to earner. In her detailed report on microcredentials, Oliver notes that '[m]any have raised the possibility that micro-credentials – non-formal signals of educational achievement – present an alternative solution to preparing for the future of work' (Oliver 2019: 3). She goes on to say that:

> employees really value work-integrated learning and curriculum that is industry-aligned and employer-validated quality. It may be the case that employees are in fact starting to value employer provision more than traditional providers with human resource leaders formally de-emphasising degrees and prioritising skills. (Oliver 2019: 13)

Of course, alignment with the world of work is not new for universities. They have long been aligned with the legal, clerical and medical professions. Polytechnics taught a wide variety of vocational subjects, and the range of such subjects taught at different higher education institutions (HEIs) keeps expanding. Work placements are integrated within many degree pathways, and there have been several other initiatives, such as the degree apprenticeships offered in England and Wales, that combine paid work with university study.

However, all these approaches are primarily designed for young people making the transition from full-time education to full-time employment. The age of these young people varies, but most undergraduate courses are designed for students under 25. Although the characteristics of this student population vary considerably from country to country, many universities will assume that their students have little experience of the world of work, few or no caring responsibilities, their primary focus during the working day should be on their studies, and any external commitments should not be prioritised over study.

These assumptions do not hold true for microcredential learners. If they are reskilling to take on a new job, or developing the skills necessary for promotion, they are likely to be studying while employed on a full-time, or part-time, basis. Their role as learner takes second place to their role as earner, so assignment schedules and deadlines will not be prioritised over work schedules and deadlines. If they are carers as well as learners, their commitments to others will also take priority.

Another characteristic of microcredentials is that, although this is not a requirement, they primarily run online. One reason for this is that the major platforms developed to host massive open online courses (MOOCs) have invested heavily in courses of this type. MOOCs attracted a lot of learners (Shah 2020; Shah 2015) but their open aspect meant these courses could usually be accessed free of charge and so brought in little money. Supplementing the MOOC offering with short, credit-bearing courses for professionals introduced a new revenue stream. The Udacity MOOC platform introduced Nanodegrees in 2014 (Shen 2014), edX trademarked its MicroMasters in 2016 (Young 2016), Coursera announced its MasterTracks at its Partners' Conference in spring 2018 (Valli 2018) and FutureLearn went live with its first microcredentials early in 2020 (Stancombe 2020).

Studying online is a new experience for many learners. The rush to remote learning during the Covid–19 pandemic meant that many had bad experiences of poorly designed online courses put together at high speed by educators who were not trained or resourced to teach at a distance. Microcredential learners therefore need opportunities to experience the benefits of online learning and to see it at its best. To do this, they need to develop the skills that support learning in this way, particularly the skills associated with self-regulation. These include goal setting, strategic planning, time management and self-evaluation. Also, just as in a physical university, they need to be given time and support to orient themselves and to find their way around their learning environment.

An issue that must be addressed by online educators is 'the gap between the understanding of a teacher (or teaching team) and that of a learner' (Moore 2019: 34). This gap was named by Moore in the 1980s as 'transactional distance' and he argues that distance education (of which online education is a subset) 'is the methodology of structuring courses and managing dialogue between teacher and learner to bridge that gap through communications technology' (Moore 2019: 34).

Not only is there a gap between the learner and the educator when studying online; there is also a distance between learners and their peers. Although this superficially seems to be a benefit – fewer opportunities for learners to engage in idle chit-chat – it has been clear for many years that students are more likely to persist with their studies if they feel involved. As Tinto (1997: 168) observes, drawing on multiple studies carried out over two decades, '[t]he more academically and socially involved individuals are – that is, the more they interact with other students and faculty – the more likely they are to persist'. On a university campus, some of these interactions take place simply because people are together in the same classroom, corridor or café. In online settings, these interactions must be planned.

One reason why microcredentials are likely to remain online is the flexibility that this offers for learners who must fit their study time around their job and family commitments. Asynchronous activities, which do not require everyone to engage at the same time, mean that online learning is largely independent of time and place. Learners have access to and can collaborate with experts and peers anywhere in the world, while participating at a convenient and appropriate pace (Harasim 1990; Wu & Hiltz 2004).

Being online means microcredentials have an international reach. For example, in her study of the MITx MicroMasters in Supply Chain Management, Moreno found that around a third of participants were from North America, with another third from Europe and Asia (Moreno 2019). This diversity means that microcredential courses need to account for an international audience. On an employment-focused course this means paying attention to any laws, standards, needs and approaches that will only apply in one country, as well as avoiding figures of speech and cultural references that only some students will recognise.

As well as extending the international reach of HEIs, online courses such as microcredentials make learning accessible to those who would not be able to access physical campuses. The World Health Organization estimates that disability affects approximately 15% of the world's population (WHO and The World Bank 2011). The Open University in the UK, which is a distance-learning institution, reports that more than 16% of its students have a declared disability. This rises to 19% of learners on its OpenLearn platform, which provides a wide variety of open educational resources, including courses (Iniesto et al. 2017). These figures suggest that online courses such as microcredentials are more likely than other courses to have to consider the needs of disabled learners, and they are also more likely to attract students with very severe disabilities who would not be able to access a physical campus.

Another aspect of online study is it does not have the physical constraints that limit numbers on a conventional course at an HEI. There is no need to restrict numbers based on the size of a lecture theatre or seminar room, or to restrict enrolment to students registered at a specific university. These courses are often hosted on MOOC platforms and, like massive open online courses, they have the potential to register massive numbers of learners. At the same time, their presence on MOOC platforms may lead to the assumption that they should be cheaper than a conventional HEI offering. Neither of these assumptions will apply in all cases. However, when they do, the course design needs to take into account that the learner/educator ratio will not be as high as on other HEI courses.

The pedagogy of microcredentials is also influenced by their potential for stackability. Rossiter and Tynan note that:

> Micro-credentials can be stacked towards larger units of competence or capability, in a format that is verified, secure and shareable with peers, employers and educational providers. (Rossiter and Tynan 2019: 2)

They add that:

> a taxonomy is desirable to demonstrate relationships, such as product 'stacks' or 'clusters,' to articulate pathways between newer alternative forms of credentials and accredited award courses and programmes. (Rossiter and Tynan 2019: 5–6)

The issue of assessment and accreditation is a substantial part of pedagogy, and a significant challenge for microcredentials, which is dealt with in Chapter 7. Here, the focus is on the requirement that microcredentials should join together to make a more substantial qualification. This requires consideration of skills and progression, which will typically need to be related to national or international requirements such as those set out in the European qualifications framework, the QF-EHEA (European Higher Education Area 2021). Frameworks like these set out requirements for skills and competencies that cannot all be developed in a short course. Just as a series of short university courses designed for first-year undergraduates cannot be snapped together to create a complete degree, a series of microcredentials cannot be stacked into a larger qualification unless the requirements of that qualification are taken into account during the design and planning stage.

Overall, there are multiple aspects of microcredentials that should be taken into account when considering how teaching and learning will take place. These are not simply cut-down versions of vocational degrees, segments of apprenticeships, or variants on company-specific workplace training. Any successful microcredential pedagogy will need to take into account that:

- cohorts are likely to be large;
- educator:learner ratios may be low;
- focus is on career, workplace and professional skills;
- learners are likely to have work and care commitments that take precedence over study;
- learners may be new to online learning;
- learners may have substantial relevant work experience;
- learners may want to stack microcredentials to form larger qualifications;
- learners require opportunities to interact with others;
- learners require skills in self-regulation;
- learners will be based in many countries;
- many learners will have disabilities that influence how and when they study;
- study is likely to be asynchronous (learners are not required to be online at the same time).

The following sections of this chapter address ways in which pedagogy can be adapted to meet some of these challenges, while subsequent chapters take a detailed look at other relevant issues, including learning design, student support, and assessment.

Pedagogies for the workplace

Shifts in society mean there is a continuing demand for courses that train workers in new skills. For example, 'developments in artificial intelligence will require capabilities that span the humanities, arts and social sciences and science, technology, engineering and mathematics' (Oliver 2019: 1). At the same time, '[d]emand for higher cognitive skills (creativity, critical thinking, complex information processing) is predicted to increase' (Oliver 2019).

Many microcredentials are designed for learners who are also earners (Selvaratnam & Sankey 2020). This means those who register may already have some degree of expertise in the subject, may have experience to draw on, and may be able to put what they are learning into practice immediately. They are more likely than younger learners to be aware of the importance of soft skills such as team working. In some cases, developing the skills and competences they need in their working life will be more significant to them than gaining academic credit or completing an entire course.

Chapter 5 introduces ways in which thinking carefully about potential learners and their contexts can be useful when designing a course. In particular, it helps with the selection of an approach to teaching and learning that is appropriate for the learners and their context. Pedagogies that are well suited to learners developing job-related skills include competency-based learning, case-based learning and conversational learning.

Competency-based learning

Competency-based learning is an approach that focuses on learners mastering a set of measurable outcomes. It therefore aligns well with the needs of those who aim to progress along well-defined career paths or who are studying subjects that are clearly structured. Progress is evaluated based on whether learners demonstrate they have acquired explicit and measurable competences that have been communicated to them clearly (Henri, Johnson & Nepal 2017). This includes the ability to apply that knowledge in practical situations, such as their day job. Learners cannot move on until they have mastered prerequisite skills, which could be split over a number of microcredentials.

Henri, Johnson and Nepal (2017) review a wide range of research about the use of competency-based learning in engineering education. Engineering curricula are highly structured, with each subject building on previous ones, so this pedagogic approach has numerous advantages because it prompts students to progress at their own pace, frequently reviewing fundamental content. The approach is associated with lower dropout rates, more positive student attitudes, and an improvement in student outcomes. It also emphasises self-directed continuous learning, which is important in the 'lifelong learning' context of microcredentials.

The approach is easiest to implement in areas that already have defined sets of competencies. The curriculum should link these with professional skills required in the field, such as teamwork, communication and the ability to work under pressure. Assessment can be used to link the different competencies, so that learners are able to explore the relationships between them, rather than treating them as discrete units.

Case-based learning

Case-based learning is another approach suited to learners developing job-related skills. It takes the form of a guided inquiry (Srinivasan et al. 2007) involving a practical case, a problem or question to be solved, and a stated set of learning objectives with a measured outcome (McLean 2016). Some of the information and content that learners require to solve the problem is presented in the course; some is discovered by them as they address the problem or question. The approach is superficially similar to problem-based learning but the process is more structured and supported. If students' approach takes them off course, facilitators bring them back to the main learning objective using guiding questions.

Students can also ask for advice from experts and are not left to their own devices. This makes links with the work environment – students find out when it is appropriate to investigate for themselves, and when it is appropriate to ask for support from others with more experience. Students also work in groups, which gives them opportunities to explore team-working skills such as group planning, timetabling and knowledge sharing. A multinational group of learners who are already working in the field may have a wealth of experience to draw on, which means that developing the skills to work with an online team may be as important to their development as the acquisition of subject knowledge.

When implementing case-based learning, educators need support to facilitate the process. 'The facilitator guides the participants in clinical decision-making by posing questions, eliciting opinions and stimulating a discussion, enabling exploration of their existing knowledge, skills and attitudes, but also to uncover gaps' (Topperzer et al. 2021). It is important that learners feel comfortable participating, and that the course environment is structured so they are willing to reflect, to share knowledge and experience, to present and discuss opposing viewpoints, and to explore gaps in their knowledge. Achieving this in an online environment requires careful attention to the use and structure of synchronous and asynchronous activities, guidance on communication and group working, modelling of appropriate behaviour by educators, thoughtful use of introductory sessions and ice-breakers, and regular reviews of group progress and interaction.

Conversational learning

Conversational learning can be applied in any field. Its particular relevance in relation to microcredentials, which typically run on MOOC platforms, is that it is a pedagogy of scale. When the first MOOC platforms were developed, there were three main ways of scaling learning. The first was by broadcasting lectures, which MOOCs could do by putting videos online. Broadly speaking, a lecture works just as well if there are 10 people or 10,000 in the audience. The second was the connectivist approach that underpinned the earliest MOOCs (Siemens 2005; Downes et al. 2008), linking networks of learners to build knowledge together. This way of structuring courses gives a lot of control to learners and is therefore challenging for people who are not already experienced self-directed learners (Milligan, Littlejohn & Margaryan 2013). The third was supported distance learning, employed at some distance-learning universities. This approach only works when there is money available to pay for tutor support.

The FutureLearn platform, which launched in 2013, was based on a fourth approach, making scale a benefit, rather than a challenge. Just as a telephone network becomes increasingly valuable as more people join, extending opportunities for communication, the aim of FutureLearn was to develop an approach that would mean that the more learners, the more value a course could offer (Sharples & Ferguson 2019). This approach makes use of the conversation theory developed by Pask (1976), which provides a scientific account of how interactions between language-oriented systems (such as tutorial groups or scientific communities) can enable a process of 'coming to know' by reaching mutual agreements.

Learning through conversation (Pask 1976) involves sharing and negotiating differences in understanding with the aim of constructing new knowledge and reaching agreements. For their interactions to be considered a conversation, learners must be able to formulate descriptions of their reflections on actions, explore and extend those descriptions, and carry forward the understanding to a future activity. An example would be two learners performing an experiment together, discussing the results and what went wrong, then planning how to re-run the experiment. Effective learning through conversation requires learners to reach agreements through a process of facilitated interaction and conversation.

Building on Pask's work, Laurillard developed the Conversational Framework (Laurillard 2002), which includes conversation at two levels: actions and descriptions. At the level of actions, a learner and one or more partners discuss a practical activity or model of the world. For example, a teacher might set a maths problem to solve or an historical event to interpret. Learners converse in the context of that model or problem, sharing experiences and interpretations. The aim is to coordinate the action so that learners' expectations and understandings mesh with the teaching materials. Teaching materials and models must be appropriately designed, relevant and provoke reflective conversation.

At the level of descriptions, learners converse about why things happen. They offer conceptions of their learning and question the understanding of others, aiming to reach agreement about their reflective understandings. At both levels, learners need to agree on clear goals and objectives. Although the process of learning through conversation is exploratory, with learners managing their own activities and reflective discussions, there is an important role for an educator in proposing goals and objectives, creating suitable activities and models to explore, and facilitating discussions.

A conversational approach to learning engages learners actively. The focus is not on passive consumption of content (watching videos and reading text) but on active engagement. This can involve conversation, collaboration, reflection, experimentation and putting ideas into practice. Learners are encouraged to relate course content to their local context, to introduce different perspectives on material that relate to their own experience, and to share relevant resources. Course activities include opportunities to discuss topics, negotiate understanding and reach agreement where possible. Guided by educators, learners connect the theories and skills introduced by the course with their lived experience and, in the process, generate new knowledge and understanding.

This approach can be employed successfully with large cohorts, works well when study is asynchronous, draws on learners' existing knowledge, and can be applied in situations where there are relatively low levels of educator support for students. However, like competency-based and case-based learning, when it is applied online, learners will require study skills in order to study effectively and have the best chance of completing a microcredential successfully.

Online study skills

Students who enrol in a bricks-and-mortar university will often begin their time there with a 'Freshers' Week' or the local equivalent. This provides opportunities to meet staff and students informally, try things out in a low-risk way, explore their new surroundings, locate resources they will need to access while working for their qualification, make connections with others and generally get settled in before starting their studies in earnest. Learners on a microcredential may only be planning to study for a few weeks, but they need opportunities to do similar things. This could involve setting time aside at the beginning of the microcredential, or including a pre-course induction period with optional activities.

This time set aside for induction can also offer study skill support for those who have never studied at post-compulsory level before, who have not done so for some time, or who are not confident about their ability to study successfully at this level. This may include advice on developing effective study strategies, reading and taking notes, thinking critically, preparing assignments and revising for assessment.

Those who have not studied online before will require support with this, and most learners will benefit from some initial guidance on how to use a specific platform and navigate the course itself. Depending on the course and their previous experience, all online learners are likely to need to set time aside to do the following things. In most cases, they will benefit from some guidance on these activities, and an acknowledgement that completing these activities will take some of their study time.

Set study goals. One goal will be to complete the microcredential successfully. However, learners are likely to have other goals, such as exploring one or two topics in more depth, gaining experience of a particular aspect, or making contact with other practitioners. Reflecting on their goals, and stating these explicitly, will help them to prioritise their work.

Manage time. Most microcredentials learners will have other commitments, so will benefit from putting important course dates (assessments due, or synchronous sessions) in a diary or calendar at the start, blocking out times for study on a regular basis, and considering how to get ahead or catch up if it is necessary to work round a commitment that cannot be moved.

Workspace. Some microcredentials learners will already have a study space available at home or in the office. Others may need to negotiate access to a space that is comfortable, not too noisy, and has access to the internet. If they do not have reliable access to a good internet connection they may need to download course materials in advance, or be prepared to study whenever the internet is accessible.

Support. It is sometimes easier to study with others, by setting up a study group or by identifying another person who can be a 'study buddy'. Microcredentials learners might be able to do this in their workplace, especially if the company has registered a group of them on the same microcredential, or they might advertise in the course chat that they are looking for someone to discuss their study with, perhaps using a medium such as WhatsApp or Zoom.

Note-taking. Online learners may prefer to take their notes online, using a tool such as OneNote, Evernote or Google Docs; on their computer or tablet; or in a handwritten notebook. The decision will partly depend on personal preference and partly on context. They need to think ahead to avoid situations where, for example, they are studying at home but their notes are on a computer at work, or when their notes are online but they have no access to an internet connection during a study session.

Self-regulation

School students are used to teachers providing the structure, resources and motivation they need to learn. When they move to higher education, they take on more responsibility for their learning, but will still rely on the institution and their educators for support with structure, resources and motivation. When studying at a distance, as most online learners do, more of the responsibility lies with the learner. This requires a new set of skills – those involved in learning to learn.

Learning how to learn involves being able to:

- decide what you need to help you learn
- manage your time
- set goals
- find valuable resources – including other people – to learn with
- choose learning strategies
- reflect on progress
- develop creative skills
- evaluate learning outcomes.

The skills involved in learning to learn are vitally important in today's society. In our rapidly changing world, there is a need for workers who are able to update their skills and who are willing to keep on learning throughout their lives.

Self-regulated learning involves learners taking responsibility for their own learning. This does not mean there is no role for the educator but it does mean that educators need to be aware of their responsibility to facilitate learning that aligns with the goals and contexts of individual learners. Zimmerman and Moylan, experts in this area, note that:

> learning in self-regulated contexts can be challenging for students due to (a) competing activities, such as watching television or conversing with friends, (b) insufficient knowledge about how to proceed, (c) difficulty in judging the quality of one's learning, and (d) insufficient

incentives. These attention, retention, self-awareness, and motivation issues have been studied as important attributes of self-regulated learners. (Zimmerman & Moylan 2009: 299)

There are various descriptions of self-regulated learning, all of which draw attention to a personal feedback loop. Self-regulated learners reflect on feedback about their performance and use this information and reflection to adjust their approach. The feedback may come from the environment – did they complete the task successfully or not? It may come from other people, such as an educator or fellow learners. It may come from self-reflection and evaluation, or from all of these elements together.

Zimmerman and Moylan (2009) identify three phases to this feedback loop, which are repeated many times: the forethought phase, the performance phase and the self-reflection phase. Each of these can be broken down into different skills. For example, the forethought phase includes goal setting and strategic planning. The performance phase includes help-seeking, task strategies and time management. Self-reflection includes self-evaluation and attribution of reasons for success or failure.

None of these skills is fixed or innate – they can all be learned, practised and improved. Studies of learning in online settings have found positive correlations between academic achievement and self-regulated learning behaviour (Littlejohn et al. 2016). For example, Cheng and Chau (2013) find that some types of activity are associated with higher achievement. These included critical thinking, elaboration (including strategies such as note-taking, summarising, and paraphrasing), organising ideas and knowledge, and peer learning (asking for help from peers when necessary). Milligan and Littlejohn (2016) describe the behaviour of highly self-regulating learners in a MOOC designed for health professionals. These learners:

have a clear understanding of what they want to learn and how it will impact their career, job or personal development. These individuals assume control of their learning, monitoring their progress and adjusting their effort to maximise the benefit they gain from their studies. These learners go beyond the core tasks of the course, searching for additional resources and engaging with others in the forums to develop their ideas and grow their learning network. (Milligan & Littlejohn 2016: 120)

While it is beyond the scope of a microcredential to develop all these self-regulation skills, they can be incorporated into courses in several ways. Most important to bear in mind, when designing a microcredential, is that skills in learning to learn are not innate and that the ones required in an online context are unlikely to be the ones that learners acquired at school or university. Therefore, microcredential learners will need support in these areas. They will not necessarily understand the importance of activities such as time management or engaging with other learners, unless the benefits of these are made explicit. Even then, learners are more likely to complete these activities if educators show they value them. This can be done by mentioning these skills in the learning outcomes, setting aside time within the course to develop them, and assigning marks or credits for learners who demonstrate they have engaged with them. One or more learning-to-learn skills can be built into the syllabus of a single microcredential, or a stackable set of microcredentials, or links to appropriate resources can be supplied for those who want to develop as lifelong learners.

Overall, attention to skills in learning to learn can be used to address the problem that learners may be new to online learning and need to adapt to this setting. Some of these skills, such as time management and reflection, will help learners to overcome the challenge of having work and/or care commitments that need to take precedence over their study. Others, such as strategic planning and help-seeking, will enable them to make use of opportunities to interact with their peers.

These skills are helpful for learners but even the most skilled learners cannot progress if they are unable to access the course or its resources. This means that educators need to pay attention to accessibility. One way of doing this is through paying attention to accessibility guidelines (see, in particular, those in W3C 2018); another is through the use of Universal Design for Learning.

Universal Design for Learning

The Universal Design for Learning (UDL) framework, initially developed in the 1990s, can help greatly when planning microcredentials. The framework promotes flexibility in learning and addresses some of the barriers to learner participation, engagement and wellbeing that can intersect for an individual learner and across diverse learner groups. The UDL guidelines (CAST 2018), which elaborate on the UDL framework, are research-informed and are frequently revised to incorporate new pedagogies, technologies and evidence about how people learn. Both the framework and the guidelines are based on research in the learning sciences. They are used to support the development of flexible learning environments that can accommodate individual learning differences.

UDL has its roots in universal design, which aims for all products and environments to be designed so that they can be used by as many people as possible without the need for special equipment or adaptation. The guiding principles of universal design include:

- equitable use
- simple and intuitive use
- flexibility in use
- tolerance for error
- low physical effort.

By extension, UDL takes the view that the curriculum should be designed to accommodate all kinds of learner. This can be achieved by providing:

- **Multiple means of engagement** with the subject and learning environment, to tap into learners' interests, challenge them appropriately and motivate them to learn. The UDL guidelines express this as the 'why' of learning.
- **Multiple means of representation** of learning materials, to give learners various ways of acquiring information and knowledge. The UDL guidelines express this as the 'what' of learning.
- **Multiple means of action and expression** in learning, to provide learners alternatives for demonstrating what they know. The UDL guidelines express this as the 'how' of learning.

In a microcredential, 'multiple means of engagement' means stimulating learners by, for example, providing varied ways of putting a theory or skill into practice, and opportunities to work both collaboratively and alone. A key focus will be on giving learners autonomy and control by offering a choice of ways to learn and heightening learners' interest by providing authentic and relevant learning experiences that relate either to their own context or to the work context for which the microcredential is preparing them.

'Multiple means of representation' means offering learning content in different formats so that learners can choose the format that they prefer. For example, when a text is included in the course, a video or audio covering the same content may appear as well. Alternatively, learners might be given a choice of ways to access learning content, for example by being asked to explore a subject using whatever resources they can find.

'Multiple means of action and expression' is also about choice. It means giving learners different options for demonstrating what they have learned, for example writing an essay, giving a presentation or recording a video. This can be challenging in a microcredential if it only includes one or two pieces of summative assessment. However, these final assignments or exams are not the only ways of demonstrating learning. Learners might be encouraged to share work in progress with their peers for comment; to contribute in different ways to a collaborative activity; or to reflect on what they have learned by creating an artefact such as a picture, video or mind map.

UDL is one of a range of inclusive pedagogies. It can be used to make microcredentials more accessible to a range of learners but it has at its roots a consideration for the needs of learners with disabilities. Thought also needs to be given to other aspects of inclusion, particularly the needs of learners who are not based in the country where the microcredential was created. This is very important for courses presented on microcredential platforms, as the experience of MOOCs has been that learners are likely to register from every country where this is possible, and the same presentation may include learners from a large number of countries (for example, Bayeck (2016) reported that students from 82 countries completed the pre-course survey on one MOOC).

Inclusive pedagogies

A systematic review of the literature on inclusive pedagogies in higher education (Stentiford & Koutsouris 2020) identified several ways of approaching inclusion. These include appreciating difference, making differences invisible, addressing the needs of diverse students, and democratising knowledge. These approaches can be applied to microcredentials in different ways.

Inclusion as appreciating difference (individuality)

Individualistic approaches acknowledge the variety of individual needs in a learning context and ensure learners are offered activities that suit them. This may result in different learning material and activities for different learners but aims to avoid marginalising particular students. These approaches are rooted in the belief that all learners can make progress under the right conditions. On a microcredential, this might include activities that learners can adapt to their own contexts, wherever they are based, or a variety of resources from which learners can make their own selection. The focus of any work on self-regulation skills within the microcredential is likely to be on helping learners to recognise and understand their own learning needs.

Inclusion as making differences invisible (commonality)

Approaches based on commonality aim to ensure the needs of all learners are met, or that they have choices about how they engage with their learning. This should allow for the same learning material and activities to be offered to everyone. The focus of work on self-regulation is likely to be on supporting learners to make appropriate choices as to how they engage with these resources. UDL is an example of a commonality approach.

Inclusion as a way of addressing the needs of diverse students (procedural approaches)

This approach acknowledges that diverse students will be enrolled on microcredentials, so focuses on ways of enabling them all to develop a sense of belonging. This might involve activities that encourage learners to share their experiences, so that the entire cohort has an opportunity to reflect on how skills and knowledge are influenced by context and culture. Microcredentials taking this approach to inclusion would acknowledge the diversity of students enrolled on the course and offer learning opportunities that students would find culturally relevant.

Inclusion as the democratisation of knowledge

Approaches focusing on democratisation of knowledge challenge perceptions of the curriculum and what students are taught. These approaches draw on historical movements that challenge the notion of education being reserved for elite social classes, and align with the aspirations of many that microcredentials could help to open up education and provide gateways to other opportunities.

> With a low entry barrier, micro-credentials could be the initial step for learners who might traditionally have been discouraged to enter the education system; they can also be the means to enable more fluid learning pathways, thereby realising the vision of lifelong learning. (European Commission 2020)

This approach to inclusion stresses that students with diverse backgrounds, circumstances and needs should see others like themselves reflected in the curriculum. This has implications for the content of the course, including the sources that are referenced, and the images that are used. Examples and resources shared by learners during one presentation of the microcredential can be built into subsequent iterations of the course, so that it not only becomes more inclusive but also richer and deeper.

Together, pedagogies for learning, the development of learners' study skills, and inclusive approaches address some of the main ways in which teaching and learning in microcredentials need to be different from other courses in order to meet the needs of the learners who are studying them. Another requirement, which straddles the boundary between learning design and pedagogy, is the desire for stackability.

Stackability

The aim for microcredentials to be joined together to earn learners more substantial qualifications is often central to how these courses are understood. The proposed EU standard for constitutive elements of microcredentials includes integration/stackability options (European Commission 2020). Oliver's (2019) description of 'An evolved 21C education system' includes 'the facility to stack and bank lifelong learning credit'. The Microcredential Roadmap created in Ireland refers several times to 'a more agile, flexible and stackable approach to training and professional development' (Nic Giolla Mhichíl et al. 2020).

Stackability implies that credits from one institution should be recognised by others, and that their value should remain constant. This would mean that learners could stack microcredentials offered by different institutions, rather than being limited to those offered by one institution. Within the European Higher Education Area (EHEA), which covers 49 countries, the Lisbon Recognition Convention sets out regulations for academic recognition. The convention was agreed in 1997, before the emergence of microcredentials, but its terms imply that microcredentials 'offered by accredited higher education institutions' would fall within its scope (MICROBOL 2020: 33).

The existence of such frameworks around the world suggests that academic credit offered by microcredentials could be transferred between institutions in different countries, but there is still work to be done to ensure that the frameworks cover these courses. In addition, as the MICROBOL project notes in the quotation above, these frameworks are designed for the transfer of academic credit. Microcredentials' position between the academic world and the world of work means that they sometimes lead to certification by professional organisations or companies. In the case of major multinationals, this makes international recognition easier in some ways, but limits stackability because the accreditation systems of different companies are not aligned.

In their analysis of accreditation approaches in the computing sector in England, Bowers and Howson (2019) demonstrate the challenges involved in aligning workplace accreditation frameworks with an institution's internal framework, the national framework and the European framework. They also outline some of the certification levels awarded by different vendors, which include administrator, engineer and professional (LPI); fundamentals, associate and expert (Microsoft); and entry, associate, professional, expert and architect (Cisco). 'Professional' is the highest grade in some of these systems, but only a midway point in others. Neither the terminology nor the levels can easily be mapped to each other.

Even within HEIs, stackability can pose problems. Qualifications are typically built from a limited set of options so that necessary skills can be acquired and evidenced over time. The set of skills required at any qualification level is usually defined at national or international level. For example, in England the Regulated Qualifications Framework sets out the criteria for qualifications at nine levels, from the most basic to a doctorate. In Europe, national qualifications frameworks for courses at university level are developed to be compatible with the framework of qualifications of the European Higher Education Area. On a global scale, qualifications are likely to be aligned with UNESCO's International Standard Classification of Education, a framework that applies uniform and internationally agreed definitions. However, once again, this is a framework that predates microcredentials, and so its criteria, which include entry requirements and course length, are not well suited to these courses.

Without the necessary over-arching frameworks in place, it will not be possible in most cases to build microcredentials that can stack with a wide variety of others. One approach will be to build sets of microcredentials within the same institution that can be combined in different ways to achieve a qualification. An example here is The Open University in the UK, which has a long history of enabling its students to select and combine modules from across the institution's curriculum to achieve an undergraduate or, more recently, a postgraduate degree (Di Paolo, Hills & Mahrra 2009). However, in that case the modules each involve 300 or 600 hours of study, so they cover more knowledge and skills than microcredentials. The courses are also levelled, so students build from an introductory level to more advanced study, whereas microcredentials are typically positioned more broadly at either undergraduate or postgraduate level. Institutions building stackable sets of microcredentials, as The Open University is now doing (see Chapter 7), need to pay careful attention to the learning outcomes of each of these, and to how these can be designed (see Chapter 5 on learning design).

Another approach will be to position microcredentials as gateways to full qualification pathways. In this case, they can make entry possible for individuals who did not previously have appropriate entry qualifications; they can enable others to make significant changes in subject area; and they can act as taster courses. This approach requires a pedagogy that introduces students to study at this level, as well as introducing them to some of the basic conventions of the discipline and specific subject area.

Conclusion

Although the definition of microcredentials has not yet been standardised, elements that are common to many of these courses require a distinctive approach to pedagogy, rather than a replication of the approaches used for other forms of qualification. One of these elements is the focus of microcredentials on career, workplace and professional skills. Another is that most of these courses are offered online and so the pedagogy must be appropriate for online learners who may have not studied in this way before and need to develop a new set of study skills alongside their coursework. Another element is associated with the intention for microcredentials to open opportunities for new groups of learners, so any cohort of learners is likely to be significantly different in its demographics from a cohort engaged in other forms of education or training. This chapter has shown how changes in pedagogy can address these issues. The following chapter considers ways of adapting and broadening pedagogy so that microcredentials really do open up learning and offer a range of new possibilities.

References

Bayeck, R. Y. (2016). Exploratory study of MOOC learners' demographics and motivation: The case of students involved in groups. *Open Praxis*, 8(3): 223–233.

Bowers, D. S. and Howson, O. (2019). *Analysis of accreditation approaches in the computing sector*. Milton Keynes: The Open University. Available at https://oro.open.ac.uk/69220

CAST. (2018). *Universal Design for Learning Guidelines version 2.2*. Available at http://udlguidelines.cast.org

Cheng, G. and Chau, J. (2013). Exploring the relationship between students' self-regulated learning ability and their ePortfolio achievement. *The Internet and Higher Education*, 17: 9–15.

Di Paolo, T., Hills, M. and Mahrra, J. (2009). Changing lives on the 'degree of choice': Older first generation learners on the Open Programme. In: BERA Annual Conference, Manchester, UK, 2–5 September.

Downes, S., Couros, A., Siemens, G. and Blackall, L. (2008). EdTechTalk#81 – The Mega-Connectivism Course (Part #1) (27 July). *EdTechTalk*. Available at https://edtechtalk.com/EdTechTalk81

European Commission. (2020). *A European approach to micro-credentials – Output of the Micro-credentials Higher Education Consultation Group – final report*. Available at https://education.ec.europa.eu/sites/default/files/document-library-docs/european-approach-micro-credentials-higher-education-consultation-group-output-final-report.pdf.

European Higher Education Area. (2021). *Qualification frameworks*. Available at https://ehea.info/page-qualification-frameworks

Harasim, L. M. (1990). Online education: An environment for collaboration and intellectual amplification. In: Harasim, L. M.

Online education: Perspectives on a new environment. New York and London: Praeger. pp. 39–63.

Henri, M., Johnson, M. D. and Nepal, B. (2017). A review of competency-based learning: Tools, assessments, and recommendations. *Journal of Engineering Education*, 106(4): 607–638.

Iniesto, F., McAndrew, P., Minocha, S. and Coughlan, T. (2017). What are the expectations of disabled learners when participating in a MOOC? In: L@S 2017, Cambridge, MA, USA, 20–21 April 2017.

Laurillard, D. (2002). *Rethinking university teaching: A conversational framework for the effective use of learning technologies.* 2nd ed. London: RoutledgeFalmer.

Littlejohn, A., Hood, N., Milligan, C. and Mustain, P. (2016). Learning in MOOCs: Motivations and self-regulated learning in MOOCs. *The Internet and Higher Education*, 29: 40–48.

McLean, S. F. (2016). Case-based learning and its application in medical and health-care fields: A review of worldwide literature. *Journal of Medical Education and Curricular Development*, 3: JMECD. S20377.

MICROBOL. (2020). *Micro-credentials linked to the Bologna key commitments: Desk research report*. MICROBOL. Available at https://eua.eu/downloads/publications/microbol%20desk%20research%20report.pdf

Milligan, C. and Littlejohn, A. (2016). How health professionals regulate their learning in massive open online courses. *The Internet and Higher Education*, 31: 113–121.

Milligan, C., Littlejohn, A. and Margaryan, A. (2013). Patterns of engagement in connectivist MOOCs. *MERLOT Journal of Online Learning and Teaching*, 9(2): 149–159.

Moore, M. G. (2019). The theory of transactional distance. In: Moore, M. G. and Diehl, W. C. *Handbook of distance education*. New York: Routledge. pp. 32–46.

Moreno, A. (2019). *Predicting student dropout in a MicroMasters program*. Thesis, MIT. Available at https://hdl.handle.net/1721.1/122250

Nic Giolla Mhichíl, M., Brown, M., Beirne, E. and MacLochlainn, C. (2020). *A micro-credential roadmap: Currency, cohesion and *consistency*. Dublin City University. Available at https://www.skillnetireland.ie/wp-content/uploads/2021/03/A-Micro-Credential-Roadmap-Currency-Cohesion-and-Consistency.pdf

Oliver, B. (2019). *Making micro-credentials work for learners, employers and providers*. Melbourne: Deakin University. Available at https://dteach.deakin.edu.au/wp-content/uploads/sites/103/2019/08/Making-micro-credentials-work-Oliver-Deakin-2019-full-report.pdf

Pask, G. (1976). *Conversation theory: Applications in education and epistemology*. New York: Elsevier.

Rossiter, D. and Tynan, B. (2019). *Designing and implementing micro-credentials: A guide for practitioners*. Commonwealth of Learning. Available at https://oasis.col.org/items/e2d0be25-cbbb-441f-b431-42f74f715532

Selvaratnam, R. M. and Sankey, M. D. (2020). An integrative literature review of the implementation of micro-credentials in higher education: Implications for practice in Australasia. *Journal of Teaching and Learning for Graduate Employability*, 11: 1–17.

Shah, D. (2015). *By the numbers: MOOCS in 2015* (21 December). Class Central. Available at https://www.class-central.com/report/moocs-2015-stats

Shah, D. (2020). *By the numbers: MOOCs in 2020* (30 November). Class Central. Available at https://www.classcentral.com/report/mooc-stats-2020

Sharples, M. and Ferguson, R. (2019). Pedagogy-informed design of conversational learning at scale. In: ECTEL, Delft, Netherlands, 16–19 September.

Shen, C. (2014). *Introducing Nanodegrees* (16 June). Available at https://www.udacity.com/blog/2014/06/announcing-nanodegrees-new-type-of.html

Siemens, G. (2005). Connectivism: A learning theory for the digital age. *International Journal of Instructional Technology and Distance Learning*, 2(1).

Srinivasan, M., Wilkes, M., Stevenson, F., Nguyen, T. and Slavin, S. (2007). Comparing problem-based learning with case-based learning: Effects of a major curricular shift at two institutions. *Academic Medicine*, 82(1): 74–82.

Stancombe, S. (2020). *FutureLearn launches microcredentials with six global partners* (11 Feb 2020). Available at https://www.futurelearn.com/info/press-releases/futurelearn-launches-microcredentials-with-six-global-partners

Stentiford, L. and Koutsouris, G. (2020). What are inclusive pedagogies in higher education? A systematic scoping review. *Studies in Higher Education*, 46(11): 2245–2261.

Tinto, V. (1997). Colleges as communities: Taking research on student persistence seriously. *The Review of Higher Education*, 21(2): 167–177.

Topperzer, M. K., Roug, L. I., Andrés-Jensen, L., Pontoppidan, P., Hoffmann, M., Larsen, H. B., Schmiegelow, K. and Sørensen, J. L. (2021). Twelve tips for postgraduate interprofessional case-based learning. *Medical Teacher*, 44(2): 130–137.

Valli, H. (2018). *Bold new initiatives from the Coursera conference* (29 March). Available at https://learninginnovation.duke.edu/blog/2018/03/bold-new-initiatives-from-the-coursera-conference/

W3C. (2023). *Web content accessibility guidelines (WCAG) 2.2: WC3 recommendation*. Available at http://www.w3.org/TR/WCAG

WHO and The World Bank. (2011). *World report on disability 2011*. Available at https://www.who.int/teams/noncommunicable-diseases/sensory-functions-disability-and-rehabilitation/world-report-on-disability

Wu, D. and Hiltz, S. R. (2004). Predicting learning from asynchronous online discussions. *Journal of Asynchronous Learning Networks*, 8(2): 139–152.

Young, J. R. (2016). *Degrees of the future – and what's at stake for students* (3 November). Available at https://www.edsurge.com/news/2016-11-03-why-udacity-and-edx-want-to-trademark-the-degrees-of-the-future-and-what-s-at-stake-for-students

Zimmerman, B. J. and Moylan, A. R. (2009). Self-regulation: Where metacognition and motivation intersect. In: Hacker, D. J., Dunlosky, J. and Graesser, A. C. *Handbook of metacognition in education*. Routledge. pp. 299–315.

CHAPTER 3

Creating microcredentials and supporting learners

It takes a team to create and run a microcredential. These are new qualifications, which do not fit neatly into the existing systems set up for undergraduate, postgraduate and vocational courses. Differences in scale, funding, learners and presentation are just some of the factors that mean microcredentials are not typical courses. Setting them up and sustaining them effectively requires thought and change in all areas of the institution, as well as new or extended partnerships with employers and professional organisations. This chapter examines the range of roles that contribute to a successful microcredential, including ways of reconceptualising the role of educator.

How to cite this book chapter:
Ferguson, R. and Whitelock, D. 2024. Creating microcredentials and supporting learners. In: Ferguson, R. and Whitelock, D. *Microcredentials for Excellence: A Practical Guide*. Pp. 51–81. London: Ubiquity Press. DOI: https://doi.org/10.5334/bcz.c. License: CC BY-NC 4.0

Roles on a microcredential

Educational institutions such as universities have tried-and-tested systems in place for running their courses. They are able to draw on decades, even centuries, of experience in the field, and are supported by national and international frameworks that specify how courses should be set up and run. Teaching staff are familiar with the qualification system, support services are in place throughout the learning journey, and learners arrive with some understanding of the way in which qualifications work and how they relate to each other. New courses can draw on the model of previous courses, with any changes being incremental. Worldwide, the higher education system is robust, withstanding numerous predictions over past decades that it is on the verge of profound disruption (Weller 2014) and even managing to negotiate the rapid pivot to online teaching required by the Covid-19 pandemic.

Microcredentials are not disruptive in the sense proposed by Christensen and his colleagues (Christensen, Johnson & Horn 2008). They are a new product, rather than a radically new business model that will overthrow the old providers. However, they are a new product that is sufficiently unlike previous products to pose a challenge to the systems currently in place to support higher education courses. Significant differences include:

- Microcredentials are typically run online and at a distance, while most higher education providers are set up to run their teaching and assessment with students co-located.
- Microcredentials differ in length but are typically much shorter than other accredited courses in higher education.

The significant levels of work involved in registering and assessing students therefore take a larger proportion of time and resources than they do on longer courses.
- Microcredential learners are based all over the world and their support needs are not the same as those of students based on campus.
- The definition of a microcredential varies significantly between institutions, so learners are not sure what to expect from their course and many staff will also initially be unsure about the similarities and differences.
- Microcredentials aligned with the requirements of employers can be difficult to align with more broadly based academic qualifications.

These are only some of the ways in which microcredentials differ from other courses, but even these differences have significant implications for learners and educators as well as for registration, assessment and support teams. Rossiter and Tynan describe a microcredentials 'ecosystem' and note that, 'If the enterprise is to thrive, it is important always to keep in mind the ecosystem's players and stakeholders, all of whom must work in harmony, appreciating and agreeing upon the value of the credential' (Rossiter & Tynan 2019: 4). The EU's Micro-credentials Higher Education Consultation Group suggested setting up cross-faculty units to offer microcredentials, supported by the university chancellor and board, to 'stimulate an institutional momentum and drive a cultural change based on a top-down dynamic but involving bottom-up processes' (European Commission 2020: 23).

Figure 1 sets out the main roles within an institution that will be impacted by the development of these new courses. Six main sets are involved.

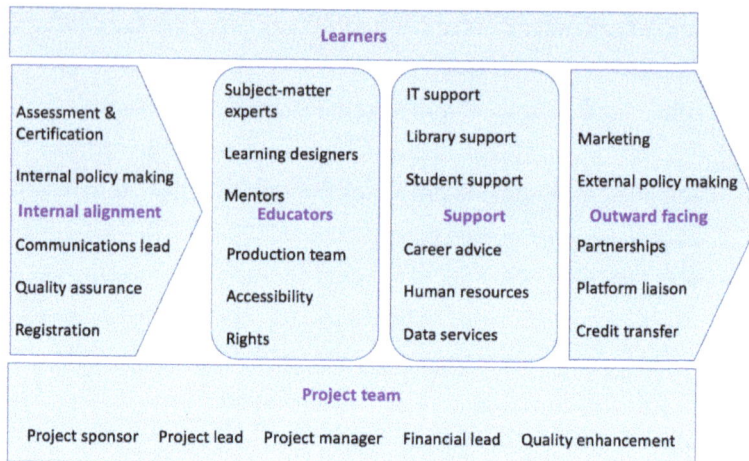

Figure 1: Key roles on microcredentials.

- **Project team** roles drive forward the microcredentials programme, forging links between other roles and developing a long-term strategy.
- **Educators** include the various groups of people responsible for developing and delivering the courses.
- **Support** covers the work of a variety of support teams, including student-focused support such as the library and the careers service, as well as staff-based support from human resources and data services.
- **Internal alignment** is concerned with ensuring that institutional services such as policies and quality assurance are extended to cover microcredentials, and that staff understand this new strategic initiative.
- **Outward-facing** roles make links with external bodies and take responsibility for marketing the courses.
- **Learners** have a role to play in defining what microcredentials become, providing input and feedback, as well

as interacting to form a learning community that extends beyond the cohorts on individual microcredentials.

Project team roles

The **project sponsor** needs to be a senior figure within the institution – the president, vice chancellor, principal or a member of the senior leadership team. Individuals who take on the role of sponsor have many responsibilities, and microcredentials are unlikely to be their only significant project. However, without wholehearted support from a sponsor at this level, it is unlikely that a major initiative such as microcredentials can be implemented successfully. This champion is needed to approve necessary changes, to make high-level decisions that impact the entire institution, and to convince others at senior management level that the project should and will succeed.

A sponsor will define, or approve, a strategic vision for microcredentials that makes it clear why they are being introduced, how they align with existing institutional priorities, and what the aims of the initiative are in the short and long terms. Possible objectives include 'to respond to student demand for more relevant future skills, to make learning personalised, to break it into smaller, bite-sized chunks, or perhaps to work more closely with industry to ensure graduates gain mastery of work-ready skills' (Rossiter & Tynan 2019: 4) It is important that project sponsors are well informed and well advised, so they have a clear and realistic view of what can be achieved.

On a day-to-day basis, the **project lead** will be responsible for microcredentials and their success within the institution. Microcredentials are so new that the project lead will need a visionary approach, looking ahead to what can be achieved in the short and long terms, balanced by the down-to-earth ability to develop deliverable plans that are strategically aligned, working together with senior managers. The project lead will bring together a strong team from across the institution.

That team requires a **project manager** who can map out the elements of the complex process of microcredential development, agreeing goals and deadlines and keeping different individuals and departments on track. This is a challenging job that involves understanding and aligning different working patterns from across the institution. The project manager defines the critical path for the project, identifying all the tasks that must be carried out, the dependencies between those tasks, and the time that each will take to complete. Managing workflow is a major task, particularly in a large organisation where existing tasks are distributed between many people and few individuals have a clear understanding of any process in its entirety. An example of this is the video production process. Academics may send videos to a production team to be edited without being aware that the team then has to wait for rights clearance on images used within the video; for a transcription to be produced, styled and proofread; and for captions to be added.

Depending on the scale of the microcredentials initiative, it is likely there will be several project managers involved, working in faculties, marketing, assessment and production. The range of processes to manage can produce conflict because different areas of an institution are likely to have very different project management styles. One department may employ a 'waterfall' approach, using a structured process with each step completed sequentially, and requirements defined at the beginning. Others might use various 'agile' approaches, working in short sprints, prioritising as they go, and regularly reviewing progress (Andrei et al. 2019). It will be up to the senior project manager to align these different approaches, so microcredentials can be developed successfully.

Another important role on the project team is the **financial lead**, who will play an important part in the development of the business case for microcredentials, the cost–benefit analysis and ongoing business planning. They will be responsible for the development and implementation of the project's financial model, working with different departments to produce indicative costs for the development of microcredentials.

The finances of an operation of this size, taking into account both internal and external markets, are complex. Financial projections will be very tentative at first because there are so many variables to be taken into account, not least the price charged to learners. 'Consumers expect short extension courses to be priced much lower than components of degrees … Because a micro-credential is a new and unknown unit of currency, the cost will be a strong consideration for the learner' (Oliver 2019: 26). Pricing of microcredentials is a delicate balance between the cost of production, the price of other credentials offered by the institution, the amount that potential learners can afford, and the need to appear competitive.

Although microcredentials may be offered worldwide, those produced by Western countries based on Western budgets are likely to be out of the price range of potential learners in many countries. On the other hand, learners may associate low prices with inferior quality. In countries where state support means that higher education is normally free or very cheap at the point of delivery, any course for which learners have to pay the market price themselves will appear expensive.

The international reach of microcredentials means the financial lead must also take into account financial and tax regulations in countries around the world. Education is often exempt from tax but the definition of education varies from country to country. For example, in the UK, online courses with little human intervention (tuition), no assessment and no academic credit are liable for value-added tax (VAT) at the standard rate, whereas courses with some human intervention, assessment and credit are exempt. That could mean, for example, a different tax treatment for a microcredential that a university offers on an external platform without awarding any academic credit other than the potential for it to be accredited as prior learning at some point in the future.

If the institution's intention is to attract learners based around the world, the financial lead will need to draw on the knowledge of a tax manager or tax adviser. They will be experienced in issues of tax compliance and will consider whether the institution needs to comply with these on a country-by-country basis. These decisions will be informed by the scale of activity expected in each country and by assessing that country's tax regime with its associated tax risks and issues. This will involve completing tax registration and tax returns wherever necessary, as well as collecting and paying any tax due.

Overall, the initial costs of setting up a microcredentials unit or ecosystem will be high, as many of the change processes need to be completed early on, before there is any certainty about revenue generation. The financial lead needs to be aware of the scale of the endeavour and should have reasonable expectations about how long it is likely to take for these courses to break even and begin paying for themselves.

The final role in the project team is **quality enhancement** (see Chapter 8 for a detailed consideration of this area). Developing microcredentials is a large-scale strategic initiative for any institution, and including work on evaluation and quality enhancement provides opportunities to assess progress and adjust ambitions. An evaluation lead can bring these existing approaches together and incorporate them into a structured consideration of the initiative as a whole that can be used by those working on the project to improve practice. More generally, evaluation work can be used by the communications lead to share progress more widely across the institution.

Internal alignment roles

In any educational institution, courses of study are underpinned by policies and regulations that define the rights and obligations of both learners and institution. These ensure that 'the learner enrols with a clear understanding of their commitment, including the effort, time, mutual obligations, benefits, costs, and terms and conditions' (Rossiter & Tynan 2019: 8). This includes 'the obligations of students and their liabilities to the higher education provider including expected standards of behaviour; access to current academic governance policies and requirements; access to services and support; resolution of grievances; information to assist international students' (Oliver 2019: 41).

In most cases, policies and regulations already in place will have been drawn up on the basis that students are intending to complete a course of study that lasts a year or more and that they will be based near the institution. This means the regulations may include timescales or attendance requirements that are unsuitable for microcredentials. They may also make commitments about resources, library access, language support, counselling or student community that are unrealistic for learners on short courses.

These regulations need early attention because they set out binding legal commitments. Policies are often numerous, lengthy and interconnected, with numerous cross-references. Some changes can be made unilaterally; others will have to go to one or more committees and may require decisions at the highest level, all of which takes time. Some revisions will need to be made by specialists in a particular area (such as accessibility, or safeguarding those who are young or vulnerable); others will need input from a lawyer. Issues will be particularly complex if the regulations for microcredential learners differ from those for other students at the institution. For example, if full-time students supplement their course with a microcredential aligned with their chosen career, it must be clear which regulations apply at which point.

Those involved in **internal policymaking** will therefore need a good understanding of the existing regulations and the wider considerations (for example, internal strategy and national law) that frame these. They also need to be clear about the ways in which microcredentials differ from other courses on offer. This means they will be reliant on the work of the **communications lead**.

It is the communications lead who has the responsibility for sharing the microcredentials vision and strategy across the institution. Why is the initiative being set up? What are its goals? What benefits will it bring, and to whom? As well as these high-level issues, staff also need more practical information. What exactly are microcredentials? Which of the many definitions and approaches have been selected by the institution? And, more concretely, how will this be implemented? Who is leading the project and who are the main contacts? Where is information about the initiative available? Ideally, this communication with staff should be an ongoing, two-way process that will engage them, inspiring some to become microcredentials champions and enabling everyone to understand the microcredentials initiative and how it is progressing.

Eventually, microcredentials will become part of 'business as usual'. However, in the short term, they need to be incorporated within the institution's key administrative processes. The first step is **registration**. This is a key stage in the learner's journey, which triggers a series of other processes. It will take time to understand all the dependencies of the registration process, how these are set up, and how they need to be changed for microcredentials. Examples include:

- Assignment of a unique ID to the learner. Have they already registered with the institution in another capacity, perhaps many years ago? If so, their records of academic achievement need to be linked.
- Collection of payment. Standard information about student grants, loans or bursaries is unlikely to apply. Policies on refunds or re-registration may be different.
- Collection of information required by the state. For example, in the UK the Higher Education Statistics Agency (HESA) requires institutions to collect and report a wide range of information about students (HESA 2000).
- Links to student regulations and policies. Links must be supplied to the revised, or newly written, regulations. Before fees are accepted, learners should be informed of their rights and obligations, including any charges or possibilities of refunds.
- Access to resources. This access may be set, by default, to a period of years. Contracts (for example, journal access, counselling services, or student discount schemes) must be checked with external providers to ensure these cover short-term learners.
- Course notifications and reminders. Defaults may need to be changed, taking into account course length.

- Triggering events later in the student journey such as careers advice, leavers' surveys, invitations to graduation ceremonies, or government reporting about completion and success rates. Each of these triggers requires review.

The task becomes more complicated if registration is outsourced to an external platform. This raises data protection issues, as information about learners is transferred between the platform and the institution. It may also introduce complications related to refunds, depending on when or why learners drop out of the course, and how they initially paid for it.

At the other end of the learner journey, assessment and certification processes are also important and will loom large in the learner experience. Pedagogic aspects of assessment and some of the practicalities of identity verification are covered in detail in Chapter 7, but there will also be a team at institutional level with responsibility for amending and administering assessment processes. Some of this work relates to putting assessment into practice on a day-to-day basis, a subject covered in some detail by Rossiter and Tynan (2019) in their practitioner guide. 'An essential requirement is to determine how the issuance of the credential will be triggered, at what point in the learning-and-earning journey, and from which technology platform or application within the system' (2019: 10).

Rossiter and Tynan also deal with the practicalities of designing a badge or other form of digital certification:

> The design of the badge should reflect the brand of the issuing organisation. The shape, colour, font and use of iconography to represent a skill are influential factors but should be chosen in the context of institutional brand guidelines and with a critical eye to determining whether these elements will contribute positively to the

impact of the badge. Badge design can also reflect the taxonomy or structure of the micro-credential portfolio. For example, the badge design may represent – through colour, shape, the use of icons or logos, etc. – the skills, the weighting or the levels of competency indicated by a micro-credential, or the relationship with industry partners. (Rossiter & Tynan 2019: 10)

Part of quality assurance work (see Chapter 8) is to ensure there are processes in place to demonstrate that a microcredential credit requires a similar amount of work at a similar standard to those required by qualifications on offer within the institution and more widely. The more robust these methods are, the more helpful they will be for the credit-transfer process, which is one of the outward-facing aspects of the microcredential initiative.

Outward-facing roles

Credit transfer is one of the concepts that underpins microcredentials, and is associated with the idea that they are – or will in future be – stackable. The intention is that microcredentials can be counted as prior qualifications that act either as a gateway to other qualifications, or can be counted towards those qualifications.

In the European context, the MICROBOL project was set up to 'explore the possible adaptation of the ECTS [European Credit Transfer and Accumulation System] Users' Guide to emphasise how ECTS can be used in the context of micro-credentials' (European Commission 2020: 27). In 2019, the Malaysia Qualification Agency launched microcredential guidelines that enable higher education providers to recognise microcredentials via credit transfer or accreditation of prior experiential learning (Ahmat et al. 2021). And, in Canada, the British Columbia Council on Admissions and Transfer (BCCAT) commissioned a detailed report that identifies and reviews both current and emerging practices in developing and accepting micro-credentials in admission and transfer (Duklas 2020).

The Canadian report notes that:

> If a micro-credential is to be considered as a bona fide credential … expectations typically exist that the learning experiences (including those represented by micro-credentials) have been structured, delivered, and assessed by trusted entities in accordance with accepted and recognized quality assurance expectations and frameworks. (Duklas 2020: 15).

Despite these national and international initiatives, Duklas found few examples of microcredentials being used for credit transfer, noting that Thompson Rivers University had announced in 2020 that it was 'among the first in the world to recognize micro-credit transfer towards a university-level qualification' (Young 2020). Whether that claim is accurate depends on the definition of micro-credit, but there are certainly few HEIs that are currently involved in credit transfer of microcredentials.

Part of the microcredential endeavour must be to develop the reputation of these courses so they are widely recognised by employers and educational institutions. Providers therefore need to take up the challenge of finding ways not only to accept their own microcredentials as academic credits that can be counted towards a qualification but also to accept microcredentials issued by other providers. This is currently a tough challenge for institutions, partly because an internationally accepted definition of microcredentials has yet to be agreed, and partly because international standards for these courses are still under development. Nevertheless, if microcredentials are to gain currency, these credit-transfer issues require serious attention from the institutions that offer them.

This is an area in which **external policymaking** is key. Institutions offering microcredentials can choose either active or passive engagement with this process. Either they can contribute to the development of national and international policy on microcredentials – discussing and agreeing on standards and regulations – or they will end up being held to the standards developed by others.

Another area of outward-facing activity is in **partnerships**. Microcredentials are intended to be aligned with professional skills and employment opportunities, so they provide an opportunity for higher education to forge new alliances with companies, industries, professional bodies, unions and service providers. Such partnerships could enable the development of microcredentials directly relevant to the needs of employers, as well as enabling both partners to develop reasonable expectations of what is possible and where responsibility lies. The possibility of building such partnerships has attracted attention at both national and international levels.

The European Commission noted that external partnerships are critical to ensuring microcredentials are responsive to employers' needs. They can help to understand market requirements, run pilot projects, bring in field-relevant expertise and reduce risk.

> Partnerships with labour market actors, including social partners and companies themselves are seen as key to the development of micro-credentials. They can reduce investment requirements and risks for individual institutions and ensure dialogue occurs around needs and priorities. External partners can contribute with expertise, and can be seen as a way forward to the uptake and promotion of micro-credentials. (European Commission 2020: 24)

In Australia (Government of South Australia 2020), a series of consultation workshops resulted in a report that called for the development and assessment of microcredentials to be co-designed and/or endorsed by industry. It also noted that the needs of industry change rapidly, so microcredential development requires rapid decision-making in order to respond to the current and anticipated demands of industry, as well as a regular review mechanism to ensure microcredentials remain current.

In New Zealand, a report commissioned by a government engineering initiative noted:

> the narrower focus of the micro-credential means that educational, industry or other organisations can develop and implement micro-credentials more easily and quickly in response to new industry needs. In the employment process, micro-credentials provide a more detailed record of a holder's actual competencies which can help them differentiate their abilities from other applicants and allow employers to identify people whose competencies match their organisation's needs. (Wilson & Hay 2018)

However, the report also identified risks associated with the narrow scope of microcredentials. If courses focus on a single competency, there is a risk that learners will only learn individual competencies without developing an understanding of how they interconnect or how the whole system works. These short courses may not offer learners opportunities to develop the higher-order thinking skills – such as analysing and synthesising information – that can be developed on longer courses that include more complex assignments. An industry/HEI partnership has the potential to make use of the benefits of microcredentials while avoiding the flaws inherent in an approach that focuses on a limited skillset that may soon be outdated.

Apart from building new partnerships, the microcredentials initiative may also be working with an external platform, such as one of the MOOC providers, which will host and publicise its microcredentials. In some cases, **platform liaison** is relatively straightforward. edX launched its MicroMasters in 2016 and Coursera piloted its first MasterTracks in 2018. There has therefore been sufficient time for these platforms to adjust their processes and assumptions to take microcredentials into account and smooth the liaison process. Other platforms have made the move more recently, host a diverse range of offerings, or have a rigid model that must be followed. In these cases, work on platform liaison becomes more time-consuming. Throughout this process it is important to be aware of where the interests of the platform and the institution align, and where they diverge. Some providers are doing little more than providing a hosting service but others have larger scale plans related to the disruption of education.

Disruptive innovation is defined as 'the process by which an innovation transforms a market whose services or products are complicated and expensive into one where simplicity, convenience, accessibility, and affordability characterize the industry' (Christensen, Johnson & Horn 2008: 11). The ideas behind disruption are set out in Christensen's influential book, *The Innovator's Dilemma* (Christensen 1997) in which he proposes that market processes are driven by two approaches: a dominating regime that defines the rules of the game and develops slowly, and a disruptive regime that uses cheaper and simpler technologies and eventually overtakes the dominant approach. The book distinguishes between sustaining technologies that are used to improve the existing market and disruptive ones that help establish a new market.

There are problems with Christensen's theory. It is not clear that any technology is inherently disruptive, or that a theory developed using case studies of companies producing disk drives can be transferred to a social endeavour such as higher education (Weller 2014). Nevertheless, the idea of 'disruption' has proved to be powerful, and education is seen to be an extremely lucrative worldwide market. If undergraduate and postgraduate degrees are the dominant market, then microcredentials could be seen as the plucky little underdogs that overcome the lumbering old university dinosaurs. It is this thinking that underpinned the edX decision to trademark MicroMasters and Udacity to trademark Nanodegrees (Young 2016). Control of the name is associated with control of the product, the standards it adheres to, and the way it is run.

This intention – to disrupt education and make a profit in the process – shapes the thinking of some of the major platforms offering microcredentials. edX, which was launched by Harvard and MIT in 2012, was sold nine years later for US$800 million (Shaw 2021). Coursera, launched in the same year, was valued at US$7 billion in 2021, despite losing nearly US$69 million in the previous year (Adams 2021). The interests and visions of platform and institution are therefore likely to be very different when it comes to microcredentials. This means that partner liaison is not a simple matter of negotiating a way of working with a technology provider. Instead, it is a process of balancing two sets of priorities and working to ensure that it is learners who benefit from this process.

One of the teams closely involved in this process is the **Marketing** team, responsible for attracting learners to these new courses, as well as to the institution's wider offering. This team faces two big challenges. The first is developing public understanding of microcredentials. The second is offering microcredentials online, to a global market.

> While reporting of learners in the millions may give the impression that the market is vast, consumers of microcredentials have a great deal of choice, there is evidence

that despite micro-credentials and degrees being available online, institutions such as universities still have strong geographical pull. (Oliver 2019: 29)

By far the biggest current challenge is developing public understanding, because if people have no idea what a microcredential is they are not going to be searching for one or making informed decisions about which one is best. There is currently no established microcredential marketing, no consistent proposition or labelling. This means that any marketing strategy needs to build awareness of microcredentials, create understanding of what they are, and help potential learners to understand their value. This needs to be done in the face of multiple competing visions of what microcredentials are.

Some microcredentials, such as the Relay/GSE 'Checking for Understanding Using Gestures', are extremely micro (four A4 pages), while others are substantial sections of master's degrees. Some offer academic credit; others do not. Some are considerably cheaper than other university study; some are more expensive, and some are eligible for government funding. Some are clearly aligned with industry or even run by multinational corporations, while others are only loosely linked with skills for employability. An analysis of 450 microcredentials by ClassCentral found little consistency, with estimates of cost and effort varying widely, and variability within each microcredential type as well as across types (Pickard 2018).

The platforms offering microcredentials do not significantly reduce the confusion because they have such a wide variety of offerings. Coursera offers MasterTrack certificates, professional certificates and university certificates alongside more conventional undergraduate and postgraduate degrees. FutureLearn offers short courses, expert tracks, microcredentials, and programmes alongside degrees (some of which are postgraduate certificates, rather than full degrees). edX offers MicroMasters, XSeries programmes, professional certificates, master's degree programmes and MicroBachelors programmes alongside its other courses.

The marketing team therefore needs to be clear what is on offer, how it is distinct from the myriad other courses on offer, and what value it offers learners. The strategic vision of the microcredentials initiative is important here because it can be used to shape marketing campaigns, emphasising aspects that the institution considers important. Microcredentials might be positioned, for example, as a gateway to wider learning opportunities; as a chance to gain skills prized by major employers; as a low-cost way of gaining high-quality education; or as a well-supported step up from using open educational resources and MOOCs.

Support roles

The main sources of support for learners on microcredentials will be their educators and mentors. However, like full-time university students, microcredential learners do not only require help with the academic side of their studies and so the microcredentials initiative must consider how their other needs will be supported and how the university's various support teams will be briefed to do this.

Online study necessarily involves queries about the use of information technologies (IT). Some learners will have basic technical needs due to lack of familiarity with the equipment they are using, outdated technology or operating systems, or limited internet connectivity. Others will regularly make use of the latest technology but only in a work or social context, so will struggle to navigate unfamiliar resources. More specifically, some will struggle to access the course, forget which email they have signed up with, fail to check their in-box for notifications, or lose their log-in details. Submitting assignments is a major stress point that is likely to produce a string of last-minute queries.

The **IT support team** needs to be aware of microcredentials, how they differ from other qualifications on offer in terms of their technical requirements, how many students are registered on them and when they can expect most queries (registration and submission dates). The team also needs to know where the responsibility lies for different types of query – with the institution or with the platform. Learners need contact details for technical support, otherwise they may bombard the institution's phone system and social media accounts with queries.

One option is to give microcredential learners a range of contacts, depending on the type of support they need. Another is to make use of centralised **student support** that learners can contact about a range of issues. This approach would cover financial support, payment issues, requests for refunds or deferrals, accessibility requests, and queries about the microcredential programme. Some learners will be in search of pastoral support, for example when mental or physical health issues impact on their studies (see Chapter 6). A clear decision is required as to whether that support will be provided.

A form of help that most university students take for granted is **library support** – helping them to find and make sense of resources, supporting the use of referencing software, and teaching information and study skills. More broadly, library support for students gives them access to a huge range of physical and online resources to which non-students have limited access because they are locked behind publisher paywalls.

Microcredential learners may not need access to library services – their course may be entirely stand-alone, with access negotiated in advance to any texts that they must access. In these cases, it is the educators who will need support from the library in suggesting relevant resources, dealing with rights access, and suggesting open educational resources (OER) that learners will be able to access. On the other hand, lack of library access can be a problem when designing postgraduate microcredentials, as postgraduate study requires learners to develop skills in finding and accessing information, as well as in carrying out their own research.

More broadly, these issues around support are linked with a decision the institution must make. Are these regular students who happen to be studying relatively short courses, or are they an entirely different group of microcredential learners? If they are students, then national quality assurance standards in some countries require them to be treated in the same way as other students, with access to all the associated wraparound services, including library access. These services come with a price attached, which increases the cost of the microcredential. On the other hand, if they are not regarded as students, quality assurance bodies will inquire how these learners can receive academic credit from a university, and learners who enrol on these credentials to test out whether university study is for them may gain an inaccurate understanding of the support that is available.

While the student/learner tension is a thread that runs through the whole microcredential initiative, the matter of library access is one of the places where it is most likely to surface. In some disciplines, a course that runs without library access is straightforward to run; in others, the prospect of running a course for academic credit on which learners have no access to journal papers, textbooks or book chapters is a challenging concept. The student/learner decision may therefore have an impact on which faculties are able to run microcredentials. On the other hand, it may prompt the institution to decide against offering academic credit and instead find a way of recognising microcredentials as evidence of prior achievement.

Decisions as to how microcredentials are recognised and accredited have career implications. As microcredentials are oriented towards starting a new job, gaining new skills or making a career change, careers advice is directly relevant to these learners. With international cohorts of learners, specific advice is difficult to provide. Nevertheless, links to job boards, recruitment sites or advice from those already working in the field can be incorporated. The institution's **careers advice** service will be well placed to help build this form of support into the microcredential offering.

Healy identifies four challenges for microcredentials learners that can be addressed by providing careers advisers to help those learners to build a cohesive career strategy that integrates microcredentials and expresses their value to potential employers:

> Firstly, microcredentials may not actually be necessary for the learner's particular goals. Secondly, learners may miscalculate the labour market demand for certain skills, or select microcredentials that do not meet explicit or implicit requirements for entry into their desired profession. Thirdly, reactive or anxious learners may accumulate microcredentials haphazardly, with little coherent purpose or strategic intent. Finally, learners may lack the job application skills needed to express the value of their microcredentials to employers or integrate them into a coherent employability narrative. (Healy 2021: 21–22)

The European Commission underlines the importance of careers guidance in this context: 'strategic career guidance could support the aims of inclusiveness in lifelong learning: individuals with lower levels of qualifications are more likely to need career guidance and are more at risk of losing their jobs due to automation' (European Commission 2020: 24). Some of this guidance can be provided by employers or by local and national employment offices, but there are also opportunities to build it into the overall microcredential offering.

Of course, the career and development opportunities offered by microcredentials are not confined to their learners. A new level of microcredential and a new set of learners open up employment opportunities within the educational institution itself. As this chapter makes clear, there are multiple internal roles that develop or emerge as the microcredentials initiative progresses. These will be supported by **human resources** work on setting up and amending contracts, recruiting and supporting staff, and providing appropriate training and development opportunities. The training needs are perhaps most acute for educators, who will be taking on a substantial amount of new work that is likely to differ significantly from their existing teaching commitments.

Educator roles

The importance of **educators** to microcredentials means their work is considered in several chapters of this book. Learning designers and the production team are covered in Chapter 5, the work of **data services** to support educators forms part of Chapter 9, and different aspects of educators' work form the basis of every chapter. Here, the focus is on the ways in which the roles of the educator change in the context of microcredentials.

This change is particularly evident for educators who normally teach in a face-to-face environment and have little experience of online education except for the emergency pivot to online teaching that was thrust upon them by the Covid-19 pandemic. Working on microcredentials is not the same as working with a group of students who would normally expect to be in physical proximity (for example, on campus or in a training room). It is a form of distance education, which functions in a different way.

Michael G. Moore has written extensively about distance education, which he has researched since the 1970s. In doing so, he has identified many roles that the educator takes on. These include: arranging for student creation of knowledge; supporting motivation, stimulating analysis and criticism; giving advice; and arranging practice, application, testing and evaluation (Moore 1993). At different times, he refers to the teacher as a:

> listener, contributor, person who deals with financial and administrative constraints, person who decides where teaching takes place, user of interactive video, provider of opportunities for dialogue, provider of appropriately structured learning materials, collaborator with design teams, collaborator with content experts, collaborator with instructional designers and collaborator with media specialists. (Papathoma, Littlejohn & Ferguson 2022)

A more recent set of teaching responsibilities compiled by Salmon and her colleagues (2017), in the context of MOOCs, extends the list. They include access and motivation, development, information exchange, knowledge construction and online socialisation. The list is extended by the responsibilities of learning mentors:

> enhancing connections between course participants, providing external links to relevant resources, building and deepening discussions, linking conversations, highlighting relevant conversations, encouraging reflection, encouraging responses, encouraging the development of external networks, and producing weekly reviews. (Papathoma, Littlejohn & Ferguson 2022)

In a face-to-face setting, most or all of these roles would be carried out by the same person. They are multiple different elements of the activity of teaching – elements that are so often combined it can be difficult to see them as separate activities. However, in a distance education setting such as microcredentials, it is helpful to disambiguate these roles, and to assign them to different people. Educators do not have to work individually, distributed one to each room in a training centre or campus. Instead, they can work together as a team. The work of designing a microcredential, presenting the material within it, supporting learners on the course, and providing feedback on assignments can be done by separate individuals.

Because the activities involved in teaching a microcredential are diverse, the teams involved in their production and presentation require diverse forms of expertise. Those involved need to be expert in the microcredential subject area, the related area of employment, microcredential design, presentation and editing of videos, legal requirements for using learning material and, ultimately, the pedagogy. Teaching on microcredentials, as with other courses on online platforms,

> involves activities that relate to administrative work (funding, allocating work to and managing different professionals), design and technical skills (video presentation and editing). These types of work and skills need to be combined with pedagogical decisions, and subject matter expertise. However, the subject matter expertise needs to be presented in new forms such as video-script writing and decisions about the use of appropriate resources (whether copyrighted or licensed under Creative Commons) are essential. (Papathoma, Littlejohn & Ferguson 2022)

Ultimately, teaching on a microcredential is about working as part of a team, recognising and drawing on the expertise of others. Narrowly defined, that team includes the **subject-matter experts**, **learning designers** and **mentors** who have the most traditional teaching roles. More broadly, it includes the **production team** and experts on **accessibility** and **rights** who make the microcredential possible. Overall, as this chapter has shown, it includes the project team, support roles and both outward-facing and internal-alignment work. The final part of the jigsaw is, of course, the focus of all this activity – the learners.

Microcredential learners

The role of the learner, and specifically of the online learner, is often presented simply as a consumer of content. Educators deliver content and learners digest it. This view is associated with an understanding of learning as the acquisition of facts or procedures, or simply as a process of memorisation (Richardson 2005) – an approach that has led to the production of many stultifyingly boring online courses that simply chain together a series of videos and require learners to watch these in sequence. As Chapter 2 on pedagogy and Chapter 5 on learning design show, learners need to play a much more active role in the learning process.

Their role can be extended to supporting the microcredentials initiative in a variety of ways. Learners can play a major part in the evaluation of microcredentials. Their activity and their performance provide some measures of the success of these courses, and this basic quantitative data can be supplemented by surveys, interviews and focus groups. Learners can be recruited as consultants when developing new microcredentials, and can support the revision of microcredentials that have already run, ensuring they remain up to date and relevant to the world of work.

Although the focus of microcredentials is on the course and learning, there is more to higher education than the classroom experience. Students form communities; they socialise; they join the students' union or students' association. When they leave, they often support the institution as alumni. Apprentices forge links with each other; they go out and they form groups. This social interaction is currently missing from the majority of microcredentials but would support their strategic aims in many cases. If microcredentials are regarded as a gateway to higher education, increasing social interaction would help to provide a more representative introduction. If microcredentials are to be stacked or used to build into a qualification, then social interaction between registration periods keeps learners engaged with the institution and reduces the need for re-recruitment. Learners who know each other outside their course may be more confident about engaging in the collaborative work required on many employment-focused microcredentials.

Some microcredentials learners certainly seek to stay in touch with each other once the course is finished. This work can be left to individuals and to social media but some institutions will see benefits in shaping and developing these interactions.

Conclusion

The roles described in this chapter show that a successful microcredentials initiative requires teamwork from across the institution, or a well-resourced unit that can draw on a range of expertise. Motivation and support of staff to engage in the development and provision of microcredentials is key to the success of the initiative. It is important to recognise that these courses are not simply another addition to the prospectus. They require change throughout the institution, and a shared sense of purpose relating to the strategy that drives them.

References

Adams, S. (2021). *Online education provider Coursera is worth $7 billion after going public* (1 April). *Forbes*. Available at https://www.forbes.com/sites/susanadams/2021/04/01/online-education-provider-coursera-is-worth-7-billion-after-going-public

Ahmat, N. H. C. A., Bashir, M. A. A., Razali, A. R. and Kasolang, S. (2021). Micro-credentials in higher education institutions: Challenges and opportunities. *Asian Journal of University Education*, 17(3): 281–290.

Andrei, B.-A., Casu-Pop, A.-C., Gheorghe, S.-C. and Boiagiu, C.-A. (2019). A study on using waterfall and agile methods in software project management. *Journal of Information Systems & Operations Management*, 13(1): 125–135.

Christensen, C. M. (1997). *The innovator's dilemma: When new technologies cause great firms to fail*. Boston: Harvard Business Press.

Christensen, C. M., Johnson, C. W. and Horn, M. B. (2008). *Disrupting class: How disruptive innovation will change the way the world learns*. McGraw-Hill.

Duklas, J. (2020). *Micro-credentials: Trends in credit transfer and credentialing*. British Columbia Council on Admissions and Transfer. Available at https://eric.ed.gov/?id=ED610420

European Commission. (2020). *A European approach to micro-credentials – Output of the Micro-credentials Higher Education Consultation Group – final report*. Available at https://education.ec.europa.eu/sites/default/files/document-library-docs/european-approach-micro-credentials-higher-education-consultation-group-output-final-report.pdf

Government of South Australia. (2020). *Micro-credentials in South Australia. Consultation outcomes report.* Available at https://www.voced.edu.au/content/ngv%3A89032

Healy, M. (2021). Microcredential learners need quality careers and employability support. *Journal of Teaching and Learning for Graduate Employability*, 12(1): 21–23.

HESA. (2000). *HESA collections.* Available at https://www.hesa.ac.uk/collection/c20051/index

Moore, M. G. (1993). Theory of transactional distance. In: Keegan, D. *Theoretical principles of distance education.* London and New York: Routledge. pp. 22–38.

Oliver, B. (2019). *Making micro-credentials Work for Learners, Employers and Providers.* Melbourne: Deakin University. Available at https://dteach.deakin.edu.au/wp-content/uploads/sites/103/2019/08/Making-micro-credentials-work-Oliver-Deakin-2019-full-report.pdf

Papathoma, T., Littlejohn, A. and Ferguson, R. (2022). Effective digital higher education. Who are the educators? In: Varga-Atkins, T., Sharpe, R. and Bennett, S. *Handbook for digital higher education.* Cheltenham: Edward Elgar.

Pickard, L. (2018). *Analysis of 450 MOOC-based microcredentials reveals many options but little consistency* (18 July). Available at https://www.classcentral.com/report/moocs-microcredentials-analysis-2018

Richardson, J. T. E. (2005). Students' approaches to learning and teachers' approaches to teaching in higher education. *Educational Psychology*, 25(6): 673–680.

Rossiter, D. and Tynan, B. (2019). *Designing and implementing micro-credentials: A guide for practitioners.* Commonwealth of Learning. Available at https://oasis.col.org/items/e2d0be25-cbbb-441f-b431-42f74f715532

Salmon, G., Pechenkina, E., Chase, A-M. and Ross, B. (2017). Designing massive open online courses to take account of participant motivations and expectations. *British Journal of Educational Technology*, 48(6): 1284–1294.

Shaw, J. (2021). *Harvard and MIT to sell edX for $800 Million* (29 June). Available at https://www.careereducationreview.net/2021/06/harvard-and-mit-to-sell-edx-for-800-million-harvard-magazine

Weller, M. (2014). *The battle for open: How openness won and why it doesn't feel like victory.* London: Ubiquity Press.

Wilson, H. and Hay, M. (2018). *Using microcredentials to enable the use of the NZDE (civil) to provide more flexible and focused response to industry requirements.* Available at https://www.researchbank.ac.nz/handle/10652/4597

Young, J. R. (2016). *Degrees of the future – and what's at stake for students* (3 November). Available at https://www.edsurge.com/news/2016-11-03-why-udacity-and-edx-want-to-trademark-the-degrees-of-the-future-and-what-s-at-stake-for-students

Young, M. (2020). *Thompson Rivers University takes lead role in global education accessibility* (9 June). Available at https://inside.tru.ca/releases/thompson-rivers-university-takes-lead-role-in-global-education-accessibility

CHAPTER 4

Planning your first microcredentials

A variety of processes and frameworks have been developed to help with the development of a microcredentials programme. These range from national guidelines to personal experiences, and each of them draws attention to aspects that should be taken into account, beginning with a consideration of the benefits of microcredentials for an educational institution and its learners. The chapter ends with a series of examples from around the world, focusing on the decisions that were made and the processes followed in each case.

How to cite this book chapter:
Ferguson, R. and Whitelock, D. 2024. Planning your first microcredentials. In: Ferguson, R. and Whitelock, D. *Microcredentials for Excellence: A Practical Guide*. Pp. 83–109. London: Ubiquity Press. DOI: https://doi.org/10.5334/bcz.d. License: CC BY-NC 4.0

Why microcredentials?

As previous chapters have made clear, the definition, role and scope of microcredentials are not yet fixed. Even in cases such as the European Union, where a definition has been developed and shared widely, it only applies in a limited number of countries and contexts. In addition, it is unlikely to be well known outside an educational setting. For example, although Colleges and Institutes Canada launched a national framework for microcredentials in 2021 (CICan 2021), research in the same year (Pichette et al. 2021) found that the majority of employers in the country were not aware of the term 'microcredential' and only 10% had a good understanding of the term.

A decision that has to be made early on is therefore what type(s) of microcredential will be developed, and what their purpose will be. 'Understanding the strategic intent will help you describe the benefits to your stakeholders, particularly to key players such as the credential earners and the reviewers or consumers of the credentials (e.g., employers and other educational institutions)' (Rossiter & Tynan 2019: 4). Different stakeholders have different needs.

> The learner wants short, practical, and up-to-date courses for their chosen career path, education institutions emphasise accreditation for building trust, employers want clarity regarding the competencies gained through micro-credentials, and government bodies expect higher graduate employability with lower tuition fees. (Varadarajan, Koh & Daniel 2023: 1).

Strategic intent might be defined in terms of national expectations about the types of curriculum and qualification that will be offered, in terms of the aims and values of the institution, or in terms of the needs and wishes of learners. Oliver (2019: 30) identifies seven types of microcredential that lead to certification, each with a different purpose.

- **Qualifying pathway:** providing a method of accessing a degree programme.
- **Granular certification of competencies within a degree:** providing data points within a degree programme.
- **Certification of experience:** mapping experience gained outside formal education against defined standards of achievement.
- **Certification of technical expertise:** providing evidence of expertise in a technical skill such as use of a specific software program.
- **Certification of complementary or additional expertise:** providing evidence of expertise that extends an individual's skillset.
- **Certification of skills update:** extending or updating an existing professional skillset.
- **Certification of personal development or personal attributes:** providing evidence of expertise in an area of personal development.

Pichette and her colleagues (2021: 8) present a different typology, which covers the mode of delivery, flexibility, student/instructor interaction, the form the credential takes (paper or digital), and the indicator of achievement. They identify four main types of microcredential: pathways to a formal qualification, updates for previous qualifications, an opportunity to gain technical skills, and an opportunity to develop transferable skills.

Both classification systems view microcredentials from the perspective of the HEI that offers them. Another approach is to work with regional government and major employers to identify local needs for skills development. This allows microcredentials to be:

> used as a dynamic response to local priorities and labour market needs – helping to streamline processes of upskilling, while making progress more tangible. Individuals gain valuable micro-credentials that demonstrate their learning, while managers and organisations can better measure the impact of workforce development activity. (Hudak & Camilleri 2018: 21)

One example of employers playing a leading role in the development of microcredentials is the Department of Education in Tennessee, USA. In 2015, the department set targets to be achieved in the following five years. An issue at the time was that 'most teachers across the state report that they are provided with inadequate resources for collaboration and professional improvement' (Tennessee Department of Education 2015: 16). The department therefore planned for the development of more effective, personalised professional learning. Microcredentials formed part of that programme and, following a pilot, the department linked microcredentials to the state's licensure advancement system, with the expectation that around a quarter of new teachers would use these courses alongside more traditional routes for career advancement (Berry, Airhart & Byrd 2016). By 2019, almost 800 educators from 25 school districts across the state were enrolled in the microcredential pilot. In addition, another nine US state education agencies were running official microcredential pilots, with five more states also experimenting with microcredentials (Berry & Byrd 2019).

Large-scale and national models

These examples of educator training in the USA indicate an increasing need for microcredentials to be integrated within national structures and frameworks. This is considered in more detail in Chapter 8, which deals with quality and evaluation. From the perspective of setting up a microcredentials programme, *The Microcredential Users' Guide*, produced by the MicroHE Consortium (Hudak & Camilleri 2018: 21–22), identifies five ways in which microcredentials can be incorporated within a wider recognition system. The focus of the guide is on higher education but the five approaches could, in principle, be used at any educational level.

1. **Microcredentials for credit transfer.** Institutions include specified microcredentials offered by other institutions as courses that can be taken for optional credits. This provides students with opportunities to gain international perspectives on a subject, or to access specialist knowledge that is not available within their home institution.
2. **Joint offers.** A consortium of institutions develops a portfolio of microcredentials that can be used to gain a larger qualification. All the courses within this portfolio are quality-assured by national agencies, and the resulting qualification is recognised by all institutions within the consortium as one that they have accredited.
3. **Clearinghouse model.** A single organisation, such as a MOOC platform, is used to host courses, build programmes and award microcredentials. This reduces the bureaucracy associated with the creation of agreements between institutions but, unless the chosen organisation is recognised as a high-quality provider of education or training, the programmes and microcredentials may be regarded by learners as low in status.
4. **National qualification frameworks.** If these frameworks are expanded to recognise microcredentials then these courses gain recognised status as well as a clear

relationship to other qualifications. This means they can be used both nationally and internationally for purposes of admission and progression. Work is already being carried out in several countries to include microcredentials within national frameworks.

5. **Recognition of non-formal learning.** Microcredentials from other institutions are not recognised by the institution where the student is enrolled. However, students can choose to have their learning on these courses assessed by their home institution. Although this superficially sounds straightforward, it creates a significant administrative and teaching burden for the home institution, which would need to provide, quality-assure and grade courses for individual learners.

Microcredentials for learners

The perspectives on microcredential production introduced above begin with the requirements of large organisations and governments. However, the perspectives of learners are also crucial. For example, microcredential programmes have been shown to have a positive relationship with students' perceived employability (Zou et al. 2023). They also develop learners' knowledge and skills, change their thinking about the subject studied and may enable a career change or provide the confidence to go on to further study (Chandler & Perryman 2023). One way of considering learner views is to consider what a short, skills-focused, accredited course has to offer for students. Another is to take a pedagogic perspective and to consider how the affordances of this type of course can be used to support student learning.

Oliver (2021) suggests that the value to a learner of a microcredential is equal to the benefits gained by that individual minus the costs incurred. She identifies four elements – motivation, education, circumstances and preferences – that are likely to influence learner perceptions of the value of a microcredential or, more broadly, of any credential. Motivations include seeking to credential existing or new skills, or an interest in gaining a credential either for personal interest or to enter or progress in a career. Educational considerations will include previous qualifications and life experience, the quality of past educational experiences, and the prerequisites for the credential. Circumstances relate to life and career stage, availability of resources to support study, ability to engage with the course, and any competing obligations, while preferences relate to course specifics such as mode of delivery, collaborative/individual approaches, or assessment type (Oliver 2021: Table 1).

Oliver's Micro-credential Learner Value Framework (2021: Table 2) provides a way of understanding the possible value of a microcredential for learners who are studying either for career advantage or for personal interest. The costs to learners relate to money and time. How much is the course and when is payment due? How much travel and effort will be required, and could this time and money be better spent in another way? Benefits cover a wider range of considerations, including:

- **Outcomes:** what knowledge and skills will be acquired, and what could these gain for the learner?
- **Certification:** what form does this take, is it widely recognised and verifiable?
- **Signalling power:** how are the platform and the provider regarded?

- **Interoperability:** does the course lead to other microcredentials or qualifications?
- **Quality and standards:** is the course accredited, quality-assured and recognised by potential employers or other institutions?
- **Assessment and feedback:** how are these carried out, to what standard, who assesses work, and is formative feedback available?
- **Engagement:** are there opportunities for meaningful feedback with educators, peers or industry?
- **Convenience:** are there flexible alternatives for engagement either online or offline?

The Learner Value Framework takes into account the ways in which learners make decisions about which qualifications to register for and which courses to take in order to complete those qualifications successfully. Another, very different, way of thinking about the production of microcredentials from a learner perspective is to start with the pedagogy. This approach begins with an understanding of how and why learning takes place and identifies how microcredentials can be used to support those processes.

Authors based at Brigham Young University and the University of Memphis (West et al. 2020) took as a starting point the increasing need for learners to become proficient at problem-solving. This, in turn, requires proficiency in argumentation, question-generation and decision-making. West and his colleagues point to the benefits of inquiry-based instruction for developing these skills because it 'emphasizes open investigations of authentic problem scenarios in a student-centered and collaborative learning classroom context' (Ku et al. 2014: 253), as well as goal-directed behaviour, causal reasoning, decision-making, motivation and self-efficacy. They also identify significant issues with implementing inquiry-based instruction: first, it is difficult to provide appropriate problems for novices with little domain knowledge and, second, ill-structured problems with no prescribed answer are difficult to assess.

West and his colleagues (2020) propose that microcredentials offer a way of addressing these issues. They argue that microlearning can motivate students to acquire both skills and domain knowledge, that micro courses offer students opportunities to build competence in areas where they are weak, and that because microcredentials are usually digital and therefore data rich, they:

> contain a wide variety of information about what the learner accomplished, including rubrics and criteria for earning the credential and endorsements from people who observed them. These affordances can provide powerful support for assessment and feedback of the student. (West et al. 2020: 829)

In particular, West and his colleagues (2020) focus on the possibilities of open microcredentials – short courses that provide learners with the knowledge and skills to gain a digital badge. Although the distinctions between digital badges and microcredentials are becoming increasingly clear, a powerful argument for digital badges has always been that use of a single technical standard by many providers means the badges are portable and so learners can assemble 'backpacks' including evidence of their abilities that is validated by multiple organisations. As courses leading to digital badges are often very short, they can be used by learners to help them prepare for a more extensive problem-solving activity.

Overall, microcredentials can facilitate inquiry-based instruction by:

> (1) facilitating how learners gain prerequisite knowledge for problem solving, (2) establishing flexible criteria

for learning and accepting flexible forms of evidence of that learning, (3) utilizing learning pathways to provide pre-approved choices for self-directed learning, and (4) creating new opportunities for learning recognition, including empowering learners to describe and claim credit for their own learning. (West et al. 2020, 835)

As well as making a pedagogic case for microcredentials, West and his colleagues (2020) briefly describe their process of developing open microcredentials. This differs significantly from other approaches described in this chapter, because they allowed students to develop their own microcredentials if a suitable one was not already available. The process for doing this was supported and scaffolded (Randall, Farmer & West 2019) and students had access to existing open microcredentials, which provided examples of high-quality projects and assessments. Students developing open microcredentials had to research the skill to be developed, draft a list of criteria that would demonstrate the skill had been developed, and then provide evidence of meeting those criteria. Quality control was provided by educators, who had to give final approval for these credentials. When educational experts later reviewed the rubrics for open microcredentials, they found that those created by learners were stronger than those created by educators.

Experiences of developing microcredentials

In most cases, though, microcredentials are produced by educators, usually working alongside other professionals. Before they begin work, the first step should be for an institution to decide to set up a microcredentials programme and to assemble a business case that underpins that decision. This is not as straightforward as it sounds. A survey of 105 post-secondary institutions in Canada found that, although 83% of those taking the survey reported that leaders at their institution were encouraging the development of microcredentials, less than 40% had a framework or strategy to guide them (Pichette et al. 2021).

Five key questions need to be answered before an institution begins to develop microcredentials:

- How do you strategically position them?
- What type of institutional leadership is required?
- What type of internal structures are required?
- What type of business model(s) are required?
- What could possibly go wrong? (Brown, McGreal & Peters 2023)

Only once those questions have been answered should there be a shift from high-level strategic decision-making to the nuts and bolts of designing and producing a course.

The following five examples are based on published accounts of how different organisations and teams have worked through the process. The following chapter will examine in more detail how this planning is put into practice.

Example 1: Microcredentials for a university – Malaysia

The Education Blueprint for Higher Education in Malaysia from 2015–2025 (Ministry of Education Malaysia 2015) did not explicitly mention microcredentials but it did set out principles that aligned well with them. These included calls for enhancements to technical and vocational education and training (TVET); intensified industry and community engagement; a framework for recognising prior learning; and enhancement of lifelong learning and online learning structures.

In this context, MARA Technological University (UiTM), the largest public university in the country, began work in 2019 to develop microcredentials and to initiate a distinctively Malaysian approach to these courses. Work began before the Malaysian government had produced full guidelines for good practices on microcredentials (MQA 2020). Although an initial guideline on micro-credentials was available at the time (MQA 2019), the advice within it was relatively limited.

Following an initial seminar to spark interest and create awareness, the university selected educators who had already been involved in the design of online courses and trained them to develop module materials and learning materials for microcredentials. Ahmat and her colleagues investigated the challenges and opportunities of microcredentials and set out the linear process followed by the university to develop them (Ahmat et al. 2021: Fig. 1). This process began with discussion, listing of potential microcredentials, and collection of materials and information. Before micro-credentials went live, they went through six development stages:

1. analysis
2. development of an instructional design document
3. script development
4. prototype development
5. development of learning management system (LMS)
6. test-run.

Once modules had been implemented, feedback was gathered and used to make improvements. Evaluation showed that the programme's success depended on several factors, including multiple stakeholders, government support, guidelines from the national qualifications agency, the marketing department, IT support, regular training, and systematic review processes (Ahmat et al. 2021).

Example 2: Microcredentials for a sector – USA

Digital Promise is a US non-profit, created with a mission to accelerate innovation in education in order to improve opportunities to learn. The organisation sees the potential of microcredentials to provide educators with:

> competency-based, on-demand, personalized, and shareable opportunities to demonstrate and be recognized for their professional learning. It's a sea change from oftentimes ineffective, traditional 'drive-by' professional development that educators experience all too commonly. (Brown 2019: 2)

By 2023, 10 US states had recognised microcredentials as a valid form of professional development for teachers to use to renew their certification (Digital Promise 2023). Since 2013, Digital Promise has been supporting this work through research, creating courses and stewarding a microcredentials ecosystem that includes hundreds of courses.

The process of developing a microcredential for this ecosystem begins when Digital Promise screens prospective issuers, looking at the ways in which their work is grounded in research. For example, the Global Financial Literacy Excellence Center developed courses that could fill the gaps in knowledge identified by its research, and the Center for Collaborative Education expanded access to its research-backed resources by running microcredentials (Brown 2019).

Before work begins on a microcredential, the issuing organisation is asked to respond to five key questions:

1. What competencies are important to educators?
2. Is the competency demonstrable?
3. What does the research suggest?
4. Once a competency has been isolated, how much evidence is the right amount of evidence, what evidence is appropriate, and how would an educator demonstrate the competency? What evidence would indicate a successful demonstration of competency?
5. What other related competencies would an educator demonstrate while they are demonstrating the selected competency? (Brady 2021)

Answering these questions thoughtfully enables an organisation to articulate a vision for microcredentials that is clear and of a high quality.

Issuers are then asked to draft microcredentials using the Digital Promise template. This covers:

- title
- competency
- key method
- method components
- supporting rationale and research
- resources
- submission guidelines and criteria
    - part 1: overview questions
    - part 2: work examples/artifacts/evidence and scoring guide
    - part 3: reflection (optional).

All research cited in the microcredentials is required to be relevant, current and openly accessible.

Digital Promise microcredentials also go through an extensive validation and evaluation process. This begins while a microcredential is being developed. Educators and experts are asked for feedback on questions and rubrics to check that questions are clear and aligned with the construct specified. When the course is running, the first 50 submissions are used as part of the validation process. Each is graded by two or more independent evaluators with an in-depth knowledge of the subject area. The grades for these 50 are then checked by a third evaluator for inter-rater reliability and the rubric is only validated if there is at least 80% agreement. If not, the rubric is investigated and clarified (Brown 2019).

Example 3: Microcredentials for a subject area – USA

Brigham Young University in the USA needed training and credentials that could help pre-service and in-service teachers become competent in teaching coding and computational thinking to young learners. Hunsaker and West documented the process of developing a microcredential that could meet this need and published their work as a detailed design case in a 16-page paper that 'outlines the project from analysis through design and development and on to pilot testing and evaluation' (Hunsaker & West 2020: 8). They noted that the project emphasised the importance of interdisciplinary collaboration. When staff from different fields began to talk to each other, 'deep and recurring collaboration among these groups strengthened the design immensely' (Hunsaker & West 2020: 15).

Early conversations among key stakeholders identified the primary audience for the project – the groups who would become the microcredential learners – as well as goals and considerations. These included material to be covered, approaches to pedagogy, development of a learning pathway that would guide learners to appropriate material, and alignment with existing university practices.

Once priorities had been developed, the designer carried out a literature review, constructed a content model and carried out a needs assessment. The literature review placed the training within the broader context of computer science education, explored developmentally appropriate practices for teaching the subject to children aged four to 12, and identified the pedagogic and technical competencies teachers would require to teach these age groups. The content model used mind-mapping software to summarise content that would need to be presented to teachers studying the module, and would then have to be assessed. This model was checked and refined by subject-matter experts and was used to identify learning outcomes. Finally, a needs assessment was carried out using a survey and interviews to establish the content would be relevant to teachers and was not covered in other courses they were studying.

The next stage was to design the microcredential. This process began with the learning outcomes and project purpose. A project summary identified key elements to be developed: four open badges; tutorials preparing learners to complete the badge requirements successfully; tutorials and job aids to support the use of robots; different learning paths for early-childhood education (ECE) and elementary teachers; and a website providing public access to learning materials.

Design processes for each of these elements were different but the process used for the digital badges provides an indication of what was involved. Building on what had been learned from the literature review and needs analysis, the team moved on to the first stage: conceptualisation. This involved identifying elements to be included in badges and tutorials, and then creating a template for both. The second stage, badge strategy, included deciding which badges would be created and the scope of each; making technical decisions; and considering a plan for maintenance. The third stage, drafting, not only produced initial versions of the badges and supporting material but also built in research-based learning strategies and produced images for the badges. The final stage, formative evaluation and revision, involved checking materials with a subject-matter expert, asking learners to review the materials, and making changes to improve learner experience.

The design process was followed by product implementation, when the materials were first used with the teachers who were to learn from them. This involved the course instructors but also the product designer, who met with the instructors pre-launch, participated in one lesson as a guest lecturer, and observed another class.

The final element of development was design evaluation, a summative process that addressed two questions: 'Did learners become competent in the intended learning outcomes?' and 'How effective did learners perceive the intervention support materials to be?' (Hunsaker & West 2020: 14). Data was collected about scores obtained on the badges, and data from a post-instruction survey was compared with that from a pre-instruction survey.

Example 4: Microcredentials for a profession – Australia

In Australia, as pressure to meet the various needs of diverse learners has increased, the need for teachers at all career stages to engage in further study has risen. In some states and territories, teachers must now provide evidence that they have spent a set amount of time on professional learning in order to keep their registration current. There is an increasing need for professional learning opportunities that fit with teachers' schedules and that can support online communities of practice.

In this context, Queensland University of Technology (QUT) began to develop a suite of microcredentials that would provide comprehensive support for the professional development of teachers in Australia. This built on Oliver's work on microcredentials (2016; 2019) and created a set of learning pathways made up of courses at Australian Qualification Framework Level 8 (graduate certificate or diploma level) that led into existing postgraduate courses.

White (2021) carried out a descriptive case study of this process, investigating how these microcredentials were developed and which design frameworks were used. Phases of the work to which she drew attention included:

- interrogating ecosystem factors
- building a learning pathway framework
- creating learning design features
- building a local/global community of practice
- ensuring work-integrated learning and assessment.

The first stage, interrogating the ecosystem, involved the development of a clear vision of the nature of learning, taking into account previous work on tools used for online learning (for example, Conole & Alevizou 2010).

> A range of ecosystem factors were considered, including building the learning pathway framework; creating the learning design features; enabling a local/global community of practice for teachers and ensuring

> work-integrated assessment tied to 'real world' cases or scenarios. Data analytics helped lead to continuous improvement. (White 2021: 703)

The learning pathway framework was developed to give teachers flexibility in how much they engaged, as well as the ability to build towards an accredited award. The learning pathways could be followed in order to work towards a graduate certificate or a master of education qualification but there were also multiple exit points for teachers who were not seeking a full postgraduate qualification. A two-hour MOOC on the FutureLearn platform provided a free introduction; a 13-hour module studied on the university's Blackboard platform came with a cost but also awarded a QUT certificate of completion; while a 62-hour module + assessment was more expensive and also awarded a QUT certificate of completion. Bundled together, the 75 study hours totalled six unit credits that could be put together to form a postgraduate qualification. Each course was open for an extended period of time, so that teachers had flexibility about when, and for how long, they engaged. Once this framework had been developed, it had to be endorsed by the accreditation and quality assurance departments of the university.

While the endorsement process was underway, academics, learning designers and technologists were working together to develop each of the features in the learning pathways. An active pedagogy was selected that would enable learners to do more than passively consume content. The aim was to instil both curiosity and creativity. There were also decisions to be made about the focus of each course, and these were made based on key areas of need for teachers, as well as expertise within the university. Overall, the learning design enabled teachers to go further with their learning by exploring different subject areas, or to go deeper by investigating a single area in more detail.

A benefit of the online design was that teachers on the learning pathways could contact others not just in their local area but also across Australia and internationally. This was a particular benefit for teachers working in rural, regional or otherwise remote areas. Several features were built into the modules to encourage peer learning and help build a community of practice. These 'included games, quizzes, blogs, vlogs, discussion boards, Padlet polls and discussion spaces and the potential for teachers to share their own resources and lessons' (White 2021: 706). Content experts and learning designers worked together to build courses that made full use of the potential of online study.

The module + assessment element of the learning pathway made it possible to earn academic credit for studying these courses. For that reason, they were not badged like the courses in Example 3 above but instead included more traditional summative assessment, marked by subject-matter experts. The award of academic credit meant that teachers could continue their learning pathway by enrolling for a full qualification.

Example 5: Microcredentials to support students – Australia

The microcredentials programme at the Royal Melbourne Institute of Technology (RMIT) was developed as a response to industry, government and university reports identifying the need for certification of skills gained through alternatives to traditional university study (Ponte & Saray 2019). The choice of microcredentials that make up the programme was influenced by Oliver's work, including her observation that '[d]emand for higher cognitive skills (creativity, critical thinking, complex information processing) is predicted to increase' (Oliver 2019: 1).

The university set up the RMIT Creds team, which collaborated with industry partners and key groups within the university to develop microcredentials that could be used to fill skills gaps. This collaboration included ideation workshops, which provided safe spaces to openly discuss and share ideas, as well as regular development meetings to ensure that content was both current and relevant.

An early initiative was a partnership with the university library to develop a series of microcredentials aligned with library resources. One of these was the information literacy credential, the foundation for a series of stackable microcredentials that enabled students to develop and evidence 'skills in planning, writing, using data, understanding and identifying emerging technologies, repurposing and sharing digital content, creating digital artefacts and writing for digital environments' (Ponte & Saray 2019: 547).

With the university committed to microcredentials, and the library/Creds team partnership in place, the process of developing the microcredential began with a concept brief. This was followed by a product proposal that fleshed out the original idea, identifying industry partners, target audience, skills to be developed, and learning outcomes that students would be supported to achieve. The structure of the microcredential was aligned with the JISC Digital Literacy Framework (see, for example, JISC 2022). Once complete, the proposal went to a central governing body of the university for approval.

Once approved, over an eight-week development period a learning designer drove discussion and creation of the microcredential. Library staff self-nominated to contribute to designing, writing, resourcing and referencing the course. The microcredential framework and structure were discussed at weekly meetings, where tasks for the coming week were identified and allocated (Ponte & Saray 2019).

Since the microcredential was launched, it has been reviewed from a pedagogical and functional perspective every 12 to 18 months by the library, the Creds team and industry partners with the support of the learning designer. Assessments and rubrics are reviewed in relation to stated learning outcomes; design features and content are critiqued; analytics considered; and student feedback gathered. A competitor review has also been carried out, based on literature and websites, to investigate how other Australian universities are teaching information literacy (Ponte & Saray 2019).

Following the microcredential's first review, it was rewritten as a new microcredential. The new version updated around two thirds of the original course content and included a new set of learning outcomes. The pedagogy was changed to include more opportunities for authentic learning that students could apply in their other courses. The credits associated with the course were increased, and the focus was shifted away from information literacy within education and towards the application of information literacy within a professional setting. The course was also added to the university's learning management system, where it could be embedded into different academic programmes (Ponte & Saray 2019).

Learning from examples

The five examples above identify structured processes that organisations and individuals have approached from different perspectives. Viewed together, there are five main stages represented in these accounts.

Gathering support. Although the published descriptions of some of the examples above begin after this stage, it is clear that there is preliminary work to be done in engaging and enthusing potential stakeholders. As noted in Chapter 3, relevant stakeholders are likely to include not only subject-matter experts and learning designers but also managers and those responsible for quality assurance, internal policy, certification, IT support, internal communications, student registration, student finance, and marketing.

Discussion and collaboration. In most cases, a great deal of work is done before work starts on an individual microcredential. This may include research and analysis, including reference to local and national guidelines and standards. Internal collaborations must be established as well as links, where appropriate, with external organisations such as employers and professional bodies. The team producing the microcredential needs to be clear who the potential learners are, what needs the microcredential could meet for those learners, what value it offers those learners, and which competencies they need to develop. Staff who have not worked on a microcredential before are likely to require training during this phase or the next.

Design and development includes both learning design and development of platform and resources. Learning outcomes and competencies must be aligned with content, activities, assessment and certification/digital badges. The pedagogic approach needs to take advantage of the affordances of online study (such as asynchronous study, global reach, experienced fellow learners, and time for reflection) and should take into account the needs and expectations of learners. Technical development may involve the construction of sites and discussion areas, providing links to external tools and resources, and making connections with existing systems such as registration and assessment.

Implementation is the phase all this work leads up to. Learners access the microcredential during this phase, and support staff in different departments across the university need to be aware of and prepared for the start of the course. Depending on the institution offering the microcredential, there may be calls on facilitators and mentors, assessment teams, wider student support, registration and finance teams, librarians, IT support and career advisers, as well as the staff who have worked on course development.

Evaluation and improvement. Although this phase is listed last here, the examples above make it clear that this process starts early with test runs, pilots and prototypes. Feedback can be gathered at any stage in the process, and a formal evaluation plan may also be in place. Crucially, this work needs to feed into improvements, looping back through the development cycle to ensure that evaluation outcomes and feedback are acted on.

Conclusion

Microcredentials take many forms and are developed and studied for multiple reasons. There is no one-size-fits-all approach to planning and development. Nevertheless, work and research on them is now sufficiently advanced for some well-established patterns and frameworks to have been developed and documented so others can use them. The five examples summarised in this chapter each provide a model that can be used in other contexts. The next chapter takes an in-depth look at the process of microcredential design and production at The Open University, a large distance university in the UK, with long-term expertise in providing online education at undergraduate and postgraduate levels.

References

Ahmat, N. H. C. A., Bashir, M. A. A., Razali., A. R. and Kasolang, S. (2021). Micro-credentials in higher education institutions: Challenges and opportunities. *Asian Journal of University Education*, 17(3): 281–290.

Berry, B., Airhart, K. M. and Byrd, P. A. (2016). Microcredentials: Teacher learning transformed. *Phi Delta Kappan*, 98(3): 34–40.

Berry, B. and Byrd, P. A. (2019). *Micro-credentials and education policy in the United States*. Available at https://digitalpromise.org/wp-content/uploads/2019/06/mcs-educationpolicy.pdf

Brady, D. (2021). *Microcredential mania: Opportunities and challenges*. Available at https://sway.office.com/Z9GVVw2AjPlIUwYW?accessible=true

Brown, D. (2019). *Research and educator micro-credentials*. Available at https://digitalpromise.org/wp-content/uploads/2019/02/researchandeducatormicrocredentials-v1r2.pdf

Brown, M., McGreal, R. and Peters, M. (2023). A strategic institutional response to micro-credentials: Key questions for educational leaders. *Journal of Interactive Media in Education*, 2023(1).

Chandler, K. and Perryman, L.-A. (2023). 'People have started calling me an expert': The impact of Open University microcredential courses. *Journal of Interactive Media in Education*, 2023(1), Article 8. DOI: https://doi.org/10.5334/jime.804

CICan. (2021). *National Framework for Microcredentials*. Available at https://www.collegesinstitutes.ca/colleges-and-institutes-in-your-community/benefit-college-institute-credential/national-framework-for-microcredentials

Conole, G. and Alevizou, G. (2010). *A literature review of the use of Web 2.0 tools in higher education. A report commissioned by the Higher Education Academy*. Available at https://issuu.com/gfbertini/docs/a_literature_review_of_the_use_of_web_2.0_tools_in

Digital Promise. (2023). *Digital promise micro-credentials for recertification*. Available at https://digitalpromise.org/initiative/educator-micro-credentials/digital-promise-micro-credentials-for-recertification

Hudak, R. and Camilleri, A. F. (2018). *The micro-credential users' guide*. Available at https://knowledgeinnovation.eu/publication/the-micro-credential-users-guide

Hunsaker, E. and West, R. E. (2020). Designing computational thinking and coding badges for early childhood educators. *TechTrends*, 64(1), 7–16.

JISC. (2022). *Higher education (HE) student profile: Six elements of digital capabilities*. Available at https://digitalcapability.jisc.ac.uk/what-is-digital-capability/individual-digital-capabilities

Ku, K. Y. L., Ho, I. T., Hau, K.-T. and Lai, E. C. M. (2014). Integrating direct and inquiry-based instruction in the teaching of critical thinking: An intervention study. *Instructional Science*, 42: 251–269.

Ministry of Education Malaysia. (2015). *Executive summary Malaysia education blueprint 2015–2025 (higher education)*. Available at https://jpt.mohe.gov.my/portal/index.php/en/corporate/policy-document/16-malaysia-education-development-plan-2015-2025

MQA. (2019). *Guideline on micro-credential*. Available at http://hea.uum.edu.my/images/2021/03/GARIS_PANDUAN_MICRO_CREDENTIALS_25OCT.pdf

MQA. (2020). *Guidelines to good practices: Micro-credentials*. Available at https://www2.mqa.gov.my/qad/v2/garispanduan/2020/GGP%20Micro-credentials%20July%202020.pdf

Oliver, B. (2016). *Better 21C credentials: Evaluating the promise, perils and disruptive potential of digital credentials*. Available at https://ltr.edu.au/vufind/Record/365528/Description

Oliver, B. (2019). *Making micro-credentials work for learners, employers and providers*. Melbourne: Deakin University. Available at https://dteach.deakin.edu.au/wp-content/uploads/sites/103/2019/08/Making-micro-credentials-work-Oliver-Deakin-2019-full-report.pdf

Oliver, B. (2021). Micro-credentials: A learner value framework. *Journal of Teaching and Learning for Graduate Employability*, 12: 48–51.

Pichette, J., Brumwell, S., Rizk, J. and Han, S. (2021). *Making sense of microcredentials*. Toronto: Higher Education Quality Council of Ontario. Available at https://heqco.ca/pub/making-sense-of-microcredentials

Ponte, F. and Saray, V. (2019). *The evolution of a micro-credential.* In: ASCILITE, Singapore, 2–5 December 2019.

Randall, D. L., Farmer, T. and West, R. E. (2019). Effectiveness of undergraduate instructional design assistants in scaling a teacher education open badge system. *Contemporary Issues in Technology and Teacher Education,* 19(4): 825–849.

Rossiter, D. and Tynan, B. (2019). *Designing and implementing micro-credentials: A guide for practitioners.* Commonwealth of Learning. Available at https://oasis.col.org/items/e2d0be25-cbbb-441f-b431-42f74f715532

Tennessee Department of Education. (2015). *Tennessee succeeds. Where are we going? How will we get there?* Available at https://eric.ed.gov/?q=source%3a%22Tennessee+Department+of+Education%22&ff1=eduHigh+Schools&ff2=pubReports+-+Descriptive&id=ED599475

Varadarajan, S., Koh, J. H. L. and Daniel, B. K. (2023). A systematic review of the opportunities and challenges of micro-credentials for multiple stakeholders: Learners, employers, higher education institutions and government. *International Journal of Educational Technology in Higher Education,* 20(1): 1–24.

West, R. E., Tawfik, A. A., Gishbaugher, J. J. and Gatewood, J. (2020). Guardrails to constructing learning: The potential of open microcredentials to support inquiry-based learning. *TechTrends,* 64(6): 828–838. DOI: https://doi.org/10.1007/s11528-020-00531-2

White, S. (2021). Developing credit based micro-credentials for the teaching profession: An Australian descriptive case study. *Teachers and Teaching,* 27(7): 696–711.

Zou, H., Ullah, A., Qazi, Z., Naeem, A. and Rehan, S. (2023). Impact of micro-credential learning on students' perceived employability: The mediating role of human capital. *International Journal of Educational Management,* 28: 13505–13540.

CHAPTER 5

Learning design and innovation in production

For most institutions, production of microcredentials is a new experience that requires a shift in production procedures. This may involve a shift from a single educator producing a course or individual lectures to a team experience of producing an online course. It may involve speeding up production methods to offer the most up-to-date thinking on fast-moving areas such as computer security or artificial intelligence (AI). It may involve partnerships between higher education institutions and professional bodies. If the new microcredentials are supposed to stack into a qualification, or into part of a qualification, then there may be a need to produce multiple courses at speed. Whatever the

---

How to cite this book chapter:
Ferguson, R. and Whitelock, D. 2024. Learning design and innovation in production. In: Ferguson, R. and Whitelock, D. *Microcredentials for Excellence: A Practical Guide*. Pp. 111–140. London: Ubiquity Press. DOI: https://doi.org/10.5334/bcz.e. License: CC BY-NC 4.0

situation, a shift to microcredentials can be a catalyst for rethinking both learning design and course production. This chapter outlines the changes implemented at our own institution, the UK's Open University, and methods we found successful when making the move to microcredentials.

The Open University

The Open University (OU) is the largest university in the UK and one of the largest in Europe. It was founded as a distance-learning institution and, for more than half a century, has offered a wide range of modular undergraduate and postgraduate degrees. It has offered wholly online courses for more than 25 years and all its modules are now wholly or partly online. In addition to its degree courses, the OU offers more than a thousand short courses free of charge on its OpenLearn platform. The university was also responsible for the creation of the FutureLearn platform, where universities and professional bodies from around the world offer a wide range of courses at different levels. Overall, the university has a wealth of experience in offering online courses at degree level, short courses, and courses aligned with professional bodies. As a result, when FutureLearn launched its microcredential programme early in 2020, the OU was among the first to offer these courses.

By the summer of 2023, the OU had developed 29 microcredentials and registered over 12,000 learners on these courses. It had also explored innovative production methods to be able to produce these courses fast and effectively.

The university is used to producing large numbers of modules. Each year, it develops around 150 new courses and these join over 350 that are already on offer. The process of doing this has developed over time and is a lengthy procedure involving market research, business case development, faculty checks, writing, filming, editing, rights checks and quality assurance. Throughout this time, teams from the internal Learning and Discovery Service (LDS) work closely with faculty members.

> The Learning Designer and Digital Development Editor roles are pivotal to the development and production of new modules and are involved right from the start, working alongside authors and faculty colleagues, to support and advise on plans. Other specialists, such as video and audio producers, interactive developers, and graphic developers, are brought in at various points in the development, as and when they are needed. (Leon & Du Baret 2022)

Innovation in production

Although this approach results in the development of high-quality courses that may be offered for several years with only minor modifications, it was not suitable for the more fast-paced demands of a microcredential programme. Under the lead of the university's head of transformation, Matthew Moran, the OU began to trial different production methods to reduce a development process, which had previously taken more than a year, to a lighter-touch method that in some cases required only six weeks to complete. As Papathoma and Ferguson (2021) note in an internal report, three approaches were trialled.

- **Six-week production.** This works well when the course is authored by skilled academics who have written other online/short courses and can draw on existing material, or when authors are available full-time throughout

the production period. Authors need to have a vision of the course, know its purpose, and have an idea of what the learning outcomes will be at the start of the production period.
- **12- to 18-week production.** This works well when academics are familiar with the platform on which the microcredential will be offered, and when sufficient time has been built into their schedules for microcredential production.
- **Editor/learning designer author content.** Academics share existing learning content with learning designers and editors, who work full-time to develop these materials into a course. Academic approval is required for the final content, tasks and assessment.

A major constraint is the amount of time available to work on a microcredential. Academics have multiple demands on their time in terms of teaching, research, management and administration. They are rarely able to set all other responsibilities aside at short notice to devote themselves to module development. Although some course shaping and rewriting can be handed to editors and learning designers, they are unlikely to have sufficient subject-matter expertise to write significant amounts of new material. Faculties therefore need to build in time for academics to concentrate on course production and to recognise how much time this takes.

Like academics, staff from LDS working on production are rarely able to concentrate on one course at a time. Editors, librarians, learning designers, project managers and video producers are typically all working on multiple projects. Matthew Moran dealt with this issue by creating a Microcredential Studio in which small teams of staff – including a project manager, a learning designer, a digital development editor and a media assistant

– concentrated all their efforts on specific microcredentials. The Microcredentials Studio developed approaches that differed from those used for the standard OU curriculum. These included:

- lightweight upfront planning;
- non-consecutive development by working on learning outcomes using a mapping document;
- working in collaboration with academics, using tools appropriate for each team;
- direct development on the platform, saving time and offering visibility of content;
- team members with cross-functional skills;
- sharing and building on existing knowledge;
- celebrating team successes;
- high levels of transparency. (Papathoma & Ferguson 2020)

An important innovation was the use of an agile approach to production. Previously, LDS had used the 'waterfall' method. This is a sequential approach to the completion of projects, used in many contexts, which works through stages one by one. In the case of course production, the stages might include designing, authoring, editing and reviewing the course, before adding it to a platform or virtual learning environment. This approach makes it relatively straightforward to schedule teams and individuals to work on different stages of multiple projects, but it is not well suited to speedy microcredential production.

Agile is a cyclic and collaborative approach originally designed for software production. The 12 principles behind it are set out in the Manifesto for Agile Software Development (Beck et al. 2021). These principles are phrased in terms of commercial software development but can be adapted to suit other situations. The approach emphasises the importance of frequent meetings and face-to-face conversations, of trusting motivated individuals to get the job done, of keeping things simple, of regular reflection, short timescales, and paying attention to good design (Beck et al. 2021).

The Microcredentials Studio implemented a type of agile known as scrum – a widely used and lightweight process framework. The key elements (Mills 2014) are:

- **Small cross-functional teams.** These should include the product owner, who has the vision and decides on the order in which things should be done, and the scrum master, who facilitates communication and removes obstacles.
- **Storytelling.** Each new feature should be associated with a short story about the user and why the feature will add value for the user.
- **Effort points.** Compare the stories and give them points according to the amount of effort that will be involved in each one.
- **Feature prioritisation.** Each sprint should end with something that can be demonstrated, so chunks of work must be small enough to fit into a sprint.
- **Sprints.** A sprint should be one to four weeks long – enough time to deal with a set amount of effort points.
- **Scrums.** A 15-minute meeting every morning, standing up, so participants are not tempted to settle in. Three questions: what did you do yesterday to help finish this sprint? What will you do today to help finish this sprint? What obstacles does the team need to overcome?
- **Sprint reviews.** At the end of the sprint the team meets to discuss what has been achieved, and to improve working practices for the future.

This approach required minor amendments – the pandemic meant that in-person standing meetings were no longer practical, so they were replaced with frequent and short meetings using video-conferencing software. Otherwise, the method worked well. The scrums proved particularly useful in making sure that everyone knew what other team members were working on, and the team could work together to remove obstacles and reduce hold-ups.

Another element of agile that was adopted by the Microcredential Studio was kanban (from the Japanese word for signboard). This is essentially a way of visualising work and managing workflow that gives team members a view of both process and progress. A project is split into individual tasks and these are displayed on the kanban board. This can be done using sticky notes on a physical board, or by using an online application such as Trello if the team is working at a distance. Individual tasks are sorted into columns. These can be as simple as to do/in progress/complete or more complex. Each column can contain an agreed maximum number of tasks – if one is full the team needs to concentrate effort there until there is space again. This highlights any bottlenecks in workflow.

In the case of the Microcredentials Studio, the kanban board is divided into eight columns. On the left is an information column, for links and resources that will be used by the team throughout the project. Next to that is the 'Course backlog' – the tasks that will need to be completed in future but are not yet being worked on – and then the 'Sprint backlog', the tasks to be worked on in the current week. Once a task is picked up from the sprint backlog it will be moved first to the preparing and authoring column, next to the developing and editing column, on into the enhancing column and the approving/quality assurance column, before making its final move into the 'Done!' column. Occasionally, if plans change, it will be moved to the very far right, in the 'Abandoned' column. As each task is picked up, the individual(s) working on it and the required completion date are added.

Using kanban, the current state of the workflow is clear to everyone. It is evident what has been finished, what is underway and what has yet to be started, as well as the tasks people are currently working on, and any bottlenecks that need to be addressed. Having the board visible during scrums can facilitate conversations and highlight problems that require discussion. The benefits of kanban include: 'efficiency, reduced email traffic and time spent in meetings, building sense of common purpose and shared understanding, and enhancing quality of outputs' (Moran 2017).

One of the reasons that agile approaches, including scrum and kanban, could be used successfully during production of microcredentials at the OU was the use of learning design to map out the different elements of the course before work began on writing it. Although learning design can be used in any context, it is perhaps most useful in online learning contexts where courses are developed by teams of specialists rather than individual educators.

Learning design

Educators have always made design decisions about how to structure the learning opportunities they create. What they have often lacked is a structured way of talking about, evaluating and sharing those decisions. This means that knowledge about what makes a great lesson, or a great course has sometimes been difficult to pass on. Learners may say a lesson was engaging, fun, fascinating or riveting – but it is not always clear what made it so, or whether that same approach would work in a different subject area or with a different teacher. That is where learning design comes in.

Mor and Craft (2012) define learning design as 'the act of devising new practices, plans of activity, resources and tools aimed at achieving particular educational aims in a given situation'. The benefits of learning design became particularly apparent during the pandemic when educators and institutions – urgently needing to move from face-to-face to remote teaching – sought guidance from others more experienced in teaching online and at a distance. Learning design offers a way of sharing ideas in a format that allows for a methodical yet swift adaptation of lessons and courses for delivery in a variety of settings and contexts, to a variety of learners.

Origins of learning design

Between 2008 and 2012, the University of Reading participated in the Open University Learning Design Initiative (OULDI), which introduced teaching staff to strategies that enabled them to think critically about their design decisions and the process of design. A subsequent report on the project (Papaefthimiou 2012) revealed the enthusiasm with which learning design was received amongst the teaching staff:

> My view is that it's revolutionised our thinking ... about learning and teaching ...The thing about the process is that it blows your mind, you know, almost like 'What can we do?' 'What would be interesting and different?' but once you've blown your mind, you've got to say 'Well, what can we actually manage here?' (Papaefthimiou 2012: 20, 31)

Since then, learning design methods like the ones used in the OULDI project have been developed and shared by educators in many countries. These methods:

- prompt educators to think about what they want learners to achieve while studying;
- help educators provide the context that will enable learners to achieve those outcomes;
- encourage educators to take into account the diversity of those learners;
- help to promote wider reflection and discussion among everyone involved in developing and producing courses, lessons and other learning opportunities.

In 2012, a group of educators met in Larnaca, Cyprus, to bring together ideas about learning design. This resulted in the Larnaca Declaration on Learning Design (Dalziel et al. 2016), which has influenced subsequent thinking in this area. The authors identified several reasons for developing and using learning design:

- to help educators become more effective in their preparation and facilitation of teaching and learning activities;
- to expose educators to new teaching ideas that take them beyond their traditional approaches;
- to help educators to describe effective teaching ideas so that they can be shared with, and adapted by, other educators;
- to share teaching ideas among educators in order to improve student learning;
- to make implicit, private teaching ideas into explicit, shared ideas;
- to provide a way of conveying an educational idea using a common framework;

- to share and develop good teaching practice;
- to support professional development to give teachers more time to work on other areas;
- to produce richer experiences for learners;
- to understand more about the nature of education.

Technology changes the contexts in which learning design takes place. For example, in online microcredentials, the structure of the educational experience is preserved. It is possible to look back at the course and see exactly what learners were asked to do, how the activities were structured and, in the case of discussions, how learners reacted. This would not necessarily be possible in a face-to-face teaching setting.

Learning design, when combined with technology, offers opportunities for educators to collaborate online to build lessons and courses together at a distance and to discuss how effective they are and how they could be improved. The Virtual University for Small States of the Commonwealth (VUSSC) is a notable example of this in practice. VUSSC is a network of 32 small-island developing states and African landlocked countries who collaborate in developing, adapting and sharing post-secondary level, openly licensed courses and learning materials in subjects relevant to the needs of people in the participating countries – including disaster management, the fishing industry and tourism (Perryman & Lesperance 2015).

Evaluation, which is a key component of the learning design process, can be easier for online courses than for face-to-face teaching and learning, due to teaching and learning activities being preserved after the course has ended. In addition, the data that are automatically generated and preserved by online systems can be used to evaluate how well things worked, where students engaged and where they did not.

The advantages of learning design, particularly in relation to online courses, mean that it is used throughout the OU when developing courses and modules. It proved to be particularly useful when developing microcredentials as it provided a framework to support the development of this new type of course. The main elements of that framework are scenarios, personas, learning outcomes and activities.

Designing microcredentials

Scenario-based design is a learner-focused approach which considers early in the design process who the learners are likely to be, how they will engage with the course, and what they may gain from it. In the case of microcredentials, it supports the shift to a new type of course and, potentially, a new type of learner. If previous courses have been designed for young people who are spending several years working towards a qualification, scenario-based design helps to identify things that will need to change when a course is developed for older learners, who may be working full-time and will only engage with the course for a few weeks or months.

Scenarios help to ground discussion around the development of microcredentials and provide a basis for talking to potential learners or even involving them in the design process. This is not always possible, but if learners on a microcredential are expected to come from a particular institution or organisation it can be very helpful to discuss goals, settings, objects, actions and events with them.

The approach highlights the importance of the following elements and related questions:

- **Actors:** who is the microcredential intended for? How diverse do you expect the learners to be? Which countries/sectors are likely to be represented?

- **Goals:** what are the goals of the microcredential? The goals of educators and learners may differ, so consider this question from both perspectives.
- **Settings:** identify one or two of the places where the learners studying the course or lesson are likely to be located. For example, learners may be studying while commuting, or during training time at work.
- **Objects:** which relevant tools and resources are learners likely to be able to access? For example, are they likely to have connectivity problems? Will they have ways of working together or sharing resources?
- **Actions:** what will learners be asked to do during the microcredential? Give a brief overview of the types of learning task they will be asked to engage with.
- **Events:** what is likely to happen while they are doing these activities? Can you foresee any potential problems?

Student personas

Scenario-based design involves thinking about the broad types of people who are likely to become learners on your microcredential. However, there is no average learner who can be slotted into any lesson. Developing personas provides a way of overcoming this problem and designing for unique people with specific characteristics, each of whom might face different barriers to learning.

Personas have been used in marketing and design for many years. More recently, they have become part of the learning design process in education, representing a fictitious person who could credibly be expected to study a particular course.

A typical persona contains basic information about the character (such as their name, age, gender, geographical location and employment status) and information about them that can help the designer, such as their likes and dislikes, goals, experiences, abilities, preferences, needs, motivations and other things that may act as barriers or blockers for that character.

Personas have value both in planning new teaching and learning activities and resources and in checking whether existing resources and learning activities still meet learners' needs. Of course, many educators already have an informal idea of the students they are designing their learning for, especially if they have been teaching for a long time. However, the unwritten, informal nature of this practice can mean that educators end up designing for the majority of students, rather than the minority of students who would benefit from more inclusive learning design approaches. In addition, they may not adjust their thinking to consider the specific needs of microcredential learners.

Designing for 'outliers' – the students who are the most different from the 'typical' student body – can result in a more inclusive learning environment for everyone. However, it can be difficult for educators to maintain a clear sense of who these students are, and their needs, while designing. Using one or more personas helps to keep the learner perspective in mind. These personas provide a way of considering how learners will engage with the course, what they expect and what could cause problems. A persona can, therefore, be considered as a tool that helps the design process.

There are different methods of generating personas. Some are data-based, drawing on information that has been collected in a related context. Others create archetypes such as 'the student', 'the postgraduate' and 'the educator'. The OU uses a fiction-based perspective, creating personas based on what is already known about learners and adding this information to a student profile template (Open University 2020). The template includes sections for background information: name, age, subjects being studied, first language and level of study. It also includes sections for:

- **Practical needs** – for example, those related to accessibility such as video and audio transcripts, captions, and alternative text for images.
- **Study motivations/career plans** – for example, career aspirations, expectations for the microcredential.
- **Previous educational experiences** – for example, highest level of previous study, any experience of studying part-time or online.
- **Study skills: strengths and weaknesses** – for example, motivation, setting goals, or paying attention to feedback.
- **Tuition likes and dislikes** – for example, in relation to collaborative tasks, reflection, synchronous/asynchronous discussion.
- **Expectations of the library** – for example, ability to access journals, e-books, databases, reference management software, or information skills training.
- **Living situation** – for example, personal circumstances, caring responsibilities, level of access to Internet and digital equipment.

Personas should be fictional characters rather than descriptions of real people. In part, this is for ethical reasons, but it also means that a set of personas can be developed that take into account important aspects of the population for which the course is being designed. For example, you might want at least one of your personas to be studying online for the first time, to be cynical about the idea of microcredentials, to be accessing the course from a different country, to be studying in their second or third language, or to require a high grade to progress in their career. These aspects can be incorporated within personas, or a persona can be built around each of them. In all cases, it is important to avoid stereotypes, so personas should be reviewed before use to make sure they resemble real people rather than caricatures.

It is usual to create a range of personas with different backgrounds or different needs. This means that, as they go through the design process, learning designers and educators can consider how these personas would react to whatever it is they are designing. For example, the bullet-pointed reflections below were noted by an educator when commenting on draft instructions for an assignment on a course relating to technology-enhanced learning. While considering these, she related them to one of the personas developed for the course – 'Adam', who works in student support, likes to be given clear instructions and is new to working at postgraduate level.

- Simplifying this part of the instructions and adding a link to the detailed guidance might be helpful for Adam.
- Adam needs clear instructions for written work. Could we use headings in this section?
- Saying that references to module materials are likely to be included implies to Adam that they are not necessarily needed. Rephrasing as, e.g., 'should include' might encourage him to try harder to integrate and reference the ideas from the module.
- We have asked learners to make a connection with practice. As someone who works in student support and is not a teacher, Adam might be wondering what this should look like.

Another educator commented on the same set of assignment instructions from the perspective of 'Liz', a persona whose study time is limited as she is a single mother of three who also works full-time as a teaching assistant.

- Reflecting on this synchronous event is an important part of the assignment. School holidays affect Liz's study time and so, bearing in mind that this event falls within the school summer holidays, knowing both the date and time at this stage would help with her planning.
- Could these elements perhaps be displayed as indented bullet points? This would help Liz break the assessment down into different chunked tasks.
- Liz likes the guidance about word count for this part of the assignment – however, this guidance is not consistent throughout this section. Could we provide guidance in terms of length of pages or rough word count for each of the sections?

Once personas have been developed that give an idea of the learners who are likely to enrol for the microcredential, it is time to turn attention to what they are expected to gain by studying it.

Learning outcomes

Learning outcomes give learners an idea of what will be expected of them during a course or lesson, and the skills and knowledge they are likely to acquire during their studies. Individuals can also use them to make decisions about enrolling for a course, considering whether they have already achieved these outcomes and whether they are interested in achieving them.

Learning outcomes are typically expressed using short clear sentences in the future tense, explaining what learners will be able to do when they complete the course successfully. They should also be SMART:

- **S**pecific – what will show the outcome has been achieved?
- **M**easurable – what aspect of the outcome can be measured?
- **A**ttainable – is the outcome both realistic and challenging?
- **R**elevant – is the outcome aligned with learners' goals?
- **T**ime-bounded – how soon should the outcome be achieved?

Developing learning outcomes provides an opportunity to think about what learners will take away from a microcredential, and the best ways of supporting them to do this. Of course, any learning experience will have unintended outcomes, or may be used by learners in unexpected ways. Learning outcomes should not act as a constraint on learning, or a barrier to following up ideas. They represent, as a minimum, what a learner will take away from the microcredential if they complete it successfully.

Learning outcomes enable learners to select an appropriate course from the many that are on offer. They can be used to help persuade an employer to fund course registration or to strengthen a CV once a learner has completed the microcredential. From an educator's perspective, they help to keep a course consistent for each cohort, even if it is taught by many educators. They can be used to evaluate whether a course or lesson is effective. They can also be used as a basis for assessment and for the construction of learning activities.

Activity types

Learning design, in terms of choice of activity types, has been shown to influence the satisfaction and retention of students (Rienties & Toetenel 2016). In the case of online learning, the focus is most commonly on two types of activity: assimilating information and assessment. Learners either read some text or they watch a video. They then answer some questions. The emphasis is on the acquisition view of learning (Sfard 1993) that is associated with the view that knowledge is passed on by experts. This approach is typically content-centric, focused on the material that will be covered rather than on what learners will be able to do once they have engaged with that content. However, although assimilative activities are positively correlated with learner satisfaction, they are correlated negatively with academic performance (Rienties & Toetenel 2016).

To avoid over-reliance on assimilative activities, the OU uses a taxonomy for learning design that characterises six different types of learning task (Open University 2021).

- **assimilative:** attending to information – activities include reading, observing, reviewing, thinking about and considering;
- **communicative:** discussing with others – activities include discussing, reporting, collaborating, questioning and describing;
- **finding and handling information:** searching for and processing information – activities include classifying, analysing, searching, visualising and using;
- **productive:** actively constructing an artefact – activities include creating, building, designing, drawing, composing and remixing;

- **practice:** applying learning in a real-world or simulated setting – activities include practising, exploring, investigating, experimenting and improving;
- **assessment:** all forms of assessment.

An aspect of learning design is discussion about how different types of activity will be balanced within the microcredential. Every course will include some assimilative activity but learners are more likely to remember information if they have engaged with it actively rather than simply reading or viewing it. The emphasis of microcredentials on skills for the workplace increases the importance of other task types. For example, most professions require practitioners to engage confidently with communicative tasks such as discussing, presenting, collaborating and reporting, so various communicative tasks are important within a microcredential. Depending on the subject area of the microcredential, productive activities, practical activities or information-based activities may also be particularly relevant.

A credit-bearing microcredential will necessarily include assessment – the OU taxonomy emphasises that this forms part of the learning process. Although a microcredential may be too short for a tutor to mark and return assignments in time for learners to benefit from feedback, computer-marked assignments such as multiple-choice questions can be used as formative assessments. Rather than simply receiving a grade, learners can be automatically provided with feedback that explains why the answer they selected is right or wrong and, if necessary, they can be pointed back to the relevant section of the learning materials (see Chapter 7).

Course content, rights and workload

Although educators begin thinking about possible course content as soon as a microcredential is proposed, a course that is led by content means that learning outcomes have to be shaped to suit that content, rather than learner needs. It can result in courses that are content-heavy, with learners spending most of their time watching and reading rather than engaging actively with the material and with each other. It may result in a course that is more aligned with educator preferences than with what learners and employers are looking for, and it can make it difficult for a team of authors to share their ideas.

Once the initial aspects of learning design are in place – scenario, personas, learning outcomes and activity types – educators are well placed to think about which content will be covered at which point. Depending on how microcredentials are structured at the institution, there may be constraints on the content that can be used, particularly in terms of access and rights issues. In a face-to-face situation, educators rarely consider copyright issues when presenting material. The situation on this varies from country to country because '[c]opyright is a territorial right, and different acts are permitted in different countries. You need to ensure that you comply with the laws of the countries in which you provide online resources' (Intellectual Property Office 2014). An online course should take into account the laws of the countries in which it is offered or its students are based. In most cases, online course materials – which will not simply be viewed in a lecture but downloaded and possibly printed and shared – should not be used without the permission of the rights holder.

The rights issue brings with it two main challenges. First, there is the cost. Depending on the source, even a small image used once to liven up a page can cost a large amount of money to reproduce. Second, locating rights holders and gaining permission to use material takes a considerable amount of time and is best done by a specialist. The OU has a rights team that works on clearing material for use but it can take weeks or even months for copyright holders to respond to queries.

Another limitation on content is library access. On courses for full-time registered students this is straightforward – they have access to the institution's library, both in person and online. In most cases, microcredential learners will only have access to online resources. If they are not registered students with full access to facilities, then they will only be able to access the resources available to the public. This is a significant barrier because important texts are often located behind a paywall. Although the obvious solution might be to register all microcredential learners as students, this brings its own problems. For the price of a microcredential, is the institution willing to give individuals access to its full library, sporting and catering facilities, careers guidance and counselling service?

Open University microcredentials make use of open educational resources (OER) wherever possible.

> Open Educational Resources (OER) are learning, teaching and research materials in any format and medium that reside in the public domain or are under copyright that have been released under an open license, that permit no-cost access, re-use, re-purpose, adaptation and redistribution by others. (UNESCO n.d.)

These resources, like this book, are released under Creative Commons licences, which specify how they can be used – whether users can distribute, remix, adapt and build upon them for commercial or non-commercial purposes. In most cases, using these resources will save both time and money. However, it is worth noting that resources are sometimes shared openly online by someone who is not the rights holder, so some checks are still necessary.

Once the course and activities are in place, it is helpful to check on the workload required of learners. With a face-to-face course it is often evident when students are overloaded, and the course can be adjusted if necessary. Online courses are less flexible. First, unless there are regular opportunities for interaction with learners, it may not be clear when they are overloaded and struggling to keep up with the course. If learners do not have a social space where they feel confident about sharing problems, individuals may feel that they are the only ones struggling to keep up, interpreting this as a personal failure rather than as a sign the course needs to be adjusted. Even if an issue with workload is identified, it can be difficult to correct. Changing a course in progress is problematic because some learners may already have completed the tasks that are to be removed or adjusted. Changing a subsequent run of the course creates quality assurance issues, because learners receive the same certificate for different amounts of work. The best solution is to avoid these problems by checking the workload before the course opens.

The amount of study hours involved in a microcredential varies by institution and the way of expressing or calculating that time varies by country. In England, an honours degree requires 360 credits, and one credit is expected to take 10 hours of study time (QAA 2013).

> The term 'notional learning time' is used to denote all time expected to be spent by a student in pursuit of a higher education qualification. This includes independent study and reading, preparation for contact hours, coursework, revision and summative assessment. (QAA 2013: 7)

OU undergraduate microcredentials are worth 10 credits, so require 100 notional study hours, and postgraduate microcredentials are worth 15 credits and require 150 notional study hours. On a 10-week undergraduate OU microcredential, learners can expect to spend around 10 hours a week studying, and on a 12-week postgraduate OU microcredential they will spend 12–13 hours a week on their study.

An evaluation of student workload (Open University 2015a) suggested that, according to the level of study, module-directed study should take from 45% to 60% of that time, with the other time set aside for independent study, preparation and revision. The situation is slightly different on microcredentials, because students are developing a more specific set of skills, but 10 hours a week at undergraduate level and 13 hours a week at postgraduate levels remain maximums for a course that is to be studied part-time.

The average reading speed of a literate adult is usually estimated at somewhere around 200 words per minute (wpm). However, reading course content takes longer because most learners will read and re-read a text, perhaps returning to earlier sections, and usually highlighting text or taking notes. The OU's student evaluation project recommended assuming a reading speed of 120 wpm for easy text, 70 wpm for medium text, and 35 wpm for difficult text. For ease of calculation and to avoid arguments about the relative difficulty of text, this is usually interpreted as 40 wpm over an entire course. So, for example, reading an 8,000-word academic paper would be assumed to take a learner more than three hours, while reading a 2,000-word section of a report would take around 50 minutes. Expert educators, who are familiar with the ideas and arguments, could skim read much faster than that, but these times are based on learners who are encountering complex ideas for the first time.

Estimating the time learners will spend watching videos or listening to audio appears straightforward, as these recordings are all accompanied by information about how long they will last. However, learners replay sections, pause to take notes or take a break to reflect on content. The OU allows three times their running time for short videos and 1.5 times their running time for longer clips. Audio clips are assumed to require twice their running time (Open University 2015b). Whichever timings are selected, using a shared spreadsheet template to calculate total activity lengths can help with course writing, especially when multiple authors are involved.

Innovation in learning design: the writers' room

The learning design process that has been developed and refined at the OU over the past 15 years works well when developing online courses. As was the case with production, the shift to microcredentials provided an opportunity to trial different approaches. In this case, Matthew Moran, the OU's transformation lead, adapted a method that has been used with great success in the creative arts – the writers' room.

In the film and TV industries, a writers' room is exactly what the title suggests, a place for a group of writers to come together to work on a script or screenplay. The original *Star Wars* script was created in a writers' room, as is *The Simpsons*.

Typically, this is a place for brainstorming ideas and creating an outline. In some cases, it is also used for fleshing out ideas into a full script. The aim is to bring people together who love what they are doing and who are excited about the project. When this approach works well, writers complement each other, bringing different skills to their joint creation.

The process has similarities with learning design, in that the entire project is mapped out before the content is added. Writers explore existing material, come up with story ideas, break those down into acts and scenes, and then share these with the producer. The producer selects one of them and takes it to the network for funding or approval.

Within the room the head (also known as the showrunner) models the process, manages time and makes decisions. A note-taker records suggestions about setting, storyline and characters, as well as recording what has been agreed. Writers discuss and agree elements of the script including characters, storylines, settings, themes and tone. They will also map the storyline out in terms of 'beats', the smallest unit of dramatic action, each one representing a large or small shift in the narrative. Together these beats establish the structure and pacing of the script as a whole.

Transferred into an educational setting, the writers' room can provide an exciting and creative collaborative space in which the people responsible for writing a microcredential can work together to map out its story structure. Instead of considering the course as a set of content on a subject, or as a path towards learning outcomes, working in this way frames it as an unfolding story that learners will want to follow to the end.

Viewed as a storyline, a microcredential can take on a three-act structure: context, journey and resolution.

Context: This begins with a situation or a problem that engages the learner – the issue that motivates the course. For example: 'We need to find a solution to the climate crisis' or 'We need better ways of supporting student wellbeing' or 'Companies are facing an increasing number of cyber attacks'. These are broad issues, so the next step is to identify a complication that the microcredential can address – 'We need to identify steps that will take us towards net zero' or 'Student mental health is noticeably worse since the pandemic' or 'Phishing attacks are increasing'. A final aspect of the context is to identify a question worth asking that the course will address – 'Is there a method of reducing carbon emissions that has been shown to work?' or 'What are the best ways of supporting the mental health of our learners?' or 'How can different parts of our organisation act to reduce the risks posed by phishing?'

Journey: Over the next 10 weeks, the course answers that question by – 'taking you through the approach that has been used successfully in Cuba (or another country or organisation)' or 'sharing the ways that learners and educators in these three very different universities have achieved this' or 'introducing a 10-step framework that has worked for these organisations'.

Resolution: Bringing together academic and practical knowledge to answer the question.

Context, journey and resolution may be completely different to the examples given here, but in each case learners are presented with a problem that engages or motivates them, they are taken on a journey that addresses that problem, and the course provides them with a resolution. As with any storyline, it is important that people are emotionally engaged. Writers can brainstorm what they want learners to experience, feel and connect with at different points in the course, mapping out an emotional journey with high points and low points, conflict and resolution.

The writers' room is a flexible form that provides a new way of approaching learning design. Microcredential teams who have tried it at the OU have given positive feedback – they like the way it offers new possibilities, centres the learner, introduces new ideas, provides a way of solving problems, speeds up the writing process, and brings the team together to have fun.

Conclusion

Ways of designing, writing and producing a microcredential will vary between institutions, depending on decisions that have been made about the length, status and purpose of these courses. The approaches described in this chapter have all been implemented successfully at the OU. Some of them have been used for many years in the development of online courses. In other cases, the introduction of microcredentials has provided an opportunity to experiment, and to introduce modified versions of techniques that have been found to work successfully in other sectors. A shift towards microcredentials opens up possibilities for change and opportunities for reinvigorating design and production processes across the institution. The next chapter expands on these possibilities by introducing ways in which mental health and wellbeing can be built into the microcredential curriculum.

References

Beck, K., Beedle, M., van Bennekum, A., Cockburn, A., Cunningham, W., Fowler, M., Grenning, J., Highsmith, J., Hunt, A., Jeffries, R., Kern, J., Marick, B., Martin, R. C., Mellor, S., Schwaber, K., Sutherland, J. and Thomas., D. (2021). *Manifesto for agile software development*. Available at https://agilemanifesto.org

Dalziel, J., Conole, G., Wills, S., Walker, S., Bennett, S., Dobozy, E., Cameron, L., Badilescu-Buga, E. and Bower, M. (2016). The Larnaca declaration on learning design. *Journal of Interactive Media in Education*, 1: 7. DOI: http://doi.org/10.5334/jime.407

Intellectual Property Office. (2014). *Exceptions to copyright: Education and teaching*. Newport: IPO. Available at https://assets.publishing.service.gov.uk/government/uploads/system/uploads/attachment_data/file/375951/Education_and_Teaching.pdf

Leon, A. and Du Baret, C. (2022). Working together in module design. *Learning Design Team Blog*, 19 April 2022. Available at http://www.open.ac.uk/blogs/learning-design/?p=1337

Mills, J. (2014). How to scrum manage. *Wired*, January 2015. Available at https://www.wired.co.uk/article/scrum-manage

Mor, Y. and Craft, B. (2012). Learning design: Reflections upon the current landscape. *Research in Learning Technology*, 20. Available at https://journal.alt.ac.uk/index.php/rlt/article/view/1364

Moran, M. (2017). *H889 Kanban*. Email message, 4 September 2017.

Open University. (2021). *OU learning design activity types framework*. Available at https://www.open.ac.uk/blogs/learning-design/wp-content/uploads/2021/10/OU-LD-Activity-Types-Framework-October-2021-FINAL.pdf

Open University. (2020). *Student profile form*. Available at https://www.open.ac.uk/blogs/learning-design/wp-content/uploads/2020/07/Student-Profile-form-v2-updated-June-2018.pdf

Open University. (2015a). *Student workload evaluation project*. Milton Keynes: The Open University.

Open University. (2015b). *Student workload evaluation project, phase 2, stage 2 findings and recommendations*. Milton Keynes: The Open University.

Papaefthimiou, M.-C. (2012). Learning design initiative at the University of Reading: Pedagogy and technological choices; Reading pilot final report. Available at http://www.open.ac.uk/blogs/archiveOULDI/wp-content/uploads/2010/12/OULDI_Reading_FINAL.pdf

Papathoma, T. and Ferguson, R. (2020). *Evaluation of Open University microcredentials: Final report of phase one*. Milton Keynes: The Open University.

Papathoma, T. and Ferguson, R. (2021). *Evaluation of Open University microcredentials: Final report of phase two*. Milton Keynes: The Open University.

Perryman, L.-A. and Lesperance, J. (2015). Collaborating across borders: OER use and open educational practices within the Virtual University for Small States of the Commonwealth.

Paper presented at the Open Education Global Conference 2015, Banff, Canada, 22–24 April 2015.

QAA. (2013). *Explaining student workload: Guidance about providing information for students.* Gloucester: Quality Assurance Agency.

Rienties, B. and Toetenel, L. (2016). The impact of learning design on student behaviour, satisfaction and performance: A cross-institutional comparison across 151 modules. *Computers in Human Behavior*, 60: 333–341. DOI: https://doi.org/10.1016/j.chb.2016.02.074

Sfard, A. (1998). On two metaphors for learning and the dangers of choosing just one. *Educational Researcher*, 27(2): 4–13.

UNESCO. (n.d.). *Open educational resources.* Available at https://www.unesco.org/en/open-educational-resources

CHAPTER 6

Student wellbeing

Traditionally, universities provide a great deal of support and facilities for students in addition to opportunities for learning. Campus-based universities are homes for students, and even institutions that are distributed across sites will offer social and sporting activities as well as opportunities for eating, shopping and finance. Together, these facilities and societies can create a feeling of belonging that ties students to their course or qualification and may later keep them engaged as alumni. Similarly, extended workplace training is also often accompanied by opportunities to work, eat and socialise together. Microcredentials break this pattern. They are relatively short qualifications,

---

How to cite this book chapter:
Ferguson, R. and Whitelock, D. 2024. Student wellbeing. In: Ferguson, R. and Whitelock, D. *Microcredentials for Excellence: A Practical Guide.* Pp. 141–172. London: Ubiquity Press. DOI: https://doi.org/10.5334/bcz.f. License: CC BY-NC 4.0

often studied online and at a distance. Learners may never meet each other or their educators and, if the microcredential is offered on a generic platform, they may have only a hazy idea of which institution is responsible for their study. Nevertheless, they are likely to encounter some of the same challenges to mental health and wellbeing as full-time students and are likely also to be facing competing demands on their time from family and workplace. This chapter focuses on mental health and wellbeing, considering the ways in which these affect microcredential learners, and how learners can be supported during their studies.

Mental health around the world

The World Health Organization reported that '[i]n 2019, 1 in every 8 people, or 970 million people around the world were living with a mental disorder, with anxiety and depressive disorders the most common' (WHO 2022). In the UK, one person in six experiences some form of mental health problem in any given year (McManus et al. 2009). In 2017, the US-based Institute for Health Metrics Evaluation (Rice-Oxley 2019) suggested that just under 300 million people worldwide were suffering from anxiety, about 160 million from a major depressive disorder, and another 100 million from a milder form of depression.

Determining accurate global statistics always involves a degree of guesswork. Many people experience more than one type of mental health problem, much of the data is reliant on self-reporting, and countries, cultures and organisations define mental health in different ways. Mental health problems often go under-reported due to a variety of factors, including social stigma. The Institute for Health Metrics Evaluation estimates that about 13% of the global population – some 971 million people – suffer from some kind of mental health problem.

Statistics about the extent of mental health problems are likely to be underestimates rather than overestimates. Even so, they make for sobering reading. In the USA, in 2017, 46.6 million adults (18.9%) were categorised as having a mental illness. Just under one quarter of these people were categorised as having a severe mental illness (Substance Abuse and Mental Health Services Administration 2018). In Europe and the Eastern Mediterranean, more than 14% of the population have some kind of mental disorder (WHO 2022: Fig 3.3).

Data for many countries is limited. However, it is clear that mental health problems are prevalent worldwide. For example, the South African Depression and Anxiety Group (2019) suggests that a quarter of medical students in South Africa have been diagnosed with a depressive disorder. A much earlier study by the WHO (2004), which compiled results of studies from around the world, gave figures for the percentage of national populations with mental health disorders that included 16% in Lebanon, and 9% in China.

Student mental health

Relatively few studies of mental health focus exclusively on the education sector, but there are some indications that rates of mental health problems are similar to or even greater than among the general population. A survey by the UK's National Union of Students reported that 78% of respondents had experienced mental health problems in the previous year and one third had experienced suicidal thoughts (Gil 2015). The following year, an *Architects' Journal* survey found that more than a quarter of UK architecture students had received medical help for mental health problems related to their course and another quarter felt they might have to seek help in the future (Hill 2017).

In 2023, the House of Commons Library published a research briefing on student mental health in England (Lewis & Bolton 2023). This revealed that the proportion of students who disclosed a mental health condition to their university had increased rapidly over the previous decade and was over 5% in 2020–21. In addition, confidential surveys had found much poorer levels of student health, with a 2022 survey by the mental health charity Student Minds indicating that 57% of respondents reported a mental health issue, and more than a quarter had a diagnosed mental health condition. A survey in 2023 by the student news site The Tab found that only 12% of respondents thought their university handled the issue of mental health well (Schifano 2023).

Evidence suggests that mental health problems have an impact on study outcomes. For example, students at a UK distance university who had declared mental health problems but no other disability were less likely to complete or pass modules than peers who had not declared a disability, but were equally likely to get good grades on modules that were completed and passed (Richardson 2015). Students with mental health problems combined with another disability were less likely to complete or pass modules than their non-disabled peers and were also less likely to get good grades.

The Tab (Schifano 2023) found that 59% of students had failed to attend a lecture or seminar due to poor mental health issues. In addition, more than a third of students had been forced to apply for extenuating circumstances because of a mental health issue.

Lister (2019) comments that 'distance learning makes it harder to see when a student is experiencing mental health issues'. This also applies to online learning. On the other hand, an educator teaching online may be the only person to whom a learner discloses their mental health issues, especially if that learner is studying in isolation. The educator may also be the first person to identify any mental health issues.

Most educational institutions, like many workplaces, have explicit strategies outlining how to handle disclosure of mental health problems, especially in situations where it appears a particular individual may be at risk of harm. These should be the first point of reference for all educators seeking guidance about how to support their learners.

The role of educators in supporting online learners' mental health has not been commonly discussed, despite there being an obvious need. The pandemic changed this somewhat, with increased attention being paid to the need for students' mental health and wellbeing to be considered when moving teaching online. However, these discussions often focus on immediate support for mental health rather than on ways of embedding mental health and wellbeing into the curriculum.

Student mental health and Covid-19

In 2020, the Covid-19 pandemic brought unprecedented challenges to all areas of society globally and had a huge impact on the mental health of young people.

In April 2020, just after the UK had gone into lockdown, an Office for Students (2020) briefing note stated that:

> All students will be facing additional challenges during the pandemic. They may contract the virus or have caring responsibilities for friends and family who fall ill. They may struggle to learn remotely or have financial problems. Some of them may be contributing to the frontline effort in hospitals across the country. Those who are still in purpose-built student accommodation may be concerned about the risk to their health

> of sharing communal areas. Students in their final year may be facing the most challenging graduate jobs market for a generation. Postgraduate students may have had to make significant changes to their programme or to pause research activity. (OfS 2020)

Calls to the student-run Nightline helpline in the UK rose sharply from the start of the pandemic, with growing numbers seeking help for anxiety, depression and suicidal thoughts (Hall 2022). A longitudinal study by the Mental Health Foundation identified young adults aged 18–24 as a population group at particularly high risk of mental health problems due to the pandemic, being 'more likely than any other age group to report hopelessness, loneliness, not coping well and suicidal thoughts/feelings' and facing 'a triple whammy of curtailed education, diminished job prospects and reduced social contact with peers' (Mental Health Foundation 2020).

Students with existing mental health issues were particularly badly affected by Covid-19. A survey of 2,438 young people with mental health needs conducted by Young Minds led to the conclusion that:

> The pandemic has had a devastating impact on many of the young people we heard from – some told us that they are deeply anxious, have started self-harming again, are having panic attacks, or are losing motivation and hope for the future. (Young Minds 2021)

Mental health and wellbeing

The wellbeing of learners, which encompasses their mental health, can also be a cause for concern. The charity Student Minds offers this definition of wellbeing:

> Wellbeing will encompass a wider framework, of which mental health is an integral part, but which also includes physical and social wellbeing. This uses a model provided by Richard Kraut, in which optimum wellbeing is defined by the ability of an individual to fully exercise their cognitive, emotional, physical and social powers, leading to flourishing. (Hughes & Spanner 2019: 9)

The organisation Advance HE focuses on student wellbeing, rather than student mental health, and gives this explanation:

> We deliberately use the term 'wellbeing' rather than 'mental health', as not everyone who experiences a decline in their wellbeing would associate that with a 'health' concern. Moreover, we wish to draw a distinction between mental wellbeing, which we all have, and a mental health problem which only some of us would identify as experiencing. We see the two dimensions as independent: a person with a diagnosed major mental health problem may experience a subjectively high level of mental wellbeing. Conversely, someone who has never received a psychiatric diagnosis may experience poor levels of wellbeing. (Houghton & Anderson 2017: 7)

The same report (Houghton & Anderson 2017) includes a model that helps to demonstrate that wellbeing and mental health are two separate issues. A student may have optimal or minimal wellbeing whether they have a psychiatric diagnosis or not. At the same time, they may have maximal or minimal mental ill-health whether they have a positive sense of wellbeing or not.

Models of mental health

When thinking about the relationships between teaching, learning and learner wellbeing, most people will have been influenced by one of the four main models of mental health: the medical, biopsychosocial, social and capabilities models.

Globally, thinking in this area is still dominated by the **medical model**. This views any mental health problem as an issue that resides with the person who has it. In this way of thinking, the responsibility for treating or resolving any issues arising also resides with that person. The medical model views mental health problems as something that can be fixed by therapy and medication. Educators may consider themselves part of this process when providing support to learners with mental health problems.

The **biopsychosocial model** proposes that biological, psychological and social factors that might contribute to mental health are interdependent. This model is similar to the medical model, in that it includes biological and psychological elements, but diverges from that model because it emphasises the influence of contextual factors and proposes that body and mind are separate. This model proposes that mental health problems are not entirely innate. Instead, they are shaped by environment, experiences, social situations and other contextual factors. From this perspective, educators should work to ensure that the teaching and learning process and environment minimise any additional triggers or stresses on students that may make existing mental health problems worse or trigger new ones.

These days, there is increasing interest in the **social model**, which takes into account the influence of multiple aspects of an individual's context on their mental health and wellbeing (Dahlgren & Whitehead 2006). This model acknowledges the influence of context on all aspects of health and has been used and adapted for many different purposes.

The model considers the following factors.

- personal characteristics including gender identification, age, ethnic group and hereditary factors;
- individual lifestyle factors such as smoking, alcohol use and physical activity;
- social and community networks including family, friends, colleagues and wider social circles;
- living and working conditions including access and opportunities in respect of jobs, housing, education, health and welfare services;
- general socio-economic, cultural and environmental conditions including disposable income, availability of work and taxation levels.

In a report focused specifically on mental health, the WHO (2022) lists the education sector as one of the required partners in delivering a multisectoral approach to mental health (alongside health, social care, child and youth services, business, housing, criminal justice, the voluntary sector, the private sector and humanitarian assistance). Together with other bodies, they continue to focus on a social determinants of health approach, with the aim of ensuring that society (including education) caters for a diversity of people, who bring with them a range of mental health problems.

Finally, the **capabilities model** posits that a person's wellbeing depends on their freedom and capability to live the kind of life they have reason to value, to be and to do the things they care about. Nussbaum (2000) identifies 10 core capabilities:

1. life – a reasonable lifespan;
2. bodily health – health, nourishment and shelter;
3. bodily integrity – freedom to move from place to place, secure against assault;

4. senses, imagination and thought – capability to imagine, think and reason, including an adequate education;
5. emotions – attachment to things and people outside ourselves, as well as freedom from overwhelming fear and anxiety;
6. practical reason – having a concept of 'good' and ability to critically reflect on life choices;
7. affiliation – ability to live with and show concern for others, and have capability for justice and friendship;
8. other species – caring about animals and nature;
9. play – ability to laugh, play and enjoy recreation;
10. control over environment – ability to participate effectively in political choices relevant to your life, and to have rights on an equal basis with others.

Constraints relating to these capabilities may be external or internal. They may relate to the environment in which a person lives, their life choices or their lack of certain skills. This makes the capabilities model a useful way of thinking about mental health in relation to learning, as solutions might lie in development of learners' skills, or in reducing environmental barriers that can impact mental health.

Barriers and enablers to wellbeing

Lister and her colleagues (2021) consider aspects of educational systems and practices in order to identify barriers and enablers to mental wellbeing in distance learning. Their study finds that many of the education-related barriers to wellbeing can also act as enablers. Whether a particular factor is a barrier or an enabler depends on the person and the context. For example, social media can support wellbeing for some people but undermine it for others.

Mental wellbeing can be classified under three headings: study-related, skills-related, and environmental, with each of those areas broken down into themes (Lister, Seale & Douce 2021).

Study-related

- curriculum – activities, content and design;
- tuition – tutorials, relationship with tutor, support and flexibility;
- assessment – feedback, grades, assessment design, types of assessment, deadlines and extensions.

Skills-related

- study skills – organising study, studying, assessment and reflection;
- self-management skills – sense of identity, managing mental health, and behaviours;
- social skills – attitude to participation, help-seeking behaviour and communication skills.

Environmental

- spaces – physical spaces, social media, isolation/community;
- people – peers, family, behaviours;
- systems – communication, support, rules, systems and administrative processes;
- life – background and life circumstances.

Each of these can be viewed as either a benefit or a barrier, depending on the context. In the case of microcredential learners, some of that context is not under the control of the course provider, but many aspects are.

Study-related aspects of learning can all be designed with learner wellbeing in mind. Universal Design for Learning (UDL; see Chapter 2) is helpful here. It provides prompts around engagement to help stimulate learners' interest and motivation for learning and suggests different ways in which information and content can be presented in order to aid the understanding of different learners. It also points out that learners differ in the ways they can navigate a learning environment and express what they know, and so the UDL checkpoints suggest different ways in which learners can compose and share ideas.

There are limited opportunities within a microcredential to develop learners' study skills, self-management skills or social skills, but elements of these can be built into the curriculum. UDL can help by suggesting ways to support planning and strategy development, facilitate the management of information and resources, and enhance learners' capacity for monitoring their progress. For skills that are beyond the scope of a short course, learners can be pointed towards relevant resources provided by the institution, or open educational resources that deal with these skills.

Some aspects of a learner's environment are out of the control of the educator or institution. However, the systems that learners encounter as they register for and work through a course can have a significant impact on wellbeing. In particular, it is important to check that these systems have been thought through in terms of microcredential learners, and that they are not faced with administrative processes designed for full-time, on-campus students, or given the double burden of working through processes associated with the institution providing the microcredential as well as processes associated with the platform on which the course is offered.

Learner journey

When planning for learner wellbeing from an environmental perspective, it can be helpful to spend some time working with different departments to identify the main administrative points in the learner journey. These can be considered under six headings: enquiry, registration, study, assessment, achievement and communication. Each of these areas has the potential to be a source of anxiety. They can also drain learners' confidence and reduce motivation if the answers to the following questions are not clear.

- **Enquiry:** where will the potential learner find out about the microcredential and what it involves? Is there an accessible website or prospectus, with opportunities to ask questions, and a clear route to registration?
- **Registration:** is a new account required with the institution or the platform? Is there a mechanism for connecting registration with any existing accounts? Are any potential sources of funding and support explained and linked to? What forms of identification are required – bearing in mind that learners may be registering from different countries? What forms of payment are accepted, which currencies are accepted – and is the price acceptable to potential learners? If they change their mind and want a refund, how will they go about this, and how will this be processed?
- **Study:** is the route to the study site clear and accessible? If the learner only has limited access to the internet, can they download the course and its resources for offline study? Is it clear how they can access library resources, their academic record, or help and support? If their circumstances change and they need to submit a special

circumstances case, ask for an extension, or transfer to a later presentation of the course, are they aware of how to do this?
- **Assessment:** how will learners submit assessed work? Which types and sizes of file are acceptable? If some of the assessment is formative, will they receive feedback in time to act on it before completing the course? How will they go about proving they are the person who did the work and achieved the learning outcomes? Is the policy on plagiarism clear (expectations about plagiarism vary around the world)?
- **Achievement:** where will results be available and how soon? What form will certification take and how will learners access it? Can it be connected to or stacked with credentials from the same institution or other providers?
- **Communication:** will learners be able to stay in touch with each other after the course ends? Will they still be linked to communities at the institution?

Responsibility for many of these areas of the environment does not rest with the educator alone (see Chapter 3 for an overview of the different roles associated with learner support on a microcredential) but it is important that someone is responsible for taking wellbeing into account at every stage of the learner journey. When planning for wellbeing on study-related and skills-related elements of the learner journey, it is helpful to consider these in relation to the key areas of identity, belonging, motivation and confidence.

Identity

A major influence on wellbeing is identity. It is widely acknowledged that having a strong sense of identity can have a positive impact on mental health and wellbeing. Within formal education, a strong sense of self can help learners of any age develop positive relationships with others, make good decisions, and cope with study-related challenges. Understanding identity can help educators design teaching and learning activities that support student wellbeing (Bliuc, Goodyear & Ellis 2017). It can also help them to support individuals in getting to grips with the process of being and becoming a microcredential learner.

Self-categorisation theory clarifies the relationship between teaching, learning and student mental health (Turner 1982). This theory distinguishes between personal and social identity. It suggests that everyone has a complex mixture of personal and social identities which develop over time as new facets are added, and existing facets are strengthened or revised.

Personal identity defines each individual as a unique person and consists of the characteristics that make them different from others. These include physical appearance, personality, values, priorities, interests and beliefs. Social identities are made up of the different groups that include the individual as a member. Some of these (such as gender, ethnic and racial background, religion and nationality) relate to demographics, while others are linked to social contexts (friend groups, classroom groups and other personal relationships). Social identities are associated with behavioural norms – members of different social groups are expected to act in specific ways.

An individual's approach to learning will partially depend on their understanding of the norms for learning connected with their social group memberships (Smyth et al. 2017). Learner wellbeing can be affected when there are clashes between the behavioural norms and apparent values of different social groups. On microcredentials, for example, there might be tensions between an individual's identity as a learner and as a worker. Or there might be tensions because the expected norms for learners in one country differ from the expected norms built into a microcredential run from another country.

Positive self-conceptions, higher self-esteem and better mental wellbeing are associated with individuals having a strong sense of personal identity (knowing who they are, what they like and how to behave in a situation); enjoying positive relationships with their groups; and being comfortable with their demographic groups and how those are represented.

In the context of education, lack of a strong sense of self can lead individuals to feel anxious when making choices about what to study and how to manage their time. It can also result in them making poor choices. For example, they may feel pressurised into socialising rather than working on an assignment. They may allow others to make decisions for them, resulting in them studying subjects they do not enjoy or participating in activities they do not feel comfortable with. This can result in them feeling disengaged from their studies. If this pattern continues, it can leave learners feeling depressed or anxious about the choices they have made. A weak sense of self can also result in a lack of confidence and may make individuals more sensitive to critical feedback on their work.

To strengthen and support the wellbeing of microcredential learners in respect of identity, educators can:

- draw attention to their achievements;
- make it clear how learners can support each other;
- design activities that strengthen learners' sense of self and wellbeing;
- ensure learners' backgrounds and aspects of their identities are represented in teaching and learning activities and in the resources.

Belonging

Associated with identity is a sense of belonging. In the context of formal education such as microcredentials, belonging is inseparable from wellbeing and academic performance. When examining the links between student identity and mental health, Skipper and Fay (2019) note that:

> Students who feel a strong sense of academic identity and belonging to their school are more likely to see themselves as part of a community and therefore seek support when experiencing challenges. This, in turn, will lead to positive mental health and wellbeing. (Skipper & Fay 2019: 4)

Learning is a social process – social interaction plays a fundamental role in the development of cognition (Vygotsky 1987). Microcredential learners may be part of a cohort from their workplace; they may be sharing their learning within a workplace; they may be building knowledge together in online forums or using online tools to collaborate on a team task. In each case, a sense of belonging to the group is important for wellbeing. Feeling they are accepted and valued by others makes it easier for them to develop meaningful and positive relationships with other learners, to participate in shared endeavours, to pursue common goals, and to develop support networks.

If learners do not feel they fit in with a particular group, or do not feel accepted by that group, this can have a negative impact on their wellbeing (Froehlich et al. 2023). This can occur if learners feel the cultural values of the group they are required to work with are at odds with their own values and interests. When learners feel they are outsiders, they may use mental energy to monitor for threats, leaving fewer resources for higher cognitive processes such as learning and tackling complex problems.

To strengthen and support the wellbeing of microcredential learners in respect of identity, educators can:

- ensure learners' backgrounds and aspects of their identities are represented in teaching and learning activities and in the resources;
- if a face-to-face course is adapted to become a microcredential accessible to international learners, check that content (for example, references to legislation or historical events) remains relevant and that the language and references will be comprehensible for learners from a different cultural background;
- create a sense of community within a cohort;
- help learners to support each other and to feel they are learning together.

Motivation

Learners need to be motivated to complete a microcredential successfully. Two types of motivation are relevant here: intrinsic and extrinsic. Intrinsic motivation comes from within. People do things because they enjoy them, find them interesting or satisfying, or consider them important to their sense of identity. When an individual is intrinsically motivated to act, for example when studying a subject that fascinates them, they feel a sense of owning their actions – actions that align with their values and interests. This supports wellbeing as it facilitates a coherent sense of self.

Extrinsic motivation relates to doing things for external reasons, such as material reward, avoiding a bad outcome (e.g. studying for a test to avoid failing) or because a particular course or certificate is required for promotion. A lot of formal learning is extrinsically motivated, with tests, grades and qualifications as motivating factors, but, if these are not combined with intrinsic enjoyment of the subject, wellbeing can be affected.

Building learners' intrinsic motivation is often a long-term process. However, educators can increase intrinsic interest by:

- sharing an enthusiasm for learning and displaying a passion for their subject and role;
- recognising learners' achievements, promoting their sense of competence;
- providing feedback that is sincere, promotes autonomy and conveys attainable standards;
- encouraging learners to connect with a wider community and relate their learning to aspects of their life that are important to them;
- designing teaching and learning activities that give learners control over their learning.

Extrinsic motivation can be developed in the short term by explaining the reasons for learning a particular topic, what it will lead to, what will be built upon it later, and why learners will find it valuable to engage with the subject. Incentives can also build short-term extrinsic motivation, enhance longer-term intrinsic motivation, and help to build confidence.

Learners' confidence can be increased by well-designed lessons and assessments that encourage and reward progress at all ability levels. When learners can see that they have achieved an objective, however small, this should provide confidence to attempt the next. It is important to be particularly supportive of, and attentive to, confidence during transitions from one educational environment to another, as learners' confidence is likely to be lower when they are in a new environment. Although learners may be familiar with individual aspects of microcredentials – skills-related development, university-level curriculum, and online communication – they are unlikely to have studied a microcredential before, so will need support to build their confidence.

Designing for wellbeing

Bringing discussion of issues such as mental health, wellbeing and anxiety into the academic domain can help to improve the student experience, and raise retention and success rates. Houghton and Anderson (2017) offer one reason why discussions around these subjects tend not to take place within formal education settings:

> Mental wellbeing issues are often not talked about; the connection with effective teaching and learning deemed to be self-evident. Do all educators not strive to create environments that are conducive to students' learning and, in the process, address the issues that might undermine students' mental wellbeing? Mental wellbeing, as a concept, can seem so all-encompassing that it stands invisible in plain sight. (Houghton & Anderson 2017: 10)

Speaking openly about mental health, and sharing experiences, can lead to greater understanding and awareness. Whatever the sector, subject or geographical context, creating open and welcoming environments where wellbeing is talked about is an important part of the educator's role, because discussion of mental health and wellbeing chip away at the social stigmas associated with the topic.

It is important that course discussion areas are safe, compassionate and supportive spaces in which learners can share their experiences (if they wish to). Educators can help by providing guidelines for discussion and modelling good practice. The box below provides an example set of guidelines. These were written by Leigh-Anne Perryman and are taken from a 12-week Open University microcredential offered on FutureLearn where they were particularly relevant, *Teacher Development: Embedding Mental Health in the Curriculum*. Similar guidelines are shared on many of The Open University's modules and microcredentials.

Guidelines for discussion

It's vital that everyone feels welcome in these discussion areas. Online discussions can easily become heated, especially as there are no visual cues giving an indication of the spirit in which a particular comment is being made. So, please be sensitive to others' perspectives and views, even if they differ from your own. If you want to voice an alternative perspective or opinion, take care to focus on the ideas expressed and not the person expressing them. Before you contribute to a discussion area, ask yourself 'am I being kind to others in what I've said?'. We're not expecting you to steer clear of discussing sensitive or contentious issues, but as the course discussions are not heavily moderated we're relying on the course community to take care of each other.

Respect others' privacy

Throughout the course, you'll be encouraged to draw on and share your own experiences. If you're an educator,

---

(Box continued on next page)

(Box continued from previous page)

> you might wish to share examples from your own practice. This could be useful for other learners, helping to give real-world relevance to the exploration of specific topics, allowing comparisons to be made across sectors, settings, nations, and cultures.
>
> Please take care to anonymise any discussion of specific people (e.g. your students, friends or family). Don't share any information that could allow the people you're discussing to be identified. Good practice is always to assume the worst – that the post you've shared will make its way to the world outside this course. In our networked age, platforms such as Twitter and Facebook allow information to be shared far and wide in an instant. This can happen by accident, even by people with the best of intentions.
>
> If you have concerns about a particular post, you have several options. Gently mentioning your worries via a reply to that post could be sufficient. Alternatively, you could use the flag system to bring the post to the attention of the FutureLearn moderators. This will submit the post for investigation by a moderator, who will then delete the post if necessary, or even block that user from posting on the course if necessary.

Curriculum infusion

As well as offering safe spaces where learners can raise issues related to mental health and wellbeing, some educators integrate or 'infuse' such content within their courses and assessment.

Curriculum infusion is fairly well established in the United States, but less so elsewhere. There are many ways to achieve it, and different disciplines and institutions have adopted a variety of approaches.

An Australian university incorporated a programme designed to promote wellbeing for indigenous people into its undergraduate social work degree. The programme was adapted for university students but its core values remained the same. Before and after the programme, learners completed questionnaires to assess their wellbeing and levels of growth and empowerment using psychological scales. These questionnaires showed significant improvements in these areas after they completed the programme.

It would clearly not be possible to include within a short microcredential all the material those students studied over the course of an entire degree, but one or two relevant elements from the themes and assessment could be incorporated.

Learners explored the following themes:

- human values and qualities
- basic human needs
- understanding relationships
- life journey
- conflict resolution
- understanding emotions and crisis
- grief and loss
- beliefs and attitudes
- managing change
- self-care. (Whiteside et al. 2017)

Learners were assessed by tasks that included:

- facilitating their own session on one of the programme topics with a group of people outside the university, such as friends, family or workmates;

- designing a presentation;
- writing a final reflection on their experience of the subject overall.

Some disciplines lend themselves naturally to curriculum infusion. Health, medicine, psychology, sports and some of the social sciences can easily have wellbeing as a core part of the content. It can be more challenging to integrate content related to wellbeing in other disciplines. However, there is growing recognition in educational contexts that mental health is a truly interdisciplinary issue and so educators are finding increasingly creative and context-relevant ways to embed it in their disciplines.

One example of this is the University of the West of England's architecture programme (Pilkington et al. 2013), in which educators are finding ways to infuse their curriculum with mental wellbeing by exploring links between green space and mental wellbeing and including a project to design a building that promotes wellbeing. An undergraduate chemistry degree at Amherst College (Chung et al. 2023) has a curriculum designed around diversity, equity and inclusion. Its subjects include reshaping the global social landscape with chemical tools, and the possibilities for chemistry as an agent of positive change. An earlier example (Olson & Riley 2009) from Georgetown University was a maths class where the lecturer incorporated datasets relating to mental health issues around nutrition, gambling and alcohol, encouraging discussion about tackling the issues while also dealing with mathematical modelling of the data.

Learner autonomy

Autonomy is related to learner wellbeing and a sense of empowerment. In contrast, disempowerment, unequal relationships, feelings of powerlessness and a sense that education is something being done to learners all have negative impacts on attainment and mental health. Over the past few decades, numerous studies have found that giving learners greater responsibility for their own learning (for example, through goal setting, or having choice over their learning activities) leads to them feeling more in control, with positive effects on their wellbeing.

UDL checkpoint 7.1 emphasises the importance of flexibility and choice for learners:

> In an instructional setting, it is often inappropriate to provide choice of the learning objective itself, but it is often appropriate to offer choices in how that objective can be reached, in the context for achieving the objective, in the tools or supports available, and so forth. Offering learners choices can develop self-determination, pride in accomplishment, and increase the degree to which they feel connected to their learning. (CAST 2018)

Learner autonomy can cover many areas, including learners having input into:

- what is learned;
- the level of difficulty or challenge;
- how this is learned – flexibility of pedagogy and process;
- what tools are used for learning;
- how learning is demonstrated;
- who they learn with;
- which resources they use to support learning;
- when they learn, and how quickly or slowly;
- their learning outcomes and objectives;
- where they learn.

The possibilities differ across sectors, subjects and contexts. Choices that are offered should be meaningful, not too complex, reflect students' interests and 'genuinely enable students to pursue different interests and preferences' (Baik et al. 2017: 19). They should also take into account that learners differ in their willingness to be autonomous and in the skills they bring. Some of the areas of learner autonomy listed above, such as where learners engage with online learning, or the tools they use to access it, are relatively straightforward to build into a microcredential, while others may increase complexity without a clear benefit for learners.

Digital wellbeing

The online aspect of most microcredentials brings its own issues related to wellbeing. Caring for digital wellbeing involves several factors:

- looking after personal health, safety, relationships and work-life balance in digital settings;
- acting safely and responsibly in digital environments;
- managing digital workload, overload and distraction;
- using digital media to participate in political and community actions;
- using personal digital data for wellbeing benefits;
- acting with concern for the human and natural environment when using digital tools;
- balancing digital with real-world interactions appropriately in relationships. (Beetham 2015)

Lister noted in a blog post that:

> The nature of distance learning attracts students with more severe mental health issues; for example, people who can't attend a campus university because they are hospitalised, have agoraphobia or severe social anxiety,

or people who may have had a bad experience at a campus university and want to be able to study in their home environment. (Lister 2019)

Online study requires the development of new skills and can involve uncertainty over matters such as assessment. These challenges may be especially acute for learners with existing anxiety. On the other hand, online study can also offer a variety of means of supporting students' mental health and wellbeing if designed and delivered appropriately.

Negative aspects of online learning for wellbeing include:

- poorly managed online discussions leading to bullying, individuals being targeted, or disconcerting opinions not being challenged;
- feeling alone or isolated due to a lack of opportunities for interaction and discussion;
- having too many online locations to keep track of when studying;
- feeling stressed when poor internet access prevents full participation;
- institutions' unreasonable expectations in relation to digital skills;
- trying to study at home or in social spaces with multiple distractions;
- difficulty separating time for study from time for family and relaxation.

These negative elements are balanced by the benefits of online learning for wellbeing, which include:

- reduced stress and pressure associated with being able to choose where and when to study;

- the satisfaction of mastering a skill or achieving a qualification when achieving the same by attending a traditional course would not be possible;
- online studies providing a focus/excitement to life in cases when studying a traditional, face-to-face course would not have been possible.
- confidence-boosting discussions or feedback that would not be achievable in a face-to-face environment.

Conclusion

Microcredentials are being introduced at a point when the importance of student wellbeing and mental health is becoming increasingly evident. This means that consideration of these elements can be built into microcredentials programmes from the start. Not only does this have the potential to improve the experience of students; research suggests it can also improve rates of success and completion. One element of the study experience that can increase stress and anxiety for learners is assessment. The following chapter considers all aspects of assessment on microcredentials, including ways of reducing the well-documented phenomenon of test anxiety.

References

Baik, C., Larcombe, W., Brooker, A., Wyn, J., Allen, L., Brett, M., Field, R. and James, R. (2017). *Enhancing student wellbeing: A handbook for academic educators*. Melbourne: University of Melbourne. Available at https://melbourne-cshe.unimelb.edu.au/_data/assets/pdf_file/0006/2408604/MCSHE-Student-Wellbeing-Handbook-FINAL.pdf

Beetham, H. (2015). Digital wellbeing. #LTHEchat, 19 June 2015. Available at https://lthechat.com/2015/06/19/lthechat-no-28-with-helen-beetham-helenbeetham-on-digital-wellbeing

Bliuc, A.-M., Goodyear, P. and Ellis, R. A. (2017). The role of students' social identities in fostering high-quality learning in higher education. In: Mavor, K., Platow, M. and Bizumic, B. *Self and social identity in educational contexts.* London and New York: Routledge. pp. 211–222.

CAST. (2018). *Universal design for learning guidelines version 2.2.* Available at http://udlguidelines.cast.org

Chung, J., Bunnell, S. L., Lopez, A. M. and Olshansky, J. H. (2023). Leveraging student–faculty–staff partnerships to implement inclusive curricular reform in chemistry education. *Journal of Chemistry Education,* 100(6): 2243–2252.

Dahlgren, G. and Whitehead, M. (2006). *European strategies for tackling social inequities in health: Levelling up part 2.* Copenhagen: WHO Regional Office for Europe. Available at https://iris.who.int/bitstream/handle/10665/107791/E89384.pdf

Froehlich, L., Brokjøb, L. G., Nikitin, J. and Martiny, S. E. (2023). Integration or isolation: Social identity threat relates to immigrant students' sense of belonging and social approach motivation in the academic context. *Journal of Social Issues,* 79(1): 264–290.

Gil, N. (2015). Majority of students experience mental health issues, says NUS survey. *The Guardian,* 14 December. Available at https://www.theguardian.com/education/2015/dec/14/majority-of-students-experience-mental-health-issues-says-nus-survey

Hall, R. (2022). Pandemic still affecting UK students' mental health, says helpline. *The Guardian,* 14 November. Available at https://www.theguardian.com/education/2022/nov/14/pandemic-still-affecting-uk-students-mental-health-says-helpline-covid

Hill, A. (2016). Survey: 25% of UK architecture students treated for mental health problems. *The Guardian,* 28 July. Available at https://www.theguardian.com/education/2016/jul/28/uk-architecture-students-mental-health-problem-architects-journal-survey

Houghton, A.-M. and Anderson, J. (2017). *Embedding mental wellbeing in the curriculum: Maximising success in higher education*. York: Higher Education Academy. Available at https://www.advance-he.ac.uk/knowledge-hub/embedding-mental-wellbeing-curriculum-maximising-success-higher-education

Hughes, G. and Spanner, L. (2019). *The university mental health charter*. Leeds: Student Minds. Available at https://www.studentminds.org.uk/uploads/3/7/8/4/3784584/191208_umhc_artwork.pdf

Lewis, J. and Bolton, P. (2023). *Student mental health in England: Statistics, policy, and guidance*. Commons Library Research Briefing, House of Commons Library. Available at https://researchbriefings.files.parliament.uk/documents/CBP-8593/CBP-8593.pdf

Lister, K. (2019). Embedding mental wellbeing in the curriculum: a new approach from the Open University. *What Works Wellbeing*, 10 December 2019. Available at https://whatworkswellbeing.org/blog/embedding-mental-wellbeing-in-the-curriculum-a-new-approach-from-the-open-university

Lister, K., Seale, J. and Douce, C. (2021). Mental health in distance learning: A taxonomy of barriers and enablers to student mental wellbeing. *Open Learning: The Journal of Open, Distance and e-learning*, 36(2): 102–116.

McManus, S., Meltzer, H., Brugha, T. S, Bebbington, P. E. and Jenkins, R. (2009). *Adult psychiatric morbidity in England, 2007: Results of a household survey*. The NHS Information Centre for Health and Social Care. Available at https://digital.nhs.uk/data-and-information/publications/statistical/adult-psychiatric-morbidity-survey/adult-psychiatric-morbidity-in-england-2007-results-of-a-household-survey

Mental Health Foundation. (2020). *Coronavirus: The divergence of mental health experiences during the pandemic*. Available at https://www.mentalhealth.org.uk/our-work/research/coronavirus-divergence-mental-health-experiences-during-pandemic

Nussbaum, M. C. (2000). *Women and human development: The capabilities approach*. Cambridge: Cambridge University

Press (The Seeley Lectures). DOI: https://doi.org/10.1017/CBO9780511841286

Office for Students. (2020). *Supporting student mental health*. Available at https://www.officeforstudents.org.uk/publications/coronavirus-briefing-note-supporting-student-mental-health

Olson, T. A. and Riley, J. B. (2009). Weaving the campus safety net by integrating student health issues into the curriculum. *About Campus*, 14(2): 27–29.

Pilkington, P., Marco, E., Grant, M. and Orme, J. (2013). Engaging a wider public health workforce for the future: A public health practitioner in residence approach to public health. *Public Health*, 127(5): 427–434. Available at http://eprints.uwe.ac.uk/18787

Rice-Oxley, M. (2019). What is mental illness? *The Guardian*, 3 June. Available at https://www.theguardian.com/society/2019/jun/03/mental-illness-is-there-really-a-global-epidemic

Richardson, J. T. E. (2015). Academic attainment in students with mental health difficulties in distance education. *International Journal of Mental Health*, 44(3): 231–240. Available at https://www.tandfonline.com/doi/pdf/10.1080/00207411.2015.1035084

SADAG. (2019). *The South African Depression and Anxiety Group: Infographs*. Available at https://www.sadag.org/index.php?option=com_content&view=article&id=3076:university-of-cape-town-the-burden-if-depression-and-anxiety-among-medical-students-in-south-africa&catid=153&Itemid=483

Schifano, I. (2023). 'They made me feel invalid': Shocking new figures show scale of student mental health crisis. *The Tab*, 2 May. Available at https://thetab.com/uk/2023/05/02/they-made-me-feel-invalid-shocking-new-figures-show-scale-of-student-mental-health-crisis-294306

Skipper. Y. and Fay, M. (2019). *'Why not me?' The extent to which students' academic identity impacts their sense of community and mental health*. SRHE Research Report. London: Society for Research into Higher Education. Available at https://srhe.ac.uk/wp-content/uploads/2020/03/YSkipper-MFay-SRHE-Research-Reoprt.pdf

Smyth, L., Mavor, K. I., Platow, M. J. and Grace, D. M. (2017). Understanding social identity in education: The modifying role of perceived norms. In: Mavor, K. I., Platow, M. J. and Bizumic, B. *Self and social identity in educational contexts*. Abingdon: Routledge.

Substance Abuse and Mental Health Services Administration. (2018). *Key substance use and mental health indicators in the United States: Results from the 2017 national survey on drug use and health*. Available at https://www.samhsa.gov/data/sites/default/files/cbhsq-reports/NSDUHFFR2017/NSDUHFFR2017.pdf

Turner, J. C. (2010). Towards a cognitive redefinition of the social group. In: Postmes, T. and Branscombe, N. R. *Rediscovering social identity*. Psychology Press. pp. 210–234. Original work published 1981.

Vygotsky, L. S. (1987). Thought and word. In: Rieber, R. W. and Carton, A. S. *The collected works of L S Vygotsky vol 1*. Plenum Press. Original work published 1934.

Whiteside, M., Bould, E., Tsey, K., Venville, A., Cadet-James, Y. and Morris, M. E. (2017). Promoting twenty-first-century student competencies: A wellbeing approach. *Australian Social Work*, 70(3): 324–336. DOI: https://doi.org/10.1080/0312407X.2016.1263351

WHO. (2022). *World mental health report: Transforming mental health for all*. Geneva: World Health Organization. Available at https://iris.who.int/bitstream/handle/10665/356119/9789240049338-eng.pdf

WHO World Mental Health Survey Consortium. (2004). Prevalence, severity and unmet need for treatment of mental disorders in the World Health Organization world mental health surveys. *JAMA*, 291(21): 2581–2590.

Young Minds. (2021). *The impact of Covid-19 on young people with mental health needs*. Available at https://www.youngminds.org.uk/about-us/reports-and-impact/coronavirus-impact-on-young-people-with-mental-health-needs

CHAPTER 7

Assessing microcredentials

Assessment is both a defining characteristic of microcredentials and one of the greatest challenges to their success. These are not simply short courses, they are short courses that lead to a credential warranting the holder has certain skills, capacities or knowledge – typically those which employers are looking for. To be able to state authoritatively that this is the case, microcredential providers must assess learners against defined criteria. Doing this in a way that will be accepted as authoritative requires expensive infrastructure. It also raises the problem of identity. How do you know who is completing the assessment if your course runs online and you have never met your learners? An additional

---

How to cite this book chapter:
Ferguson, R. and Whitelock, D. 2024. Assessing microcredentials. In: Ferguson, R. and Whitelock, D. *Microcredentials for Excellence: A Practical Guide.* Pp. 173–216. London: Ubiquity Press. DOI: https://doi.org/10.5334/bcz.g. License: CC BY-NC 4.0

challenge is the expectation, which is often included in definitions of these credentials, that learners will be able to 'stack' microcredentials from different providers. This implies some degree of alignment between those providers, which requires additional infrastructure as well as complex negotiations.

Assessment

Assessment is required for accreditation to be awarded in a way that is both meaningful and trustworthy. When massive open online courses (MOOCs) became a worldwide phenomenon (Pappano 2012) it seemed possible that short online courses could be offered without a complex accreditation system because the value they offered to those who signed up lay in the opportunities for learning that they offered, rather than an opportunity to evidence that learning. Some MOOCs operated without any assessment; others used multiple-choice tests that could easily be gamed by individuals searching the internet for the answers or simply working through the same free course multiple times (Northcutt, Ho & Chuang 2016). Without reliable evidence that individuals had gained skills or knowledge from a course, providers instead offered certificates of participation or completion. These recognised that an individual had engaged in some way with the course but did not go any further. In other cases, the course itself was offered free of charge, but assessment and accreditation came at a price.

For some people, these approaches work well because they join a course to gain skills and knowledge rather than a piece of paper. However, those people typically have no need of a certificate because they already have one, or several. Although MOOCs initially appeared to be a way of opening up education for everyone, enrolments are heavily skewed towards those who already have one or more degrees (Cannell & Macintyre 2014; Meaney 2021). Opportunities to develop knowledge and skills are valuable but, for those who want to access new employment opportunities, the opportunity to gain accreditation may be even more important. This need for accreditation has been one of the factors that has pushed MOOC providers to shift to Nanodegrees (Shen 2014), MicroMasters (Young 2016), MasterTracks (Valli 2018) and microcredentials (Stancombe 2020).

Assessment is valuable to employers because it leads to accreditation, which offers a way of filtering job applicants quickly. It is valuable to job applicants for much the same reason. More broadly, though, what is its value to learners? Although credentialing focuses attention on the high-stakes assessment, often an exam, that takes place at the end of a course, there are actually three types of assessment, each with a different purpose: assessment for learning, assessment as learning, and assessment of learning.

Assessment for learning gives educators and learners information about what learners know. This means that educators can target future teaching and feedback to address any areas in which a particular learner needs further development, while learners can determine areas of study that need additional attention. This type of assessment may take place before or during a course and can make a significant contribution to learner achievement and attainment (Black & Wiliam 1998). Before a course, it may take the form of diagnostic assessment intended to identify learners' existing knowledge, skills, strengths, needs, interests and learning preferences. Such assessment will often collect information from multiple sources, including the learner and previous educators.

Assessment during a course of study can provide information that helps learners improve their knowledge and skills, for example by an educator adjusting their teaching methods, giving the learner additional resources, or providing resources in a different format. In a microcredential that provides limited tutor support, assessment for learning can be used to automatically assign a learner to a certain route through the course or it may prompt learners to return to material they have not yet fully understood. Incorrect responses to multiple-choice questions can lead to hints about the correct approach to take, or signposts to relevant parts of the study materials.

Assessment as learning emphasises the role of learners, engaging them in self-assessment so they can participate actively in directing their own learning. This approach, which often uses reflection-based activities, can involve educator-supported activities such as:

- Self-reflection: learners reflect on their own understanding and progress and set specific, measurable and achievable goals for their learning.
- Self-monitoring: learners monitor their progress towards their goals and adjust their learning strategies as needed.
- Self-evaluation: learners evaluate their own understanding and progress, then provide feedback to the educator and/or their peers.
- Feedback-seeking: learners actively seek feedback from the teacher and/or their peers to improve their understanding and progress.

By taking an active role in their learning, learners can become more invested in the material they are studying and more motivated to act. At the same time, they develop skills that are valuable both in the workplace and in other learning situations.

In the case of microcredentials, some students may decide they do not need to complete the assessment. This may be because they do not need the credential to evidence their learning; they are not working towards a more extensive qualification that requires them to gather evidence of previous learning; or they have joined the course for the knowledge and skills it offers, rather than for a certificate. It is therefore useful to emphasise within the course the roles of assessment as and for learning, making it clear that assessment and learning are not necessarily separate activities.

Assessment of learning, or summative assessment, is generally used to confirm what learners know and can do, whether they have achieved learning outcomes, and whether they can be assigned credit for the work they have completed. It can also be used to rank learners in order of ability.

Assessment of learning in a microcredential may involve a variety of activities, such as:

- **Tests and exams:** Written assessments that measure student understanding of the material. These may include multiple-choice, short answer and essay questions.
- **Final projects:** Hands-on or applied assessments that measure student understanding of the material and the ability to apply it in a real-world context.
- **Portfolios:** Collections of student work that demonstrate their understanding and progress over time.
- **Observation:** This method is only possible in some microcredentials and involves observing and evaluating students as they engage in tasks or activities that demonstrate their understanding of the material.

These three types of assessment – for learning, as learning and of learning – can be used in combination throughout a course of study and tailored to different learning outcomes.

Learning outcomes and competency frameworks

All three types of assessment can be aligned with learning outcomes. These specify what learners should be able to do once they have completed the course (see Chapter 5 for more on learning outcomes). In the case of a microcredential, they may form an element of the final badge or certificate, specifying what the learner is able to do. Given the huge range of credentials and microcredentials on offer around the world, learning outcomes provide a useful guide for any employer who is unsure what a certain course covers.

This means that assessment of learning should always be aligned with learning outcomes. If some learning outcomes go unassessed or some assessment tasks require skills that are irrelevant to the stated learning outcomes, this signals a lack of alignment between curriculum elements that may reduce learners' study performance. It is important that learners have an opportunity to demonstrate they possess the skills and knowledge associated with the course, particularly as these may be explicitly linked to the skills and competencies required for specific jobs.

Competencies are the behaviours and technical abilities needed for people to perform effectively at work. An individual's competency, their ability to perform effectively within a given context, 'can be measured by assessing key performance indicators that define and provide a map of the expected areas and levels of performance' (George 2022).

A 'competency framework' sets out and defines each competency required by individuals working in an organisation or as part of that organisation (George 2022). Examples include the European e-Competence Framework, which classifies 40 competences for professionals working in areas related to information and communication technologies (ICT). The UNESCO Competency Framework includes 'a set of related knowledge, skills and abilities that result in essential behaviors expected from those working for the Organization' (UNESCO 2016). Published more recently, the European Sustainability Competence Framework (Bianchi, Pisiotis & Cabrera Giraldez 2022) comprises 12 main competences, organised in four areas: embodying sustainability values (such as supporting fairness), embracing complexity in sustainability (such as systems thinking), envisioning sustainable futures (such as adaptability) and acting for sustainability (such as political agency).

These frameworks can be used to inform the development of a curriculum that will enable learners to achieve the required outcomes (see Chapter 2 for more details about the pedagogy of competency-based learning). In the context of microcredentials, not only can these frameworks be used as a guide for course development but the competencies covered by them can also be used as metadata tags that will help learners to find relevant courses in online prospectuses when using search engines (Braxton 2023).

Assessment in a digital age

The majority of microcredentials are offered online, which may pose challenges when systems are set up for students who are taking exams on site or handing coursework to tutors who have worked with them face to face. However, since the Covid lockdowns, most institutions have gained some experience of technology-enabled assessment, while others have been working in this way for many years.

Technology-enabled assessment includes use of a computer (or, more broadly, a digital technology) as part of any assessment-related activity. It is also referred to as e-assessment, computer-aided assessment, computer-assisted assessment, technology-based assessment or technology-enhanced assessment – these are all terms that can be used to search for practical support or research in the area.

This is not a new phenomenon. The presidential address to the American Educational Research Association (AERA) in 2007 drew on more than a decade of research in this area and included computer-assisted assessment authoring systems, computer scoring of written responses using optical character reading, speech recognition technologies to analyse learner discourse, and knowledge mapping, as well as assessment using computer games, virtual worlds, mobile phones and game platforms (Baker 2007).

Using technology in assessment has many benefits (Oldfield et al. 2012), including:

- assessment of skills that cannot be assessed in other ways;
- feedback that is perceived to be impersonal and non-judgemental;
- immediate feedback;
- improved cost-effectiveness;
- increased efficiency;
- more authentic assignments;
- new possibilities for the design of assignments;
- opportunities for repeated practice;
- students being able to check their understanding without having to wait for an educator;
- students being able to make mistakes in private.

On the negative side, though, technology-enabled assessment can:

- become constraining;

- prompt educators to teach to tests that can be automatically marked and assessed;
- mislead learners with badly phrased questions or a selection of wrong answers;
- waste teachers' time with a requirement to produce challenging questions, pitched at the right level, paired with a series of answers that are all equally plausible;
- make it easy for learners to game the system;
- enable learners to access previous answers;
- open up possibilities for plagiarised responses.

Technology-enabled assessment encompasses a wide range of tools and methods. In the context of microcredentials, these include the following.

- **Adaptive testing:** computer algorithms adjust the difficulty level of questions based on a student's responses, providing a personalised and efficient assessment experience.
- **Automated essay scoring:** uses natural language processing and machine learning algorithms to evaluate students' written responses.
- **Computer-based testing:** uses computer software to deliver and grade tests, quizzes and other assessments.
- **Electronic portfolios (e-portfolios):** digital representations of a learner's experiences and achievements. Creating and curating collections like these requires learners to develop organisation, planning, reflection and communication skills.
- **Multiple-choice questions (MCQs):** frequently used form of computer-based testing in which students must select their answer from several options.

- **Online exams:** although some countries and institutions require examinations to take place in person, since the Covid lockdowns online versions are increasingly common.
- **Online quizzes:** delivered and completed online, often using learning management systems, apps or specific educational software. These may include multiple-choice questions, questions that require one-word or one-sentence responses, or images to be labelled.
- **Peer assessment:** using a rubric, and usually with training and educator support, students are automatically assigned the work of others to provide feedback on. Learners become familiar with course content and requirements, with what to look for in good work, and with providing feedback. However, students do need to be aware of these learning opportunities, which should be well aligned with learning outcomes.
- **Simulation and gaming:** uses interactive simulations and games to evaluate student understanding of complex concepts and problem-solving skills.

Two of these approaches, MCQs and online exams, are frequently used in microcredentials. The following sections consider the possibilities they offer and the issues they present.

Multiple-choice questions

Multiple-choice questions (MCQs) have a simple format. The stem contains the question or sets up a problem. Distractors offer possible answers that are incorrect, while the key (or keys) gives the right answer. Students are asked to identify the correct answers while avoiding the distractors.

MCQs are well suited to an online learning environment. Once a computer has been programmed to identify the correct answers, these questions can be marked almost instantaneously. In some cases, MCQs are underpinned by a question bank,

> a collection of uniquely identified questions that allows the selection of questions to create tests based on various predefined criteria. Questions are tagged with descriptors such as: the difficulty of the question, topic, academic level, and the skill or knowledge component addressed. (Bull & Dalziel 2003: 173)

Question banks make it possible to set every student a different variant of the same test, making it difficult to copy the responses of others or to search online for a fully completed quiz. When quiz banks are used formatively, they can also be set to adapt to a student's ability level, with each question selected based on whether previous responses were correct.

A downside of question banks is that they require a large amount of initial input. In the case of some mathematical or statistical subjects, similar questions can be generated automatically once realistic parameters have been set. In other areas, generative AI can help with this task, but is likely to require a lot of sense-checking. It can also be difficult to assess the difficulty of questions, as questions that are phrased in a similar way may vary from easy to impossible to answer. Despite these challenges, many exam boards and educational publishers have created robust question banks that are accessible at a price.

A criticism that has been levelled at MCQs is that they encourage the view that learning simply consists of the acquisition of facts. This is more likely to be true when the questions posed resemble those in trivia quizzes rather than ones that require deeper understanding of the material. As learners spend much of their time practising for assessment, there is a danger that they will tend to adopt a surface approach to learning, gathering facts rather than seeking a deeper understanding. Likewise, teachers will be inclined to teach material that can be assessed using MCQs, rather than encouraging a detailed consideration of the material.

Draper (2009) argues there is no reason that technology-enabled assessment should have a negative impact on learning, because learning benefits do not depend on the choice of technology (in this case, MCQs) but on the teaching method that is paired with the technology. He suggests several ways of using MCQs to support deep learning. These include:

- **Assertion-reason questions.** These begin with a statement and offer a range of explanations of why it is true or false. A correct answer requires an understanding of the different explanations and how they apply to the case.
- **Considering each answer in depth.** Students are asked to respond to the MCQ but also to note for each answer why it is right or wrong. These notes can form part of their study or may be submitted as another element of the assessment.
- **Brainteasers.** Questions are based on the course material but are designed to challenge learners. For example, physics students might be asked what would happen to someone in a lift that was plummeting after its cable had snapped. If the person jumped just before the lift crashed, is it more likely they would (a) be killed or badly injured (b) escape with minor injuries (c) survive unscathed? Posing a question like this to a class via a polling system can assess understanding of the principles and forces

involved and form the basis for subsequent discussion. This approach is most suitable when tutor support is available within the microcredential.
- **Creating questions.** As part of a tutor-marked assignment, students are asked to produce MCQ items that would be suitable for their peers to answer. To design good questions, they need a deep understanding of the subjects they are testing. The questions they produce can be graded based on their lack of ambiguity, alignment with course learning outcomes, appropriate level of difficulty (neither too easy nor too hard), justifications supplied for each item and whether the answers marked as correct are accurate. The best questions could be incorporated within subsequent runs of the course.
- **Including questions in a presentation.** Students working in small groups can be asked to present their work to the class, including a certain number of MCQ items that others in the class respond to using a polling tool or electronic voting system.

A sixth approach is confidence-based marking (Draper 2009). In this form of the MCQ, students not only select a preferred answer but also indicate how confident they are that their answer is correct. Marks are then assigned on the basis not only of whether the answer is correct but also of confidence that the answer is correct. Assigning marks in this way makes it less likely that students will simply guess. It also indicates areas where many students are having problems and which students have misunderstood material.

One method of doing this is to assign students a certain number of marks for each question. They can then allocate these marks as they wish. An example is an MCQ test in which each question has four possible answers, and the students all have four marks to distribute for each question. The correct answer to Question 1 in this test is (b).

- Some students are confident that answer (b) is correct, so each of them allocates four marks to that answer. In this case they are right, so each of them receives four marks for Question 1.
- One student is unable to decide between answers (a) and (b), so assigns two marks to each of them, and receives two marks for answering (b).
- Another student has no idea, and distributes marks evenly, allocating one mark each to answers (a), (b), (c) and (d). They receive the one mark they allocated to answer (b), but they have also clearly indicated their uncertainty to the tutor.
- A final student is falsely confident of the correct answer. They assign all their marks to answer (c) and therefore receive no marks. By allocating marks in this way, they indicate that they have a misconception, which the teacher can then address.

A related approach allows students several attempts at a question. If they get the answer right first time, they receive full marks for that question. If wrong, they receive a helpful piece of feedback, perhaps one that points them to the relevant course material. If they are right the second time, they receive half marks. If their second answer is wrong, they receive no marks but an explanation of the correct answer is provided. This works well on a large scale but the educator must write explanations for every answer, which makes this approach labour-intensive at the small scale.

No matter how MCQs are used, it is important to avoid common mistakes when writing questions.

- **'All the above'.** If students recognise two correct answers, then they can move straight to this option without considering any others.
- **Clear pattern to correct answers.** Students will be looking for patterns in the arrangement of distractors. Test setters often avoid putting the correct answer early on, meaning (c) and (d) are more likely to be correct.
- **Final distractor is obviously wrong.** It can be difficult to come up with plausible distractors, with the result that the last one is clearly incorrect.
- **Grammatical clues.** If the verb in the question implies the correct answer will be plural, then distractors should also be plural. If use of 'an' implies the correct answer begins with a vowel, then distractors should also begin with vowels.
- **Including absolutes.** Students know that things are rarely true or false in all situations, so words like 'always', 'never' or 'none' indicate the presence of a distractor.
- **Negative wording.** Students may miss the negative word and give the wrong answer because they have misread the question rather than because they do not know the correct answer.
- **'None of the above'.** Does not give students an opportunity to demonstrate that they know the correct answer.
- **Off-topic distractors.** One of the distractors is clearly from outside the subject area, which means students can eliminate it as an option.

- **Off-topic questions.** One or more questions does not relate to the course. This can happen when the course is amended after the MCQs have been written.
- **Random success.** If each question has four options and one correct answer, a student who always gives the same answer in response – all (b)s, for example – is likely to score around 25%. Make this random success more unlikely by requiring students to identify two or more correct answers to some questions.
- **Response length.** If the correct answer is long and detailed, distractors should also be long and detailed.
- **Testing recall.** In an online course, a search of course materials will provide a quick answer to a question that tests recall. Instead, ask learners to interpret information, draw inference or predict results.
- **Testing the wrong thing.** Questions about where information appears in the course or how it is presented, rather than about knowledge that relates to learning outcomes.
- **Trick questions.** Questions that are designed to catch students out reveal little about their understanding of the subject and may leave them feeling cheated of the opportunity to gain full marks.
- **Two distractors are synonymous.** If one is true, the other will also be true, which means they can be assumed to be distractors if students know there is only one correct answer.
- **Using the correct terms more often.** If a term appears in multiple answers, students will assume that the answers without it are likely to be distractors.

- **Verbal association.** One or more words in the stem is picked up in one of the answers, suggesting that the two are closely related and that answer is likely to be correct.

Although MCQs are challenging to write well, they have an important role to play in assessment for and as learning as well as assessment of learning.

Because microcredentials are relatively short courses, with some running for 12 weeks and many even shorter, it is difficult to incorporate an online exam at any point except the end, so online exams in this context are almost invariably used as a summative assessment of learning.

Online exams

In a systematic review of 61 articles about students' views on online exams pre-pandemic, Topuz and Kinshuk (2021) found that online exams do not impact students in the same way as in-person exams. The most positive aspect of online exams was students' reduced anxiety about assessment, while the most negative aspect was students' concerns about the technical aspects of the exam.

The Quality Enhancement and Innovation team at The Open University surveyed more than 1,000 distance students about their perceptions of online exams (Aristeidou et al. 2023). Four in five participants preferred to have exams online rather than face-to-face. Students liked the convenience of not having to travel to an examination hall, which can be stressful and time-consuming, especially for students who have to travel for hours if they do not live near a study centre.

Students in the survey highlighted ways in which online exams can benefit students who are less advantaged, such as those with mobility or mental health issues. Benefits for all included students being in control of their environment and able to accommodate other commitments, such as arranging childcare or requiring less time off work. Some students looked at the bigger picture and commented that online exams can contribute to sustainability, as students do not need to use transport to get to the examination hall.

However, there are also downsides to online exams. Students will need a strong and consistent internet connection. In countries where internet connection and electricity supply are intermittent, maintaining a reliable connection throughout the exam period can be hard. Depending on how the exam is invigilated, students may need to have access to a device with a webcam and a microphone or will have to install the hardware and software necessary for scanning and quality control of any handwritten submissions. The design of the online exam interface can also impact students negatively, raising anxiety levels if they cannot backtrack to earlier questions or are given insufficient time to complete their answers (Novick et al. 2022).

Therefore, before designing online exams, it is important to think carefully about the technology that students can access. Microcredential students may be based in countries with different infrastructure and time zones; they may have disabilities that impact how they can engage with an online exam; they may have care commitments that make it difficult for them to spend uninterrupted time on an exam; and they may not have access to a dedicated study space. In addition, unlike most campus students, they may lack recent exam practice and opportunities to develop exam study skills.

Exam proctoring

In some cases, a high-stakes exam is an essential part of a microcredential, perhaps because it is a required component of professional recognition. This raises two significant issues. How can the institution be sure that a completed exam paper is the unaided work of the named student, and how can the institution be sure that students did not have access to the information resources and support that are available to them in everyday life?

In examination halls, these issues are addressed by the use of invigilators or 'proctors'. These are responsible for checking student IDs, collecting mobile phones and other study aids, preventing communication and enforcing timekeeping. Proctors are not infallible, but their actions make it highly probable that the exam scripts handed in are the unaided work of the named student.

In an online setting, some problems can be removed or reduced by good assessment design. Questions that test understanding can be completed by students who have access to their normal technology and resources. Questions that require some sort of personalised response, for example quotes from contributions a student has made in the past, make it more likely that the individual sitting the exam is the same individual who worked through the course.

If an online equivalent of the examination hall is necessary, online proctoring provides a way of making this a rigorous process. There are three main approaches. For full proctoring, an invigilator proctors the exam using webcam footage. At the start of the exam, each student displays their surrounding environment, showing it is clear of study materials. Proctoring may take place live or by reviewing recordings. Random proctoring uses software to take pictures of students at random times during the examination; these pictures are analysed automatically to check that the same person is pictured each time, and reports are sent to an examiner. Automated proctoring requires little or no human intervention – an automated system encodes behaviours as normal or suspicious.

In a 2020 report that covers online assessment and verification practices, Sanzgiri and Habib (2020) outline an additional approach, TESLA, that is not yet in regular use but that combines tools already in use separately. This system includes:

- **face recognition:** as with random proctoring, still and video images are analysed and compared;
- **voice recognition:** recordings of the student's voice made during the exam are compared with each other and with previous recordings;
- **plagiarism checks:** the text submitted is automatically compared with published material and with work submitted in the past;
- **key-stroke patterns:** patterns of press and release times for different computer keys are compared with previous patterns.

Although students are used to major restrictions on their behaviour and a high degree of surveillance in an examination hall, moving these practices to their home environment highlights how intrusive and problematic these restrictions can be. Swauger (2020) provides a detailed overview of the main issues. These include but are not confined to:

- systems that flag loud noises as suspicious may be triggered if the student does not have a dedicated workspace where they can work in silence;

- systems that flag movement as suspicious may be triggered if a student is caring for children or pets, or if they are unable to sit still for long periods of time;
- systems that require identifying documents to be held stationary in front of a camera in order to identify an individual may be triggered if the student lacks fine motor skills;
- systems that have been trained on white students may fail to detect the faces of students with black or brown skin;
- systems that rely on video footage recorded in a student's home environment create an atmosphere of surveillance and suspicion.

The challenges of online exams are so great for both students and institutions that alternative forms of final assessment are preferable. These typically require individual students to submit an extended piece of work, or collection of work, which will then be assessed by educators. Asking students to relate their responses to their own setting, to course materials, and to forum discussion or activities during the course are techniques that help to establish that the person submitting the assessment is the same person who completed the course.

An advantage of technology-enabled assessment is that it opens up new possibilities for assessing authentic activity. Pieces of written work can be shared online, as can presentations, videos and images. Assessed work can be developed for an international audience as well as for an examiner. Projects can be developed in collaboration with people in other parts of the world, even if they are assessed separately. Nevertheless, the majority of assessed work is still disposable, written for no one but the assessor or examiner.

Wiley (2016) advocates for 'renewable assessments' that are designed to add value to the world, perhaps by developing or modifying something that others can use. Carefully designed renewable assessments embedded within microcredentials have the potential to benefit students because they are meaningful and can be used to demonstrate expertise beyond the course. They can meet some of the needs of employers by aligning the microcredential with the world of work. They can also support the verification process by establishing multiple links between a student and the work they submit for assessment.

Closely related to renewable assessments are ecological (or authentic) assessments. These typically measure a learner's ability to apply knowledge and skills in real-world, meaningful contexts. Unlike traditional assessment methods such as multiple-choice tests or written exams, ecological assessments aim to provide a complete picture of a learner's understanding and competence by requiring them to use their knowledge in practical, hands-on ways. Ecological assessments typically emphasise the process of learning, not just the result. They include projects, simulations, case studies, portfolios and recordings of performances.

An advantage of renewable and ecological/authentic assessments is that they reduce opportunities for cheating and, by making tasks more relevant and valuable for learners, reduce some of the motivations for cheating. Tasks that must be answered in different ways by different students, that relate to known details about the context of those students, and that involve structured reflection on course experiences do not generate responses that can be shared verbatim on the internet and submitted by multiple students with only minor adjustments.

Artificial intelligence (AI)

Since the public release of ChatGPT in late 2022, there has been concern that students will use generative AI (tools that use artificial intelligence to produce material such as text, images, computer code or videos) to complete assignments. As these tools have become more commonplace, universities and other educational institutions have drawn up guidelines for their use.

Banning the use of AI tools entirely is not a viable option for several reasons. AI is now embedded in tools that students are expected to use to complete assignments, such as Microsoft Office. AI tools can help students to produce good-quality work without having a significant impact on the content – for example, Grammarly reviews aspects of writing such as spelling, punctuation and clarity. In some cases, AI tools are offered by the university, in order to help students structure their essays or reflect on progress. Many universities use AI tools themselves, for example employing Copycatch and Turnitin to identify potential cases of plagiarism.

More broadly, educational institutions are preparing students for a world in which AI tools are widely available. In many jobs, they will be expected to use these tools – programmers already make extensive use of generative AI to help them with their work. Students need to be aware of the tools that they can use, and how they can use them both effectively and ethically.

With these ideas in mind, assessment design needs to take account of the fact that students are very likely to have access to generative AI tools while being assessed, unless they are placed under high levels of surveillance. These tools can be very helpful to students when producing essays and reports, completing online coursework, or working on online quizzes, standardised tests or book exams (Williams 2023). Students can be taught to use these tools appropriately. On the other hand, it is relatively difficult to use generative AI unnoticed when creating a novel artefact, solving an original problem, sitting a proctored closed-book exam, or carrying out a task that involves working with others (Williams 2023). If students are expected to work without using generative AI tools, then assessment needs to be designed in such a way that these tools will not be helpful – and students should be aware of regulations about use of these tools.

When introducing or revising microcredentials, it is important to check that the institution's policy on generative AI is up to date and fit for purpose. Some of the checks that are possible when teaching face to face cannot be carried out with learners who are studying remotely, connected to the institution for only a few weeks, and required to submit only one or two pieces of work for assessment. Microcredential students have very little time available to read university regulations and policies, so expectations about the use of generative AI should be clearly set out within assessment requirements and reviewed, if possible, with every presentation of the course.

Group assessment

The majority of microcredential assessment will focus on the performance of individuals. Group work and assessment present challenges in any environment and online groups face a series of challenges when working together. The differing participation patterns of students, taking full advantage of the flexibility offered by asynchronous learning, means that any significant change in a group's direction can cause significant problems for those who do not log in frequently (Ferguson 2009). Additionally, students who have never met in person and who are working together for the first time will be unaware which members of the group can be relied on, who will need support and who is likely to engage.

The problems of free-loaders and team members who do not pull their weight are common in the workplace, but they feel particularly acute for students when assessment is key to gaining a credential or qualification. In the workplace, there are management structures and working practices in place that can be used to support teams. In student group work, these are usually lacking and students may not have been taught strategies that they can use to overcome the problems associated with working together.

Unless a group develops and sticks to clear reporting guidelines, it is often not clear to members which of them are working hard and which are unlikely to meet deadlines. These uncertainties increase anxiety around assessment.

Despite these difficulties, there are times when group work is necessary and has a clear pedagogic value within microcredentials. Collaboration enables people to share ideas and perspectives, challenge and defend ideas, and develop a line of reasoning. Many jobs require applicants to be able to demonstrate that they possess competences such as teamwork, collaboration and leadership. Some microcredentials are run in a blended setting, some are incorporated within a wider qualification, and others include cohorts from the same workplace.

Cooperation provides opportunities to split a workload that would be unmanageable for an individual. Group work offers opportunities to develop skills that are important in the workplace, such as work planning, progress monitoring and dispute resolution. Yet when it comes to collaborative assessment, group members are often concerned that they will not be marked fairly

– they will either be marked down for the failings of others, or colleagues will take the credit for their hard work.

There are many ways of assessing group work. The list below sets out the main options. Students should be clear which method will be used to assess their work and why that method has been selected.

- **Shared group mark:** the group hands in one piece of work and all group members are awarded the same mark for it.
- **Group average mark:** parts of the task are submitted individually by different students and marked separately. Group members receive an average of these marks.
- **Group average mark – based on process:** each student's contribution is assessed using predefined criteria and evidence from observations and records. The mark awarded to group members is the average of these marks.
- **Individual mark – allocated task:** each student is given a task that makes up part of the final group product and is marked on that task.
- **Individual mark – individual report:** group members work together on the project. Students submit individual reports on that work and receive a mark for their report.
- **Individual mark – examination:** exam questions are based on the group projects, so questions can only be answered by those who have been fully involved.
- **Individual mark – based on process:** each student's contribution is assessed using predefined criteria and evidence from observations and records.
- **Individual mark – analysis of process:** students submit and are marked on a paper that assesses the group process, including their own contribution and that of peers.

- **Combination of group and individual:** a mark is assigned to the group but is adjusted for individual students, based on their contribution.
- **Student distribution of pool of marks:** the educator awards a set number of marks for the project and group members decide how to distribute those marks between themselves.
- **Students allocate individual weightings:** the educator gives a shared group mark that is adjusted according to a peer assessment factor.
- **Peer evaluation – random marker:** parts of the assessment are randomly distributed among group members, who must mark the work they have been assigned, based on a set of assessment criteria. The marks they assign are moderated by an educator.
- **Peer evaluation – average:** students evaluate the contribution of other group members using predetermined criteria. The final mark is an average of all marks awarded.
- **Self-evaluation – moderated:** students use predetermined criteria to evaluate their own contribution. The marks they decide on are moderated by an educator.

Concern about assessment can be a serious block to progress. It is therefore important to be clear about how it will be carried out in a way that gives everyone an equal chance of success. It is also essential that assessment relates closely to the learning outcomes of the microcredential. If these state that those who complete the course successfully will have team-working skills, it is reasonable to assess students on these. On the other hand, if collaboration has been selected simply as the best way of helping students to understand subject matter, then it is individual understanding of subject matter that should be assessed. Whichever is the case, if the assessment is formative – involving assessment for learning or assessment as learning – then feedback is an important element of it.

Feedback

If a student submits an assignment partway through a course and the mark counts towards their final grade, then it is assessment of learning. If they receive detailed feedback on that assignment, indicating both where they could have improved and links to aspects of the course coming up, then it also operates as assessment for learning. Feedback is therefore an important part of making assessment valuable for the learner and has been shown to be one of the most important influences on learning gain (Hattie 1999).

Effective feedback helps students to understand how they are progressing towards their learning goals and what they need to do next. It not only clarifies how well they are doing but it also enables them to improve their performance and can provide confidence and motivation. Assessment is most useful for learners when the feedback they receive is relevant, constructive, accessible, consequential and timely.

The short timescales of microcredentials mean there are limited opportunities for students to receive feedback from educators. Composing, submitting and marking an assignment all take time, especially because educators are likely to have many other responsibilities and will not necessarily be able to mark an assignment as soon as it is submitted. In addition, some microcredentials have large student cohorts, making a fast turnaround very difficult. This means some feedback is likely to consist of automated responses. These can be set to go far beyond a correct/

incorrect binary, instead identifying common errors, providing encouragement, pointing to relevant sections of the course material, and providing further explanations.

As learning analytics (which use data to support learning and teaching) become more sophisticated, there are increasing opportunities for the provision of automated feedback. This has the advantage that it is timely – there is little or no delay between submission of work and receiving feedback. It is also non-judgemental – students are happier to show work in progress to a computer program than to a human. They also feel confident to submit and resubmit work without the worry that they are overloading or annoying a teacher.

The *On Task* open-source tool has been used across courses and universities to provide students with personalised messages and feedback (Pardo et al. 2022). The system can send personalised messages to groups of learners based on rules defined by the educator (for example, students who have not yet submitted an assignment, or students who have not yet clicked on the link for a certain set of material). These messages can contain blocks of text that are visible to certain subsets of learners, so each learner receives a personalised message based on their activity, which reinforces or builds upon previous feedback messages.

Despite its advantages, automated feedback is an approach that works best in subject areas where answers are clear and can be presented succinctly, in a standard way. Opportunities for automated feedback on longer, free-text answers are very limited. Nevertheless, it can work very effectively with multiple-choice questions, which is one of the reasons these are so frequently used for assessment within microcredentials.

Whitelock and her colleagues (Whitelock & Watt 2007) developed a system for assessing the pattern between feedback and the assigned grade using Bales's (1950) 'interactional categories' system, which distinguishes between 'task-oriented' feedback intended to improve the content of future work, and the 'socio-emotive element' provided to maintain student motivation. Bales's (1950) system has four main categories:

- positive reactions – socio-emotive category
- attempted answers – task-oriented category
- questions – task-oriented category
- negative reactions – socio-emotive category.

The system recognises that, in any setting, feedback on performance can energise, encourage and motivate students or leave them feeling demoralised.

The balance of comments should change as the mark awarded decreases. Students who receive the lowest marks need more direct teaching and so the number of teaching comments should increase. However, praise should be given where it is due to encourage and motivate students to complete their studies. Feedback in the 'questions' category can be used both to stimulate further reflection and to point out constructively where there are problems with a response.

Writing multiple-choice questions, selecting appropriate answers and distractors, and devising feedback for each potential response is a time-consuming process but it is well worth it. Learning cannot happen without feedback, so learners need a clear picture of the progress they are (or are not) making. When assessments and feedback do not inform instruction or when they are not given to the students in a timely manner, learning cannot change because students do not know what to do differently. They need feedback that is explicit, timely, informative and accessible. Especially important is feedback that allows them to monitor their own progress effectively and to use that information to guide their own effort and practice.

However, even in cases where assessment is well designed and feedback appropriately targeted, students may struggle for reasons connected with wellbeing, mental health and accessibility. Issues that might be raised and addressed in a face-to-face environment, such as an obvious accessibility challenge, may be more difficult to identify online. Other issues, which might have become apparent over the course of a student's multi-year university career interacting with multiple educators and other staff members, may be neglected during the short span of a microcredential. For these reasons, it is important to build attention to wellbeing and accessibility into assessment from the start.

Test anxiety

Students often bring with them a negative experience of assessment. They recall it being 'done to them' at school and may associate it with being punished if they did not do well. Many people – up to one in five – experience extreme anxiety and stress during and before a test. Hundreds of studies carried out over more than 70 years have demonstrated a direct relationship between higher test anxiety and lower test performance (Von der Embse et al. 2018). Anxiety can be amplified in specific subject areas, particularly mathematics. Maths anxiety is a strong emotional reaction that occurs when someone needs to solve mathematical problems or manipulate numbers. It provokes tension and anxiety that can be debilitating and correlates with poor performance.

In a longer course or qualification, there are various strategies for reducing test anxiety. These include opportunities to seek emotional support externally, role-playing exercises or simulations to increase coping skills, and activities designed to help students develop internal controls and coping skills. On a microcredential, there may not be opportunities for any of these approaches, so assessment and feedback should be designed to reduce anxiety levels wherever possible, so that students are able to demonstrate what they have learned without being overwhelmed by anxiety.

A strategy for assessment that supports wellbeing should help learners to manage stress and anxiety, employ inclusive assessment, and create a supportive assessment design. These factors are closely linked to general good practice, making sure assessment is relevant, authentic and well designed.

Whenever possible, educators should consider whether learning outcomes could be assessed in different ways, including the type of assessment, required output, and time given to complete the task. Expectations should be transparent, including unambiguous mark schemes and clarity about word counts. Sharing the assessment schedule with learners well in advance enables them to plan their workload and means that clashes with major holidays, festivals or other important events can be avoided. Authentic assessments that are valued, relevant and valid can be created by using realistic or real-world data or scenarios.

The following suggestions for supporting wellbeing and accessibility in relation to different types of assessment draw on the Universal Design for Learning guidelines (CAST 2018).

Numerical assessment

- Allow students extra time to complete their assessment.
- Assess understanding of tools and related methods separately to the application of those tools and methods.
- Present information in stages, allowing students to complete each stage separately if they wish.

Multiple choice/short answer

- Give students as much time as possible to complete the assessment task.
- If the test is formative, provide supportive feedback.
- Switch between multiple-choice and short-answer questions.
- To avoid unnecessary confusion, follow the MCQ guidelines listed earlier in this chapter.

Visual/presentation/participatory/spoken assessment

These forms of assessment are very demanding for some learners, especially those with pre-existing anxiety. In the case of online microcredentials, this type of work will typically need to be submitted as a recording or a presentation. For some students, this will require them to learn to use a new set of software and technology.

- Consider whether the assessment is in line with the learning outcomes of the course. Were students expecting to spend hours becoming familiar with presentation software to be able to submit an assignment?
- Include options for work in multiple formats, such as posters or scripts.
- Make it clear whether both content and presentation will be assessed or only content.
- Make time in the curriculum for students to become familiar with new software and technology (not everyone has used PowerPoint or created a video).
- Provide support for students who are unfamiliar with the tools they will need to use, including opportunities for risk-free practice before submitting a final piece.

- Take into account the needs of students who have limited sight or hearing, and those with social anxiety. Including multiple options for presentation means they can demonstrate their skills and understanding of content without having to overcome additional barriers.

Written assessment

- Assess work in separate stages, so learners can gradually build a piece of work in response to ongoing feedback.
- Give learners assistance with planning and time management.
- Minimise the pressures of tight deadlines by allowing learners to complete self- and peer-assessment exercises over time, or to compile a portfolio of evidence or reflection over time.
- Offer flexible deadlines, if possible.
- Offer opportunities to present information in alternative formats such as oral presentations, posters, leaflets or scripts.
- Provide a list of sources or a presentation of key readings.
- Where possible, provide feedback on plans or drafts of written work.

Online exams

- Familiarise students with exam technologies and processes.
- Embed assessment-related study skills activities early in the study journey.
- Promote a shared understanding of academic integrity. Views on plagiarism vary considerably worldwide, so,

if a microcredential is offered internationally, ensure students are aware of and understand the rules at your institution.
- Make extra time in exams, alternative formats of exam papers, rest breaks in exams or use of assistive technology available to students with certain types of disability.

The main theme in all the above adjustments is flexibility, particularly in listening and responding to learner needs. Using a range of assessment approaches, wherever possible, gives all learners a more equitable chance of success in demonstrating their learning. In all cases, it is important to ensure that the skills being assessed are relevant to the course or lesson learning outcomes and that the assessment task information and instructions are given to learners in multiple formats.

Accrediting and stacking microcredentials

A final challenge associated with assessment in microcredentials is accreditation. Elements of this are covered in Chapter 3, which points to the role that internally aligned microcredential team members play in dealing with assessment and certification processes, as well as the roles of outward-facing team members who deal with external policies and credit transfer. These outward-facing team members will also be dealing with the national and international quality standards that are covered in the next chapter.

The need for quality assurance when assessment leads to accreditation requires a great deal of resources. Markers must be trained and, if several people are marking the same microcredential, their marking needs to be standardised. Outcomes must be compared across the department or faculty, and across the institution, to ensure consistency. An external examiner or assessor is required to ensure marking within the institution aligns with that at other institutions. In addition, assessment questions and rubrics may require regular updates, plagiarism checks will need to be carried out, there are likely to be student requests for special circumstances (such as serious illness or bereavement) to be considered, and many microcredentials will need to demonstrate that their assessment aligns with the latest version of external professional schemes or certificates.

Alongside this work, identity (ID) checks are needed to reduce the possibility of cheating and ensure that credit is awarded to the correct person. This can be done using basic platform ID verification, university registration, interviews (online, on-site or recorded) or proctored exams (Iniesto et al. 2022). A survey of how ID checks were carried out across European MOOC providers revealed considerable variation. FutureLearn certification programmes required learners to register with a university as a non-degree student. The Spanish/Portuguese platform MiríadaX used random proctoring, taking pictures of learners at random times while completing an exam; the French platform FUN employed full proctoring on some exams, and the EduOpen platform made use of on-site interviews (Iniesto et al. 2022).

All this work is valuable for learners who need to be able to produce evidence that they have gained academic credit. However, this work is also time-consuming – delaying results for weeks or months – and requires a lot of effort from expert professionals, which raises the price of microcredentials. However short the microcredential, all these processes are required if quality-assured academic credit is to be issued. This reduces the economic viability of very short courses because the associated administrative work is too time-consuming and expensive. As a result, some microcredentials use a simplified process and award digital badges rather than academic credit.

As Chapter 1 noted, a digital badge is an online record of achievement that includes information about the achievement, the community that recognised that achievement and the work carried out to achieve it. Digital badges have two elements: an image file that represents the badge, and an electronic record of the award's criteria and validator (Hauck & MacKinnon 2016). In some cases, they are awarded automatically once certain criteria are met, while in other cases they are linked to more traditional assessment approaches. Badges from different providers can be gathered on websites such as LinkedIn or in electronic backpacks, creating an individual record of competencies that have been acquired or demonstrated.

If a microcredential does award academic credit, then there is an expectation that this will be 'stackable' or will become so in the future. Stackability 'means that micro-credentials can be accumulated and grouped over time, building into a larger, more recognisable credential' (Lantero, Finocchietti & Petrucci 2021: 31). In some cases, this is seen as an essential aspect of microcredentials: 'The basic idea behind the awarding of micro-credentials is to "stack" a series of certificates or courses in a related area' (Lang & Sharp 2023: 4). However, a Europe-wide study identified 16 countries where microcredentials were not stackable, often owing to national legislation (Lantero, Finocchietti & Petrucci 2021).

'Stackable microcredentials could be organized either around development ladders of advancing skill levels or around patchwork areas of complimentary credentials' (Ifenthaler, Bellin-Mularski & Mah 2016: 429). There are problems with both approaches. The patchwork approach allows individuals to select courses in any order so that gaps in knowledge can be filled.

However, qualifications typically include an element of progression – more is asked of a final-year undergraduate than is asked of a first year. Study skills introduced at the start of a qualification may be reinforced later but will not be taught again from the beginning. However, if students can take courses in any order, this progression is lost, meaning each short course must devote some time to introductory material in case learners have not encountered it before. On the other hand, a 'skills ladder', which requires courses to be taken in a particular order, may force experienced learners to pay to enrol in courses that go back over areas with which they are already familiar.

The Open University (OU) in the UK now offers some qualifications that can be completed by stacking microcredentials with other courses. Its Postgraduate Certificate in Academic Practice (PGCAP) is made up of four microcredentials offered on the FutureLearn platform – but this qualification is only open to members of staff (Rienties et al. 2023; Sargent et al. 2023). For non-staff members, four microcredentials can be used to earn sufficient academic credits to make up a third of the university's Masters in Online Teaching (MAOT). However, the intention is that microcredentials will be 'clickable' – series of them can be studied to build a set of skills and knowledge. They are not currently 'stackable' – they cannot be combined to complete full OU qualifications. The university requires at least two thirds of credits on any master's qualification to come from longer courses, and students are required to complete a 'capstone' module that demonstrates their capacity for individual study and scholarship.

Although the ability to make up qualifications by stacking a variety of courses from different expert providers is attractive, most providers are finding that this cannot be done at a price that would make these qualifications attractive to learners. As noted above, the quality assurance measures required to award academic credit require a lot of resource. If universities must then spend time checking the syllabus and requirements of other providers' microcredentials then the costs spiral out of control. Educational providers need to 'develop and adopt at scale a much more joined-up taxonomy and recognition system for skills and credentials across countries, education systems and industries' (World Economic Forum 2021: 33).

This is easier said than done – international systems that bridge sectors take time and effort to develop. At present, 'there is very little economy of scale' (Usher et al. 2023). The difficulties are summarised by the UK's Quality Assurance Agency for Higher Education:

> there are challenges in a learner designing and accumulating in a modular manner, particularly if the credit is achieved across a number of different providers. Under current pricing arrangements, it is likely to be more expensive. Other challenges include the risk that a learner struggles with a sense of belonging, and continually has to navigate different systems and Recognition of Prior Learning processes. The time and effort involved in familiarising themselves with a range of different approaches, resources and support services might also impact on the space available for extra-curricular skills development. (QAA 2022: 7)

Conclusion

Overall, assessing and accrediting microcredentials pose multiple challenges. The vision of a wide range of short courses on offer from multiple expert providers that can be stacked to build a widely recognised qualification is resource-heavy, time-consuming and expensive in practice. However, assessing and accrediting individual microcredentials is more straightforward, and principles of good practice for online assessment and feedback support these processes. As with other aspects of microcredentials, assessment must take into account learners' relatively short engagement with the educational provider, the wide range of contexts in which they are studying, and the possibilities and constraints of online study. Around the world, national agencies and institutions are working on frameworks for quality and evaluation that can help to ensure assessment and accreditation are carried out to high standards. This work is the subject of the next chapter.

References

Aristeidou, M., Cross, S., Rossade, K.-D. and Wood, C. (2023). Online remote exams in higher education: Distance learning students' views. Paper presented at INTED 2023, Valencia, Spain, 6–8 March 2023.

Baker, E. L. (2007). 2007 presidential address—The end(s) of testing. *Educational Researcher*, 36(6): 309–317. DOI: https://doi.org/10.3102/0013189X07307970

Bales, R. F. (1950). A set of categories for the analysis of small group interaction. *American Sociological Review*, 15: 257–263.

Bianchi, G., Pisiotis, U. and Cabrera Giraldez, M. (2022). *GreenComp: The European sustainability competence framework*. Luxembourg.

Black, P. and Wiliam, D. (1998). *Inside the black box: Raising standards through classroom assessment*. Granada Learning.

Braxton, S. N. (2023). Competency frameworks, alternative credentials and the evolving relationship of higher education and employers in recognizing skills and achievements. *The International Journal of Information and Learning Technology*, 40(5).

Bull, J. and Dalziel, J. (2003). Assessing question banks. In: Littlejohn, A. *Reusing online resources: A sustainable approach to e-learning*. London: Kogan Page. pp. 171–181.

Cannell, P. and Macintyre, R. (2014). Towards open educational practice. Paper presented at the EADTU Annual Conference: New Technologies and the Future of Teaching and Learning, Krakow, Poland, 23–24 October 2014.

CAST. (2018). Universal design for learning guidelines version 2.2. Available at http://udlguidelines.cast.org

Draper, S. W. (2009). Catalytic assessment: Understanding how MCQs and EVS can foster deep learning. *British Journal of Educational Technology*, 40(2): 285–293.

Ferguson, R. (2009). The construction of shared knowledge through asynchronous dialogue. Thesis (PhD). The Open University. Available at http://oro.open.ac.uk/19908

George, S. (2022). Competence and competency frameworks. Available at https://www.cipd.org/uk/knowledge/factsheets/competency-factsheet/#gref

Hattie, J. (1999). *Visible learning: A synthesis of over 800 meta-analyses relating to achievement.* Abingdon: Routledge.

Hauck, M. and MacKinnon, T. (2016). A new approach to assessing online intercultural exchanges: Soft certification of participant engagement. In: O'Dowd, R. and Lewis, T. *Online intercultural exchange. Policy, pedagogy, practice.* Abingdon: Routledge. pp. 209–234.

Ifenthaler, D., Bellin-Mularski, N. and Mah, D.-K. (2016). *Foundation of digital badges and micro-credentials.* Switzerland: Springer.

Iniesto, F., Ferguson, R., Weller, M., Farrow, R. and Pitt, B. (2022). Introducing a reflective framework for the assessment and recognition of microcredentials. *OTESSA*, 2(2): 1–24.

Lang, G. and Sharp, J. H. (2023). Micro-credentials in US higher education: An empirical analysis. *Information Systems Education Journal*, 21(1).

Lantero, L., Finocchietti, C. and Petrucci, E. (2021). *Micro-credentials and Bologna key commitments: State of play in the European Higher Education Area.* MICROBOL. Available at https://www.enqa.eu/wp-content/uploads/Microbol_State-of-play-of-MCs-in-the-EHEA_19.02.2021.pdf

Meaney, M. J. (2021). Essays on the design of inclusive learning in massive open online courses, and implications for educational futures. Thesis (PhD). University of Cambridge. Available at https://api.repository.cam.ac.uk/server/api/core/bitstreams/d1dde49e-4c55-4f87-85a8-c346968b1c27/content

Northcutt, C. G., Ho, A. D. and Chuang, I. L. (2016). Detecting and preventing 'multiple-account' cheating in massive open online courses. *Computers & Education*, 100: 71–80.

Novick, P. A., Lee, J., Wei, S., Mundorff, E. C., Santangelo, J. R. and Sonbuchner, T. M. (2022). Maximizing academic integrity while minimizing stress in the virtual classroom. *Journal of Microbiology & Biology Education*, 23(1).

Oldfield, A., Broadfoot, P., Sutherland, R. and Timmis, S. (2012). *Assessment in a digital age: A research review.* Bristol.

Pappano, L. (2012). The year of the MOOC. *New York Times*, 2 November. Available at http://www.nytimes.com/2012/11/04/education/edlife/massive-open-online-courses-are-multiplying-at-a-rapid-pace.html

Pardo, A., Mirriahi, N., Gašević, D. and Dawson, S. (2022). A model for learning analytics to support personalization in higher education. In: Sharpe, S., Bennett, S. and Varga-Atkins, T. *Handbook of digital higher education.* Cheltenham: Edward Elgar. pp. 26–37.

QAA. (2022). *Characteristics statement: Micro-credentials.* Gloucester: Quality Assurance Agency for Higher Education. Available at https://www.qaa.ac.uk/docs/qaa/quality-code/micro-credentials-characteristics-statement.pdf?sfvrsn=32bda081_4

Rienties, B., Calo, F., Corcoran, S., Chandler, K., FitzGerald, E., Haslam, D., Harris, C. A., Perryman, L.-A., Sargent, J., Suttle, M. D. and Wahga, A. (2023). How and with whom do educators learn in an online professional development microcredential. *Social Sciences & Humanities Open*, 8(1): 100626.

Sanzgiri, J. and Habib, M. (2020). *Compendium on good practices in assessment and recognition of MOOCs for the EU labour market.* EMC-LM. Available at https://emc.eadtu.eu/images/publications_and_outputs/EMC-LM_Compendium_on_good_practices_final.pdf

Sargent, J., Rienties, B., Perryman, L.-A. and FitzGerald, E. (2023). Investigating the views and use of stackable microcredentials within a Postgraduate Certificate in Academic Practice. *Journal of Interactive Media in Education*, 2023(1): 1–12. DOI: https://doi.org/10.5334/jime.805

Shen, C. (2014). *Introducing Nanodegrees* (16 June). Available at https://www.udacity.com/blog/2014/06/announcing-nanodegrees-new-type-of.html

Stancombe, S. (2020). *FutureLearn launches microcredentials with six global partners* (11 February). Available at https://www.futurelearn.com/info/press-releases/futurelearn-launches-microcredentials-with-six-global-partners

Swauger, S. (2020). *Our bodies encoded: Algorithmic test proctoring in higher education* (2 April). Available at https://hybridpedagogy.org/our-bodies-encoded-algorithmic-test-proctoring-in-higher-education

Topuz, A. C. and Kinshuk. (2021). A review of literature to understand students' perceptions regarding online assessments. Paper presented at the 3rd Pan-Pacific Technology Enhanced Learning Conference, online.

UNESCO. (2016). *UNESCO competency framework*. Available at https://unesdoc.unesco.org/ark:/48223/pf0000245056

Usher, A., Wilson, I., MacLennan, T. and Izhanova, A. (2023). *Approaches to stackability of micro-credentials: Options for Ontario*. Ontario: Ontario Council on Articulation and Transfer (ONCAT).

Valli, H. (2018). *Bold new initiatives from the Coursera conference* (29 March). Available at https://learninginnovation.duke.edu/blog/2018/03/bold-new-initiatives-from-the-coursera-conference

Von der Embse, N., Jester, D., Roy, D. and Post, J. (2018). Test anxiety effects, predictors, and correlates: A 30-year meta-analytic review. *Journal of Affective Disorders*, 227: 483–493.

Whitelock, D. and Watt, S. (2007). Open Mentor: Supporting tutors with their feedback to students. Paper presented at the 11th CAA International Computer Assisted Assessment Conference, Loughborough, UK, 10–11 July 2007.

Wiley, D. (2016). *Toward renewable assessments* (7 July). Available at https://opencontent.org/blog/archives/4691

Williams, P. (2023). AI, analytics and a new assessment model for universities. *Education Sciences*, 13(10): 1040.

World Economic Forum. (2021). *Upskilling for shared prosperity.* Geneva: World Economic Forum.

Young, J. R. (2016). *Degrees of the future – and what's at stake for students* (3 November). Available at https://www.edsurge.com/news/2016-11-03-why-udacity-and-edx-want-to-trademark-the-degrees-of-the-future-and-what-s-at-stake-for-students

CHAPTER 8

Quality and evaluation

This chapter examines the definitions of 'quality' that become operationalised as a suite of standards in both national and international contexts. These standards are a necessary consideration for providers of accredited qualifications and so the question of whether they are sufficient kitemarks for the more recent stackable microcredential qualifications is explored, together with their validation through the process known as 'evaluation'.

How can we know quality when we see it?

Educators are usually confident about judging their students' work and awarding the submitted assignments suitable marks.

How to cite this book chapter:
Ferguson, R. and Whitelock, D. 2024. Quality and evaluation. In: Ferguson, R. and Whitelock, D. *Microcredentials for Excellence: A Practical Guide*. Pp. 217–262. London: Ubiquity Press. DOI: https://doi.org/10.5334/bcz.h. License: CC BY-NC 4.0

They can judge the value and the quality of students' performance of the task in hand, which is communicated as a mark. This process usually works well for formative assessment but with higher-stakes examinations, where double marking occurs, there is not always agreement. This is particularly true in the arts and even architecture, where ranking assignments has been found to lead to more agreement and provides a better metric for quality (van den Heuvel & Bohm 2023). Therefore, 'seeing' even for arts experts is not necessarily believing, which suggests one of the continuous problems around quality is not recognising it intuitively but employing an agreed, robust set of metrics or key performance indicators that can be used to review it systematically. Why is this important? The answer lies within a continuous improvement cycle of educational provision where the analysis of relevant metrics forms a foundation for quality advancement. Furthermore, with newer qualifications such as microcredentials, the elements of trust and transparency can be evidenced by quality assurance processes (Orr, Pupinis & Kirdulyte 2020).

There is also a political and ethical dimension to quality standards, as illustrated by Europe's aspiration to achieve the European Education Area by 2025 with 'high quality digital learning quality to increase the relevance quality of European education and Training' (European Commission 2020). The following section unpacks the notion of quality through a discussion of its measurement using both international and national standards.

International quality standards

A range of existing quality standards were initially designed for face-to-face teaching and learning and a number of quality assurance tools have been specifically developed to ensure the quality of online education, for example E-xcellence (see Rosewell et al.

2017). In addition, a range of stakeholders, not least students when choosing where to study, take note of ranking systems. However, Brasher et al. (2022) note that current ranking systems are of limited value for most potential undergraduate students, particularly with reference to online education, as these systems have been slow to include online teaching metrics into their analytics. These are valid points to bear in mind when microcredentials are delivered online. It is important to examine the basic quality frameworks and standards that already exist before discussing the quality recommendations of microcredentials, as these are being produced by higher education establishments that comply with existing regulatory guidelines.

A clear generic example is provided by the European Association for Quality Assurance in Higher Education (ENQA); a set of Standards and Guidelines for Quality Assurance in the European Higher Education Area (ESG 2015) is based upon four principles for quality assurance:

- higher education institutions have primary responsibility for the quality of their provision and its assurance;
- quality assurance responds to the diversity of higher education systems, institutions, programmes and students;
- quality assurance supports the development of a quality culture;
- quality assurance takes into account the needs and expectations of students, all other stakeholders and society.

These principles leave scope for individual circumstances and cultures, which can be reflected in the education policies of degree-awarding institutions. They also allow delegation of regulation and external quality assurance reviews to be undertaken by national bodies.

Moving on to unpacking these principles, 10 standards are proposed, as follows:

1. generation of a policy for quality assurance, which links to all the principles;
2. a design and approval process should be in place;
3. student-centred learning, teaching and assessment need to be explicit;
4. a process for student admission, progression, recognition and certification is required;
5. ensuring that teaching staff are competent;
6. learning resources and student support should be available;
7. information management should include the analysis of relevant data to maintain progress;
8. public information should be available;
9. programmes should be monitored on an ongoing basis and periodically reviewed;
10. there should be cyclical external quality assurance, usually undertaken by a national quality assurance agency.

All these standards are valid for any quality assurance system and at the heart of the quality process sits the seventh standard, the need to collect and analyse reliable data for decision-making and to identify what is working well and what requires further attention. The European guidance recommends evaluation of the following:

- content of the programme in the light of the latest research in the given discipline, thus ensuring that the programme is up to date;
- changing needs of society;
- students' workload, progression and completion;
- effectiveness of procedures for assessment of students;

- students' expectations, needs and satisfaction in relation to the programme;
- learning environment and support services and their fitness for purpose for the programme.

This means that effective processes to collect and analyse information about courses and qualifications need to feed into an internal quality assurance system. The following are typical key performance indicators:

- profile of the student population;
- student progression, success and dropout rates;
- students' satisfaction with their programmes;
- learning resources and student support available;
- career paths of graduates.

Other quality guidelines from Australia and the UK (QAA 2023) exhibit similar principles, noting that the information gathered by individual institutions for external appraisal and self-regulation in these countries depends, to some extent, on the type and mission of the institution. Australia, however, includes research and research training (see the Australian Government's Tertiary Education Quality and Standards Agency; TEQSA 2021). Canada does not have a national university accreditation system. Instead, all education is regulated provincially but universities tend to belong to Universities Canada, which establishes standards of quality for all Canadian degree programmes (Universities Canada 2023).

International microcredential quality standards

It is clear from the final report of the Micro-credentials Higher Education Consultation Group (European Commission 2020) that the rationale for an European approach for microcredentials is to increase personalised learning for all and widen learning opportunities both in higher education and vocational education and training (VET) establishments. The aspiration is to mainstream microcredentials' use with respect to both an economic and social mission perspective.

It was agreed that a standards framework for microcredentials should align with national (NQF) and European (EQF) qualifications frameworks, that Member States could consider adapting their own national qualifications frameworks to include microcredentials, and that an important step in this process was to agree a transparent definition, which is:

> A micro-credential is a proof of the learning outcomes that a learner has acquired following a short learning experience. These learning outcomes have been assessed against transparent standards. (European Commission 2020)

In summary, the European recommendations for a microcredential quality framework in 2020 were that it should include:

- a defined list of critical information elements to describe microcredentials;
- alignment with national qualifications frameworks (NQFs) and the European Qualifications Framework (EQF): defined levels, standards for describing learning outcomes;
- quality assurance standards;
- defined credits: European Credit Transfer and Accumulation System (ECTS), defined learning outcomes and notional workload;
- recognition: for further studies and/or employment purposes;

- portability: issuing, storage and sharing of microcredentials;
- platform solutions for the provision and promotion of courses leading to microcredentials;
- incentives to stimulate the uptake of microcredentials.

A very important consideration that allowed the notion of microcredentials to progress was that all HEIs following ESG (Standards and Guidelines for Quality Assurance in the European Higher Education Area) quality assurance procedures could be regarded as 'trusted providers of micro-credentials'. Additionally, where microcredentials are delivered online, the tool developed by the E-xcellence project (Rosewell et al. 2017) may be used as a reference point. There was clear recognition that microcredentials are also issued by non-higher education providers, that quality assurance is essential and that the ESG could, in principle, be used in these circumstances.

One example of how this framework has been applied is provided by the Netherlands through an 'Acceleration Plan' (2022). Within this plan, 32 higher education institutions (10 universities and 22 universities of applied sciences) have been taking part in a national microcredentials pilot under the direction of the Making Education More Flexible zone. The Universities of the Netherlands and the Association of Universities of Applied Sciences of the Netherlands have produced a quality framework, a starting point which can be refined and which is open to further interpretation as the universities work through it together.

1. The guideline for microcredentials is that these are educational units that are no smaller than 3 EC and no larger than 30 EC [one European Credit (EC) represents 28 study hours].

2. The education certified by a microcredential is substantively related to the institution's education and/or research portfolio. This may be existing education as well as newly developed education or research.
3. It is clear who the intended target group of the education is, what prior knowledge is required from the participants, what the entry requirements are (if any), and how these are tested.
4. The educational programme, the educational environment and the quality of the team of teachers enable the incoming participants to achieve the intended learning outcomes.
5. The learning outcomes and the educational level and scope of the microcredential are made clear. The participating institutions describe this in an unambiguous manner, in line with European agreements (Bologna) and developments in Brussels.
6. In principle, institutions recognise the (validated) learning outcomes of microcredentials that have already been attained and/or are being attained elsewhere. Whether this leads to intake and/or exemption remains within the mandate of the examination board or another body designated by the institution.
7. The tests support the learning process of the participant and the assessment is valid, reliable, transparent for participants and sufficiently independent. (Acceleration Plan 2022)

A set of minimum requirements for internal quality assurance is guaranteed by the ESG and microcredentials are to be offered in line with the lifelong vision of the awarding institution. This is similar to HEIs providing a policy for production, presentation and assessment of any of their microcredentials advertised to potential students.

There is a consensus building around quality standards for microcredentials that should be adhered to by any recognised body which has received a quality kitemark. However, there are also other considerations such as the stackability of these credits towards a diploma or degree, and whether a transcript of these credits should be available to future employers.

A study was undertaken by the Higher Education Quality Council of Ontario (HEQCO), an agency of the Government of Ontario that undertakes evidence-based research to assist with the improvement of post-secondary education in the province. As part of its microcredential awareness investigation, HEQCO surveyed 201 Canadian employers, 161 representatives from 105 Canadian post-secondary institutions and 2,000 prospective students (Pichette et al. 2021). Their findings included the following suite of 'quality markers'.

- **Relevant:** consulted or involved industry/community;
- **Accredited:** recognised or issued by a professional accrediting body;
- **Standardised:** meets a government-set quality standard;
- **Assessed:** learner must demonstrate skills/knowledge to earn the credential;
- **Flexible:** pace and/or structure of learning can be personalised;
- **Stackable:** can be 'stacked' or combined toward a larger credential, e.g. a diploma or degree. (Pichette et al. 2021: 16)

These quality markers were viewed favourably by all the stakeholders and provide kitemarks that match other recommendations from international bodies, in a clear and concise manner that would ease transferability of these types of credentials between institutions (Bates 2021), supporting lifelong learning.

National quality standards

In the UK, the Quality Assurance Agency for Higher Education (QAA) has produced a characteristics statement for microcredentials that means a set of general guidance is provided for higher education providers when developing a new provision such as microcredentials. It describes 'outcomes and attributes of microcredentials in a UK-wide context, many higher education providers will use them as an enhancement tool for the design and approval of short courses, and for subsequent monitoring and review' (QAA 2022).

Important considerations for the UK context include advice about how to manage the implementation of standards (which, in essence, follow EU standards) and, more importantly, the implementation and evaluation of a quality enhancement process. The QAA (2022) highlights the following areas for careful thought:

- admissions decisions, and the role of recognition of prior learning;
- approaches to course design and approval that are agile and not overly burdensome while still being robust;
- swift confirmation of outcome and award following completion of assessment;
- effective monitoring and review;
- student engagement in quality management.

Before moving on to questions of managing and evaluating the quality of microcredentials, as required by these quality standards, it makes sense to zoom out of this level of detail and look at the context of some of these quality enhancement frameworks.

Contexts

A European approach to microcredentials will allow higher education institutions to offer such courses on a larger scale and in a comparable manner throughout Europe, ensuring agreed quality standards, and facilitating their recognition and portability across the EU (European Commission 2020: 4).

The definition of microcredentials produced by Europe's MICROBOL project (MICROBOL 2020) made reference to quality assurance in line with the Standards and Guidelines for Quality Assurance in the European Higher Education Area (ESG).

A need for just-in-time training is not easily met by a course that must go through rigorous quality assurance processes to demonstrate it meets local and national standards.

Although there is a lot of work to be done in this area, there is also the political will to achieve it, as evidenced by government initiatives supporting quality assurance and standards agencies to incorporate microcredentials within their work (see, for example, QAA 2022). At the same time, online platforms are developing pathways to study that do not necessarily lead to academic credit but do lead to industry-relevant certification.

Microcredentials need to:

- be aligned with multiple existing frameworks as well as across countries and continents;
- strike a balance between requirements for high-quality just-in-time training and the time required to carry out quality assurance processes.

The final role identified in the microcredentials project team in Chapter 3 was quality enhancement. Developing microcredentials is a large-scale strategic initiative for any institution, and including work on evaluation and quality enhancement provides opportunities to assess progress and adjust ambitions. One approach is to align aims with key performance indicators (KPIs) so that progress towards an aim such as 'attract more international learners' can be linked with specific targets such as: '1,000 registrations from countries in South America in the next calendar year', 'more than 50% of those who complete a microcredential successfully will be based in another country' or 'microcredentials offered in Mandarin will recruit as well as those offered in English'.

KPIs like these enable at-a-glance summaries of progress but quality enhancement also needs a more reflexive consideration of what has happened, what has worked well and what could be done better. Agile approaches to project management incorporate regular retrospectives, so some teams involved in microcredentials will be reflecting and developing as the initiative progresses. Other teams will have standard reporting processes that prompt them to evaluate their work and to identify opportunities for quality enhancement. An evaluation lead can bring these existing approaches together and incorporate them into a structured consideration of the initiative as a whole that can then be used by those working on the project to improve practice.

As with any course that awards academic credit at higher education level, microcredentials must be aligned with national and international frameworks. This means the normal quality assurance checks must be applied or adapted to fit them. The institution will need to be able to assure both learners and regulatory bodies that microcredentials are as rigorously checked as any other credit-bearing course and that their standards are in line with those applied to other academic courses. In Europe, for example, all courses offered by higher education institutions must undergo internal quality assurance by the institution in question. In addition, either each course or the higher education institution as a whole is required to undergo periodic external quality assurance (e.g. accreditation, audit, review). (European Commission 2020: 14)

Processes are needed to demonstrate that a microcredential credit requires a similar amount of work at a similar standard to those qualifications on offer within the institution and more widely.

Ways of doing this will vary between institutions but might include, for example, external reviewers on microcredentials, reputable external examiners, second or third marking, scrutiny by academic committee, and agreed policies for assessment and awards that apply specifically to microcredentials. The more robust these methods are, the more helpful they will be for the credit-transfer process, which is one of the outward-facing aspects of the microcredential initiative.

A 2020 study of microcredentialing research and pilots across Canada, with a focus on their utility for admission and transfer into higher education, noted that:

> If a micro-credential is to be considered as a bona fide credential … expectations typically exist that the learning experiences (including those represented by micro-credentials) have been structured, delivered, and assessed by trusted entities in accordance with accepted and recognized quality assurance expectations and frameworks. (Duklas 2020: 15)

A part of this quality assurance is evaluation, which the Hewlett Foundation's Evaluation Principles and Practices (Twersky & Lindblom 2012: 3) define as a 'systematic' approach, stating that 'evaluation is an independent, systematic investigation into how, why and to what extent objectives or goals are achieved'.

Evaluation

Defining evaluation

However, evaluation can be a contentious issue and not all definitions agree on its purpose Gullickson (2020). Therefore, for any type of evaluation, agreement about what the term means is an essential first step to scoping the work and resources involved, together with an appraisal that considers whether the evaluation has met its objectives. It can be useful to examine some definitions of evaluation before coming to a final decision as these can prompt reflection about what can be achieved and then acted upon once the evaluation has taken place.

While the definition from the Hewlett Foundation that appears at the end of the previous section emphasises systematic elements, evaluation can be seen as a judgement of value and worth. Scriven (1991: 53) states that 'evaluation is the process of determining merit, worth, or significance'. The findings can also aid reflection and point to future improvements. This definition could well apply to an educational pilot study, where the findings lead to a stop/go decision.

Another definition has arisen in which the essential feature is not one of judgement but of learning. Two major philanthropic bodies that fund education-related projects support the latter. The W.K. Kellogg Foundation (2017: 1) defines evaluation as a process of 'systematically generating knowledge that can support learning, quality improvement and good judgement in decision-making', adding that 'evaluation also can align purpose, action and impact to ensure that longer-term change at the societal level unfolds progressively'. In its *Evaluation Handbook*, the foundation

(2012: 2) suggests that evaluation should 'strengthen projects during their lifecycle' and, whenever possible, provide 'outcome data to assess the extent of change'.

Attwell (2017), focusing specifically on the evaluation of online learning, reiterates the notion of evaluation as a learning process, defining it as:

- a joint learning process for all involved, generating useful and relevant information and knowledge;
- a theoretical and practical approach, which feeds back into ongoing change processes in organisations and projects;
- a systematic process to assess the relevance, efficiency and effectiveness of policies, projects and programmes.

Evaluating online teaching

Online teaching and learning have broken new ground in that they have explicitly introduced new pedagogies and technologies, the impact of which has been evaluated and shared. These findings have influenced which new technologies or large-scale implementations receive funding or support at institutional or even national level.

There is a wealth of data that can be used to evaluate online teaching. This includes:

- learning analytics findings about students' and educators' use of online platforms such as virtual learning environments (VLEs);
- recordings or records of students' discussions;
- observations of online teaching sessions.

Online teaching also has its evaluation challenges. The context in which a student is engaging with online teaching will not be apparent to the evaluator but could be of considerable significance in helping to understand the learner's experiences, attitudes, behaviour and study performance. Also, some evaluation methods, such as focus groups, can be more challenging to conduct online.

Online teaching evaluations have much in common with evaluations of face-to-face teaching. However, some aspects of online teaching and learning require specialist knowledge, such as the accessibility of online resources for students with sight or hearing difficulties. A holistic approach to evaluation is a good way forward:

> A holistic assessment goes beyond course design; it acknowledges the nuances that make a course unique, including input and contributions from students, developments in the field of study, and current events. Most valuable are students' perceptions of their learning and of the course experience. A good course assessment considers the course over a period of time, and considers interactions between instructor and students, students and students, all of which create artifacts that can be studied and analyzed (Thompson, 2005). Artifacts might include, emails or forum posts of student questions, dialogue within forums, feedback from group interaction, end-of-course student surveys, LMS reports on student interaction patterns, student assignment results, and more. Course artifacts give valuable clues to a course's quality, more so when collected from two or more course iterations and analyzed collectively. (Morrison 2015)

Types of evaluation

There are various types of evaluation and a clear point of differentiation is whether an evaluation is **discrete** or **ongoing**. A discrete evaluation has a clear beginning and end to its timeline. An ongoing example would be the collection of students' performance metrics such as assessment grades or VLE activity. The type of evaluation can also be classified in terms of the people conducting the evaluation. These might be internal staff, external examiners or a team of staff allocated to a particular project, including statistical analysts.

Different types of evaluation may take place while any course is being run or any new initiatives are being introduced. These include:

- **Performance evaluation** reports on progress towards intended goals, identifies problems and assesses whether an initiative and the resources it uses are being managed well.
- **Process (or formative) evaluations** probe the nature and quality of the implementation of an initiative. Formative evaluations are conducted during a project and identify its strengths and weaknesses. The results will typically be used to instantiate change and development and will often be carried out internally by a member of the project or course team.
- **Summative evaluations** take place after the event. These include:
    - Outcome evaluations, which aim to establish how well an initiative or programme is working overall, rather than being the basis for immediate action. Oliver (2000: 5) notes that summative evaluation 'is often an external process concerned with judgement rather than improvement', though some outcome evaluations will inform the development of an initiative before its next iteration.

○ Impact evaluations, which consider what has happened as a result of an initiative. Intended and unintended impacts are analysed together with how change was achieved.

Why evaluate?

Educational evaluation can have value both in terms of the results of an evaluation and the process itself. Although Tyler's definition of educational evaluation is still used and described as 'the process of determining to what extent the educational objectives are actually being realized' (Tyler 1950: 69), Ramsden's (2003: 209) definition makes explicit that all good teaching involves not only reflection but also the evaluation of practice. He states that 'evaluation is an analytical process that is intrinsic to good teaching'. There are also regulatory licensing authorities that require evidence from evaluation that good teaching and learning are both taking place. These add another reason for sound evaluations to be conducted in agreement with national regulatory frameworks and standards.

Approaches to evaluation

First steps in planning an evaluation

A number of key planning considerations should be considered in conjunction with the evaluation focus and units of analysis. One way of refining the focus of an evaluation topic is through identifying its unit of analysis – the entity that is being analysed in the evaluation. In this way, every aspect of the evaluation will be open to inspection, allowing decisions to be made about the evaluation timing, the people involved, stakeholders, cost, evaluation criteria, data collection approach, methodology and methods and the ethical considerations that will need to be managed.

The Kellogg Foundation (2017: 53) identifies six possible units of analysis for its funded projects. These categories can be applied to any online teaching-related evaluation, such as a microcredential course, and the descriptors would be comparable to those found below.

- **Individuals.** The evaluation focuses on the changes that individuals experience. These individuals could be microcredential learners, educators or other stakeholders such as national education policymakers.
- **Course, programme or educational initiative.** In this case, the focus is to understand whether the microcredential course or initiative is effective. This means identifying what does and does not work, together with the knowledge and skills required for educators to deliver the course or initiative and/or how the course or initiative could be improved. A formative evaluation may be particularly suitable in this instance.
- **Organisation** (for example, an entire higher education establishment). The evaluation focus could investigate changes within an organisation's priorities, culture, policies and institution-wide practices such as the introduction of microcredentials into the curriculum.
- **System** (for example, one for submitting assessments online). The evaluation will be based on a clear idea of the parts of the system that are being assessed and any changes in outcome that are to be expected. For example, where an assessment submission system has been changed to an online format, the evaluation might

consider how this has affected assessment submission rates and pass rates.
- **Policy** (for example, the nationwide introduction of a particular approach to microcredentials).
- **Community** (for example, a network of tutors delivering a new microcredential and supporting each other using social media). With this type of investigation care should be taken to clearly define the nature of the community in focus.

An evaluation can focus on one or more of these units of analysis at the same time. The size and scope of the evaluation will be informed by a number of considerations but should not lose sight of its originally funded objectives. Twersky and Lindblom (2012: 16) warn that evaluations should 'NOT sacrifice relevance by having evaluation findings be delivered too late to matter'. Good planning and keeping deliverables to schedule are essential components of a successful evaluation that provides value for money.

Developing a logic model

'A logic model is a graphic display or map of the relationship between a programme's resources, activities and intended results, which also identifies the programme's underlying theory and assumptions' (Kaplan & Garrett 2005). It acts as a road map that represents the relationships between all the components of the model, which are usually: resources, activities, outputs and outcomes.

Logic models visually explain a project's purpose, strategy and expected results. They help to provide clarity and identify cause and effect, including available resources to build a good plan of work, supporting the adaptability of a project's resources and overall planning. Effective logic models make an explicit, often visual, statement of the activities that will bring about change and the expected results for the community and its people. They keep participants moving in the same direction by providing a common language and point of reference.

A logic model should convey its information on a single page. An example of a logic model that was produced by the W.K. Kellogg Foundation (1998) has five elements, represented by a line of coloured boxes arranged in a horizontal line. These five elements cover both planned work (resources/inputs and activities) and intended results (outputs, outcomes and impact). The chain of reasoning behind the ordering of these elements is:

1. **Resources and impacts.** Certain resources are needed to operate your programme.
2. **Activities.** If you have access to these resources and inputs, then you can use them to accomplish your planned activities.
3. **Outputs.** If you accomplish your planned activities then you will, hopefully, deliver the amount of product and/or service that you intended.
4. **Outcomes.** If you accomplish your planned activities to the extent that you intended, then your participants will benefit in certain ways.
5. **Impact.** If these benefits to participants are achieved, then certain changes in organisations, communities or systems might be expected to occur. (Kellogg 1998)

It is important to note that '[l]ogic models are not evaluation tools; they are learning and management tools that should be used throughout the life of a strategy, initiative or program. A logic modelling process should facilitate effective planning, implementation, evaluation and improvement of your effort' (Kellogg Foundation 2017: 113).

The question you might ask is: 'If logic models are not evaluation tools, as they look more like management instruments, why are they important to designing an evaluation?' The answer is that the process of creating a logic model is considered to be valuable as it requires programmes to fully and clearly articulate both vision and aims, thus introducing a more structured approach to evaluation, setting out a clear hypothesis to be tested.

A specific example of a logic model is given below. It was prepared by Perryman (2021) for one of The Open University's microcredentials, *Online Teaching: Evaluating and Improving Courses*. It splits outcomes into two – short-term and intermediate – and contains an additional section in which possible evaluation questions for the course have been derived from the logic model. This worked example demonstrates how, for the purpose of evaluations, logic models give a basis for understanding how a particular programme or initiative works and its impact. This comprehension can inform all stages of the evaluation process, including the design, development of evaluation criteria and questions, data collection methods and data interpretation.

Logic model for the *Online Teaching: Evaluating and Improving Courses* microcredential.

- **Inputs:** human resources, financial resources, organisational systems, ICT [information and communications technology] and AV [audio-visual] equipment, external platforms and staff.
- **Activities:** producing the course and AV, presenting the course, recruiting and registering learners, facilitating the course, managing the assessment process.

- **Outputs:** number of learners on the course, number of learners completing the course, number of learners passing the course, number of comments in discussions.
- **Short-term outcomes:** participants achieve the course learning outcomes and gain knowledge, understanding and skills related to evaluating online teaching.
- **Intermediate outcomes:** participants conduct/plan evaluations in their own institutions, online teaching is improved on the basis of evaluation findings.
- **Long-term impact:** students at course participants' institutions benefit from improved online teaching, these students' study outcomes improve, these students' life chances improve. (Perryman, 2021)

Evaluation questions derived from the logic model.

- **Inputs:** Were the inputs sufficient and timely?
- **Activities:** Was the course developed as planned? How was the course promoted? Did the course recruit the target number of learners across identified categories? Were those learners registered effectively? Did the mentors facilitate the course as required? Was the assessment process carried out according to the required university processes and procedures?
- **Outputs:** How many learners were registered on the course? How many learners completed the course? How many learners passed the course? How many comments were made in the discussion?
- **Short-term outcomes:** Did course participants achieve the course learning outcomes in terms of knowledge, understanding and skills?
- **Intermediate outcomes:** Have course participants used their skills in conducting / planning evaluations in their

own institution? Have these evaluations been effective? Is there evidence that online teaching has been improved on the basis of the findings of these evaluations?
- **Long-term impact:** Is there evidence that students at course participants' institutions have benefited from improved online learning? Have these students' study outcomes improved? Have these students' life chances improved? (Perryman, 2021)

Evaluation questions, indicators and standards

In the Perryman logic model, the evaluation questions build on salient guiding principles, which include questions around data collection, data analysis and data reporting. There are also some general evaluation criteria that can assist with devising appropriate questions. Evaluations usually address one or more of these criteria, the exceptions being exploratory or descriptive evaluations. Nonetheless, the general criteria assist with an initial phase of question development and include effectiveness, appropriateness, implementation, efficiency, equity and need. From these general criteria, questions can be formulated, such as 'how are the intended outcomes being achieved?' This would match an effectiveness evaluation.

The types of evaluation question that are developed are also related to the type of evaluation that has been chosen, these being either formative or summative. It is important, however, to keep in mind not only the type of evaluation but also its purpose, evaluation criteria and stakeholders.

Formative evaluations take place while a course or initiative is in progress. The Open University undertook formative evaluations as it developed and presented its microcredentials. The first year's evaluation considered progress over the year in relation to the agreed aims of the project (Papathoma & Ferguson 2020); the second evaluated production methods used for microcredentials as well as the learner and educator experience (Papathoma & Ferguson, 2021), while the third considered impact, pedagogy, assessment, and the balance between theory and practical skills (Chandler, 2023).

Formative evaluation questions relate to the 'activities' or 'outputs' stage of a logic model. Some questions that are relevant include:

- How is the programme/microcredential/project being implemented? Subquestions may focus on the enquiry and registration processes: are prospective learners' queries answered promptly? How were learner expectations managed? Was there too much content in the courses for the allocated study time?
- How appropriate are the processes compared with relevant quality standards? Subquestions could cover any of the aspects of online teaching mentioned in related standards.
- Is the programme/microcredential/project being implemented correctly? Subquestions may be asked about how the course mentor/study adviser role was performed and whether this was found to comply with the guidance provided.
- Are as many participants being reached as intended and have any related targets been met (e.g. relating to ethnicity, gender or socio-economic status)?

Summative evaluations ask questions at the end of an initiative or programme of courses. The evaluation questions for the first phase of the OU summative evaluation (Papathoma & Ferguson

2020) of its microcredentials were based upon the agreed aims/purpose of the initiative, which, in turn, determined its effectiveness and impact. These types of evaluation are often referred to as 'outcome evaluations' or 'impact evaluations'. The types of summative question that were asked by the OU included:

- How well did the project/microcredential work? Subquestions focusing on specific aspects of the initiative included: how did the innovative approach to the development and delivery of course content work? This is an important question that also relates to the cost of the resources that produced the innovative content.
- Did the project/microcredential/programme achieve, or contribute to, its intended short-term, intermediate and long-term outcomes? Subquestions probed: did the project access international markets? Which countries favoured this form of learning and why?
- For whom, in what ways and in what circumstances? These subquestions focused on new and different learner populations.
- What external factors may have contributed to, or prevented, impact and in what ways/which circumstances? Subquestions focused on the impact of the availability/non-availability of technology and the support given by the study advisers.

Indicators are specific, measurable and observable statements that provide clearer definitions of outcome statements. Indicators guide the rest of the evaluation plan including the selection of data collection methods, the design of the evaluation instruments (e.g. the survey and interview questions used), the choice of data analysis methods, and consideration of what has occurred or changed in the evaluated initiative, leading to further questions, such as how these changes happened.

Indicators can be quantitative, such as metrics that include the number of students who submitted a particular assessment or passed a course. On the other hand, qualitative indicators focus on variables such as attitudes, perceptions and beliefs. Indicators can relate to any part of an initiative and its logic model or initial descriptions.

There are three categories of indicator. Input indicators relate to the 'inputs' or 'resources' part of the logic model. An example from this group could relate to microcredential production costs, which are checked to see if they remained within the agreed budget. Process indicators measure the activities and related outputs to ascertain whether the initiative was implemented as planned. Some evaluations only use output indicators as their process indicators. This is based on the assumption that, if the original outputs have been achieved in a satisfactory manner, it is more than likely that an initiative's activities have been correctly implemented. Other evaluations may use separate indicators for activities and outputs. Outcome indicators measure whether the initiative achieved the expected outcome and impact identified in the logic model in the short term, intermediate term and longer term. Therefore, pre and post indicators need to be measured before an initiative starts and again at the end of that initiative. If that is not possible, then an indicator probably needs to rely on self-reported data about whether the expected changes took place.

It is likely that each activity or outcome will have more than one indicator and some indicators will be more time-consuming than others to enact. Indicators that rely on observing an educator's practice will be more time-consuming to collect evidence for than those relying on self-reports of changed practice collected via a survey. For online teaching-related evaluations, these indicators can be drawn from existing standards and benchmarks, as discussed below.

'Standards' refers to the level of performance required for specific indicators.

> 'Standards' can refer to an aspect of performance, or to the level of performance, or to a combination of both. The level of performance can be specified tightly or described in terms that will vary according to the context. These standards can be considered minimum levels required, or levels required to be considered 'best practice'. (Rogers, cited in Fang 2017)

A review of standards by the International Council for Open and Distance Education (ICDE) noted in 2015 that:

> There are many existing schemes and models for quality assurance of open, distance, flexible and online education, including e-learning. They share many common features and many are designed to offer flexibility for institutions to adapt to suit national and institutional contexts. The most common structure encountered presents criteria for performance in aspects of institutional management, curriculum design, student support and other elements of educational provision, further subdivision into performance indicators and indications of sources of evidence. The most general categorisation of activities is Management (Institutional strategy, visions, and resourcing) Products (processes of curriculum and module development) and Services (student, and staff support, information resources etc.). Some models apply numerical scoring criteria with target performance levels others rely on more subjective assessment of performance. There are models that require performance assessment of 20–30 items others in excess of 100. (Ossiannilsson et al. 2015: 2)

An important message from this report is that the ICDE recognised that the institutional context is likely to inform the choice of standards, or quality model that will be used in an e-learning evaluation. With respect to standards for online teaching and learning, Attwell's (2006) observation continues to be true: many online learning evaluation studies focus on the technology used rather than the pedagogy and learner experience.

As discussed at the beginning of this chapter, there is an extensive selection of standards and frameworks developed for different purposes and in differing contexts, from which can be derived generic advice about variables that need to be addressed for quality assurance and quality enhancement purposes. These have been summarised by ICDE as:

- **'Multifaceted** – systems use a multiplicity of measures for quality, and will often consider strategy, policy, infrastructure, processes, outputs and more so as to come to a well-rounded view of holistic quality.
- **'Dynamic** – flexibility is built into systems, to accommodate for rapid changes in technology, as well as social norms. For this reason, they rarely refer to specific technological measures, and rather concentrate on the services provided to users through that technology.
- **'Mainstreamed** – while all the quality tools surveyed aim at high-level quality improvement, this is intended to trickle down throughout the institution and be used as a tool for reflective practice by individual members of staff in their daily work.
- **'Representative** – quality systems seek to balance the perspectives and demands of various interested stakeholders, including students, staff, enterprise, government and society at large.

- '**Multifunctional** – most systems serve a triple function of instilling a quality culture within an institution and providing a roadmap for future improvement, as well as serving as a label of quality for outside perspectives.' (Ossiannilsson et al. 2015: 31)

Involving people and stakeholders towards an equitable evaluation

As stakeholders play an important role in any evaluation process, developing a logic model should be a collaborative process. Each stakeholder is likely to have different opinions about elements of the logic model, especially about the mechanisms of change featured in any initiative. The process of collaboratively developing a logic model therefore requires careful facilitation to avoid conflict and allow diverse voices to be heard. These are important considerations when considering educational equity.

Educational equity is realised when there is fairness and justice for all students. This means that each student is able to develop their full academic and social potential, with the requisite support. It is therefore crucial to listen to all voices in an equitable evaluation, especially to voices that might otherwise be neglected. This can be achieved through guidelines that have been produced and which embody the concept advanced by Gorski (2016b) as equity literacy. The concept of equity literacy is important because it describes the skills and attitudes that facilitate the creation of sustainable learning environments for all. Gorski (2016a) also argues for a framework that instantiates equity literacy that can overcome some of the disparities that arise from some culture-centric guidelines.

More recent work from the Equitable Evaluation Initiative (EEI) offers a set of guidelines. The EEI set out to explore, prototype and advance a new frame for evaluative thinking, a five-year initiative that started in 2019. Its framework was expanded in May 2023 and its three principles are:

Principle one

Evaluation and evaluative work should be in service of equity:

- Production, consumption, and management of evaluation and evaluative work should hold at its core a responsibility to advance progress towards equity.

Principle two

Evaluative work should be designed and implemented commensurate with the values underlying equity work:

- Multiculturally valid, and
- Oriented toward participant ownership.

Principle three

Evaluative work can and should answer critical questions about the:

- Ways in which historical and structural decisions have contributed to the condition to be addressed,
- Effect of a strategy on different populations, on the underlying systemic drivers of inequity, and
- Ways in which cultural context is tangled up in both the structural conditions and the change initiative itself. (Equitable Evaluation Initiative 2023)

These guiding principles are worth considering when designing any educational evaluation.

Ethical evaluation

An ethical evaluation involves standards of conduct that promote integrity, honesty and respect for all the actors involved. According to Barnett and Camfield's (2016) definition, an ethical evaluation is 'a set of principles of right conduct that is supposed to govern practitioners' behaviours'. In an educational evaluation context these correct behaviours would fall within the normative ethics domain.

There are general ethics principles that can guide an education-related research study as provided by funding bodies, such as those published by the Australian Council for International Development (ACFID 2015) and the British Council Research and Evaluation Ethics Policy (British Council n.d.). These documents highlight the following considerations:

- informed consent;
- privacy protection and confidentiality of data;
- protection of participants' rights;
- doing no harm;
- data management and storage;
- transferring data electronically and keeping data safe in transit;
- dissemination and impact of the research.

Farrow (2016) concurs with these principles and offers a comparison of three different sets of ethics guidelines from the ESRC (2015), BERA (2011) and BPS (2010) in relation to informed consent, independence, integrity, privacy and data security, full disclosure, respect for participant autonomy and the avoidance of harm / minimisation of risk. It is important to note that the principles that guide ethical practice in online research are similar to those for other research undertaken with human subjects: respect for autonomy, justice and beneficence (Kitchin 2007).

According to Gupta (2017), autonomy refers to the notion that each individual has the right to privacy and dignity. Justice refers to the notion that all research participants should be treated fairly, equitably and decently during the research process, while beneficence requires researchers to evaluate harms or risks to their participants and to attempt to minimise these and maximise the benefits to them (Kitchin 2007). Within the context of online research, 'the risk of harm can arise with disclosure of a participant's identity or other sensitive information that could expose them to the risk of embarrassment, reputational damage, or legal prosecution' (Gupta 2017).

Evaluators also need to be aware of the ethics of disclosure, for example with regard to students' engagement in discussion forums, where subjects may indulge in 'confessional' activity and 'online disinhibition' (Joinson 1998; Suler 2004). There is also much oversharing of personal information on social media sites, calling into question the matter of informed consent with respect to such information. This means that potential harm could be done by using this type of data, an issue that should be discussed while planning such an evaluation. A good resource to use during this planning phase is that of van den Berg, Hawkins and Stame (2022) in their *Ethics for Evaluation*, which provides a theoretical framework focusing on evaluations **doing no harm**, **tackling bad** and **doing good**.

Evaluation models

One of the most commonly used evaluation models is that of Kirkpatrick, which was developed in the 1950s and has been upgraded to a 'new world' version (Kirkpatrick Partners 2020). It can be used to measure both long- and short-term impact and has been employed by Lin and Cantoni (2017) and by Goh, Wong and Ayub (2018) as a framework for evaluating MOOCs. The current features of this model include:

- **Level 1: reaction** – learners' feelings about the learning experience; and the more recent additions:
    - Engagement – 'The degree to which participants are actively involved in and contributing to the learning experience';
    - Relevance – 'The degree to which training participants will have the opportunity to use or apply what they learned in training on the job.'
- **Level 2: learning** – the increase in knowledge, skill and changes in attitudes resulting from the learning experience; and the more recent additions:
    - Confidence – the belief in being able to apply the knowledge, and
    - Commitment to applying that knowledge.
- **Level 3: behaviour** – the implementation of acquired knowledge/skills in employment/other contexts; and the more recent addition:
    - Required drivers: 'Processes and systems that reinforce, encourage and reward performance of critical behaviors on the job.'
- **Level 4: results** – the broader impact of the training on an organisation (or, by extension, any other environment

or stakeholders, though this is not covered in Kirkpatrick's original model); and the more recent addition:
- Leading indicators: 'Short-term observations and measurements suggesting that critical behaviors are on track to create a positive impact on desired results.' (Kirkpatrick Partners 2020)

Perryman (2020: 15) finds a problem with the model with respect to addressing 'the significance of contextual factors in enabling or inhibiting impact at Levels 3 and 4' and suggests that it does not offer a particularly nuanced approach to analysing complex relationships between cause and effect, or to capturing and understanding the impact of context on learners' experiences, and on changes in their attitudes and behaviour.

Kalz et al. (2015) developed a specific model survey instrument from the MOOCKnowledge Project. This project was an initiative of the European Commission's Institute of Prospective Technological Studies (IPTS), which aimed to provide data on participants studying MOOCs, in order to evaluate the impact of different groups studying MOOCs within a European context. Since the MOOCKnowledge model identifies variables that may explain the impact of a project or course on different groups of learners who have followed an identical course, it can assist course designers and providers to assess variables that could affect long-term impact goals.

Theory of change

The theory of change (ToC) was derived from the field of theory-driven evaluation (Chen 1990; Coryn et al. 2011) and then popularised by Weiss (1995). Its purpose is to make explicit underlying assumptions associated with a given initiative. This allows the evaluation team to understand the goals and intentions of the project's designers. Reinholz and Andrews (2020) state that the benefits of ToC come through 'making the underlying rationale of an initiative explicit, it can be interrogated, assessed and revised systematically as it is being implemented'.

The ToC is often produced as a diagram that illustrates the interventions that will be applied to achieve the preconditions and long-term outcomes for the project. In this way the activities are clearly articulated and the diagram will assist with choosing interventions in a systematic and rigorous manner. Furthermore, it can demonstrate how an intervention has contributed to a chain of results that produced the intended or actual impacts. A ToC is therefore more complex than the logic model described earlier, with a more detailed exploration of the relationships embodied within the logic model. It also offers a framework to investigate cause and effect and to compare change mechanisms from various and diverse contexts.

A practical example of applying the ToC to an educational technology initiative is that undertaken by Perryman (2020). She employed a theory-of-change-based evaluation to the massive open online course on technology-enhanced learning (TEL MOOC) produced by the Commonwealth of Learning and Athabasca University. The evaluation report reveals extensive short-, medium- and long-term impact on TEL implementation and open educational practices across 32 countries. It also draws attention to the variables that limited the impact of this initiative, such as infrastructure problems and institution-related, cultural and technological barriers.

> A theory of change approach was adopted as the basis for the evaluation due to its affordances in offering a systematic framework for investigating the complex

relationship between cause and effect that must be unravelled when conducting a long-term impact study, and for investigating the mechanisms of change in very diverse contexts. (Perryman 2020)

Since it is difficult to prove attribution for many interventions, Perryman (2020) in her evaluation adopts a contribution analysis (see Mayne 2012). Contribution analysis is a methodology used to identify the multiple factors that could be responsible for the short-, medium- and long-term impact of a given intervention such as a course or educational initiative. Contribution analysis does not conclusively prove an intervention has contributed to a change or set of changes. Instead, its prime function is to reduce uncertainty (Mayne 2008: 1).

The TEL MOOC ToC used three clusters of possible contributory factors (A, B and C), which were identified from the existing literature:

- **Cluster A** – making a potential contribution to the impact of TEL MOOC on participants in terms of changes in their attitudes and behaviour,
- **Cluster B** (identical to Cluster A) – making a potential contribution to the impact on TEL MOOC participants' colleagues' attitudes and behaviour, and on institutional/policy change, and
- **Cluster C** – making a potential contribution to the longer-term impact on stakeholders other than the course participants and their colleagues (Perryman 2020: 42).

The benefit of this approach of identifying possible contributory factors in advance of the evaluation was that these were taken into account in the design of the survey and interview questions. This ensured that analysis would not neglect these variables, giving more confidence to findings from this study.

Dissemination

There are multiple dissemination routes for any evaluation findings. The primary one for funders is usually a report but this may be accompanied by academic articles, conference presentations, media stories or outputs on social media. There are important factors to consider when sharing findings, including ensuring the report title can be easily found by search engines (a numerical internal report title will not be picked up by a search engine). The evaluation website can be designed to maximise the potential for visitors by using search engine optimisation (SEO) techniques. These can be complex but registering the site using keywords is a good start.

All these factors are important when using an institution's own institutional repository. The Open University supports Open Research Online (ORO), a platform in which its academics are required to deposit their research publications. Although a project may have a website, this may only exist for the duration of the research and using an institutional repository will guarantee longer term access to associated work. Peers can also be encouraged to publicise findings to their various networks.

Writing a blog and creating an account on a platform such as LinkedIn, BlueSky, Threads, Mastodon or Twitter/X will not only publicise the project but could also make the prospective audience aware of the evaluation methodology and findings. These types of message will also form an alert to the release of the final report. Other social media outlets, such as Instagram, facilitate the creation of an image-based narrative for the evaluation.

Facebook can be useful for community engagement, while tools such as Snapchat and TikTok also suit the needs of specific audiences and age groups.

Findings can also be shared as data via open data repositories, such as Figshare. This enables other users to combine the project data with their own and also with other data sets. This increases the impact of the evaluation. Events can be arranged around the release of the report, which will in turn increase social media exposure and generate more interest in the evaluation findings.

Dissemination activities can be fun and a range of unusual dissemination formats have been used. For example, the OU organises annual 'Bake your PhD' competitions, in which doctoral researchers bake goods that visually represent their research (these can be viewed on X using the hashtag #BakeYourPhD). By 2024, the annual Dance Your PhD organised by the American Association for the Advancement of Science together with the Science journal had run 16 times, with the entrants available to view on YouTube.

Further thoughts

Having discussed the role of policies and standards to ensure quality, together with checking the quality through different types of evaluations, several questions remain about how microcredentials are viewed and embedded within a tertiary education ecosystem. McGreal and Olcott (2022) suggest that the advent of microcredentials provides an opportunity for a strategic reset. There are, of course, risks to any new venture and microcredential creation can involve the breaking up and repurposing of previous parts of the curriculum. Brown and Nic Giolla Mhichíl (2021: 3) argue that microcredentials can be a 'wolf in sheep's clothing' and strongly suggest that an important starting point for any institution is to agree a strategic microcredential institutional framework. The development of this needs to be a high priority for the senior leadership team with due diligence around costs and market share of potential students that match government policies around skill gaps that can be addressed through microcredential production and presentation. Brown et al. (2023) offer practical advice for constructing and implementing a strategic framework with an examination of the business models that could be adopted. There is still a way to go but microcredentials offer learners a way to engage with new employment opportunities, especially with the fast growth of AI in the workplace, but only if the price is right. The final chapter of the book looks to the future and examines what may lie ahead for microcredentials.

References

Acceleration Plan. (2022). *Microcredentials pilot.* Acceleration Plan: Educational Innovation with ICT. Available at https://www.versnellingsplan.nl/en/Kennisbank/pilot-microcredentials

ACFID. (2015, February). *Guidelines for ethical research and evaluation in development.* Australian Council for International Development.

Attwell, G. (2006). *Evaluating e-learning: A guide to the evaluation of e-learning.* Evaluate Europe Handbook Series Volume 2. Available at http://pontydysgu.org/wp-content/uploads/2007/11/eva_europe_vol2_prefinal.pdf

Attwell, G. (2017). *Evaluating eLearning.* Available at https://www.slideshare.net/GrahamAttwell/evaluating-elearning-104938005

Australian Government. (2021, November). *National microcredentials framework.* Australian Government, Department of Education, Skills and Employment.

Bates, T. (2021). *Understanding microcredentials: A report from HEQCO* (31 May). Available at https://www.tonybates.ca/2021/05/31/understanding-microcredentials-a-report-from-heqco

Barnett, C. and Camfield, L. (2016). Ethics in evaluation. *Journal of Development Effectiveness*, 8(4): 528–524. DOI: https://doi.org/10.1080/19439342.2016.1244554

Brasher, A., Whitelock, D., Holmes, W., Pozzi, F., Persico, D., Manganello, F., Passarelli, M. and Sangrà, A. (2022). Comparing the comparators: How should the quality of education offered by online universities be evaluated? *European Journal of Education*, 57(2): 306–324. DOI: http://doi.org/10.1111/ejed.12497

British Council. (n.d.). *British Council research and ethics evaluation policy*. British Council. Available at https://opportunities-insight.britishcouncil.org/sites/siem/files/field/file/news/research_and_eval_risk_and_ethics_policy.docx

Brown, M. and Nic Giolla Mhichíl, M. (2021). *Micro-credentials untethered: A wolf in sheep's clothing?* Dublin City University. Available at https://irelandseducationyearbook.ie/downloads/IEYB2021/YB2021-Higher-Education-08.pdf

Brown, M., McGreal, R. and Peters, M. (2023). A strategic institutional response to microcredentials: Key questions for educational leaders. *Journal of Interactive Media in Education*, 2023(1).

Chandler, K. (2023). Microcredentials evaluation phase 3 final report (internal report). Milton Keynes: Open University.

Chen, H. T. (1990). *Theory-driven evaluations*. Sage.

Coryn, C. L., Noakes, L. A., Westine, C. D. and Schröter, D. C. (2011). A systematic review of theory-driven evaluation practice from 1990 to 2009. *American Journal of Evaluation*, 32(2): 199–226.

Duklas, J. (2020). *Micro-credentials: Trends in credit transfer and credentialing*. British Columbia Council on Admissions and Transfer. Available at https://eric.ed.gov/?id=ED610420

Equitable Evaluation Initiative. (2023). *Framework* (21 May). Available at https://www.equitableeval.org/framework

ESG. (2015). *Standards and guidelines for quality assurance in the European Higher Education Area (ESG)*. EURASHE.

European Commission. (2017). *European pillar of social rights.* Available at https://ec.europa.eu/info/strategy/priorities-2019-2024/economy-works-people/jobs-growth-and-investment/european-pillar-social-rights_en

European Commission. (2020). *A European approach to microcredentials – Output of the Micro-credentials Higher Education Consultation Group – final report.* Available at https://education.ec.europa.eu/sites/default/files/document-library-docs/european-approach-micro-credentials-higher-education-consultation-group-output-final-report.pdf

Fang, M. (2017). Design a study for determining labour productivity standard in Canadian armed forces food services. In: *Proceedings of the 6th International Conference on Operations Research and Enterprise Systems (ICORES 2017).* pp. 219–227.

Farrow, R. (2016). A framework for the ethics of open education. *Open Praxis,* 8(2): 93–109.

Goh, W. W., Wong, S. Y. and Ayub, E. (2018). The effectiveness of MOOC among learners based on Kirkpatrick's model. In: *Redesigning learning for greater social impact: Taylor's 9th Teaching and Learning Conference 2016 Proceedings.* Singapore: Springer. pp. 313–323.

Gorski, P. (2016a). Rethinking the role of 'culture' in educational equity. From cultural competence to equity literacy. *Multicultural Perspectives,* 18(4): 221–226. DOI: https://doi.org/10.1080/15210960.2016.1228344

Gorski, P. C. (2016b). Equity literacy: More than celebrating diversity. *Diversity in Education,* 11(1): 12–15.

Gullickson, A. (2020). The whole elephant: Defining evaluation. *Evaluation and Program Planning,* 79: 101787. DOI: https://doi.org/10.1016/j.evalprogplan.2020.101787

Gupta, S. (2017). Ethical issues in designing internet-based research: Recommendations for good practice. *Journal of Research Practice,* 13(2): D1.

Joinson, A. N. (1998). Disinhibition and the internet. In: Gackenbach, J. *Psychology and the internet: Intrapersonal, interpersonal, and transpersonal implications.* Academic Press.

Kalz, M., Kreijns, K., Walhout, J., Castaño-Munoz, J., Espasa, A. and Tovar, E. (2015). Setting-up a European cross-provider data collection on open online courses. *International Review of Research in Open and Distributed Learning*, 16(6): 62–77. https://doi.org/10.19173/irrodl.v16i6.2150

Kaplan, S. A. and Garrett, K. E. (2005). The use of logic models by community-based initiatives. *Evaluation and Program Planning*, 28(2): 167–172.

Kellogg Foundation. (1998). *Logic model development guide.* W K Kellogg Foundation.

Kellogg Foundation. (2012). *Evaluation handbook.* Available at https://bja.ojp.gov/sites/g/files/xyckuh186/files/media/document/wk-kellogg-foundation.pdf

Kellogg Foundation. (2017). *The step by step guide to evaluation.* Available at https://www.betterevaluation.org/sites/default/files/WKKF_StepByStepGuideToEvaluation_smaller.pdf

Kirkpatrick Partners. (2020). *The Kirkpatrick model.* Available at https://www.kirkpatrickpartners.com/the-kirkpatrick-model/

Kitchin, H. A. (2007). *Research ethics and the internet: Negotiating Canada's TriCouncil policy statement.* Fernwood.

Lin, J. and Cantoni, L. (2017). Assessing the performance of a tourism MOOC using the Kirkpatrick model: A supplier's point of view. In: *Information and Communication Technologies in Tourism 2017; Proceedings of the International Conference in Rome, Italy, January 24–26, 2017.* Springer. pp. 129–142.

Mayne, J. (2008). *Contribution analysis: An approach to exploring cause and effect.* ILAC Brief No. 16. Rome: The Institutional Learning and Change Initiative.

Mayne, J. (2012). Contribution analysis: Coming of age? *Evaluation*, 18(3): 270–280.

McGreal, R. and Olcott, D. (2022). A strategic reset: Microcredentials for higher education leaders. *Smart Learning Environments*, 9(9): 1–23.

MICROBOL. (2020). *Micro-credentials linked to the Bologna key commitments: Desk research report.* MICROBOL.

Available at https://eua.eu/downloads/publications/microbol%20desk%20research%20report.pdf

Morrison, D. (2015). How 'good' is your online course? Five steps to assess course quality. *Online Learning Insights* (26 May). Available at https://onlinelearninginsights.wordpress.com/tag/how-to-evaluate-course-quality

NZQA. (2022). *Micro-credential approval, accreditation and listing*. New Zealand Qualifications Authority. Available at https://www.nzqa.govt.nz/providers-partners/approval-accreditation-and-registration/micro-credentials/#heading2-0

Oliver, M. (2000). Evaluating online teaching and learning. *Information Service & Use* 20(2–3): 83–94. DOI: https://doi.org/10.3233/ISU-2000-202-304

Orr, D., Pupinis, M. and Kirdulyte, G. (2020). *Towards a European approach to micro-credentials: A study of practices and commonalities in offering micro-credentials in European higher education*. NESET Report. Publications Office of the European Union. DOI: https://doi.org/10.2766/7338

Ossiannilsson, E., Williams, K., Camilleri, A. and Brown., M. (2015). *Quality models in online and open education around the globe. State of the art and recommendations*. International Council for Open and Distance Education (ICDE). Available at https://files.eric.ed.gov/fulltext/ED557055.pdf

Papathoma, T. and Ferguson, R. (2020). *Evaluation of Open University microcredentials: Final report of phase one*. Milton Keynes: The Open University.

Papathoma, T. and Ferguson, R. (2021). *Evaluation of Open University microcredentials: Final report of phase two (internal report)*. Milton Keynes: The Open University.

Perryman, L.-A. (2020). *TELMOOC long-term impact evaluation study*. Commonwealth of Learning. Available at https://oasis.col.org/items/f6dd8b4c-6eb5-45e9-8cad-038bda4e1e68

Perryman, L.-A. (2021). *Logic model and possible evaluation questions for the production of 'Online Teaching: Evaluating and Improving Courses'*. Milton Keynes: The Open University.

Pichette, J., Brumwell, S., Rizk, J. and Han, S. (2021). *Making sense of microcredentials*. Toronto: Higher Education Quality Council of Ontario. Available at https://heqco.ca/pub/making-sense-of-microcredentials

QAA. (2022). *Characteristics statement: Micro-credentials*. Gloucester: The Quality Assurance Agency for Higher Education. Available at https://www.qaa.ac.uk/docs/qaa/quality-code/micro-credentials-characteristics-statement.pdf?sfvrsn=32bda081_4

QAA. (2023). *The UK quality code for higher education*. The Quality Assurance Agency for Higher Education. Available at https://www.qaa.ac.uk/docs/qaa/quality-code/revised-uk-quality-code-for-higher-education.pdf?sfvrsn=4c19f781_24

Ramsden, P. (2003). *Learning to teach in higher education*. 2nd ed. Routledge.

Reinholz, D. L. and Andrews, T. C. (2020). Change theory and theory of change: What's the difference anyway? *International Journal of STEM Education*, 7(2). DOI: https://doi.org/10.1186/s40594-020-0202-3

Rosewell, J., Kear, K., Williams, K., Rodrigo, C. and Sánchez-Elvira, A. (2017). E-xcellence methodology: Lessons learned over ten years of development and implementation. In: Ubachs, G. and Konings, L. *Proceedings of the Online, Open and Flexible Higher Education Conference: Higher education for the future: Accelerating and strengthening innovation*. Milton Keynes: The Open University. Available at https://conference.eadtu.eu/download2399

Scriven, M. (1991). *Evaluation thesaurus*. 4th ed. Sage.

Suler, J. (2004). The online disinhibition effect. *Cyberpsychology and Behaviour*, 7(3): 321–326.

TEQSA. (2021). *Higher education standards framework (threshold standards) 2021*. Australian Government, Tertiary Education Quality and Standards Agency (TEQSA).

Thompson, K. (2005). *Constructing educational criticism of online courses: A model for implementation by practitioners*. Unpublished dissertation (PhD). University of Central Florida.

Twersky, F. and Lindblom, K. (2012, December). *Evaluation principles and practices: An internal working paper*. The William and Flora Hewlett Foundation. Available at http://www.hewlett.org/wp-content/uploads/2016/08/EvaluationPrinciples-FINAL.pdf

Tyler, R. W. (1950). *Basic principles of curriculum and instruction*. University of Chicago Press.

Universities Canada. (2023). *Quality assurance*. Available at https://www.univcan.ca/universities/quality-assurance

van den Berg, R. D., Hawkins, P. and Stame, N. (2022). *Ethics for evaluation: Beyond 'doing no harm' to 'tackling bad' and 'doing good'*. Routledge, Taylor & Francis.

van den Heuvel, L. and Bohm, N. L. (2023). *Exploring the reliability, time efficiency, and fairness of comparative judgement in the admission of architecture students*. European Society for Engineering Education (SEFI). DOI: https://doi.org/10.21427/WEY8-JZ69

Weiss, C. H. (1995). Nothing as practical as good theory: Exploring theory-based evaluation for comprehensive community initiatives for children and families. *New Approaches to Evaluating Community Initiatives: Concepts, Methods, and Contexts*, 1: 65–92.

CHAPTER 9

Microcredentials futures

In this final chapter, we look at what the future may hold for microcredentials. The chapter begins by examining some of their current expected trajectories, looking at the different visions proposed by those who are developing them or influencing that development. It goes on to examine the different factors that will influence progress towards those visions, identifying some of the challenges that lie ahead. It ends by looking at recent developments in teaching and learning that could, in future, be incorporated within microcredentials.

How to cite this book chapter:
Ferguson, R. and Whitelock, D. 2024. Microcredentials futures. In: Ferguson, R. and Whitelock, D. *Microcredentials for Excellence: A Practical Guide.* Pp. 263–296. London: Ubiquity Press. DOI: https://doi.org/10.5334/bcz.i. License: CC BY-NC 4.0

Visions of the future

Education, particularly education like microcredentials that is enabled by the use of technology, is a complex system. It includes communities, technologies, and practices that are informed by pedagogy (Scanlon et al. 2013). In order to succeed in the long term, each of the elements in this complex must be taken into account as the innovation is developed, modified and finally embedded. A vision of the future helps to shape the trajectory of development and also inspires those involved to take on and overcome challenges.

As previous chapters have emphasised, there is currently no single agreed definition of microcredentials. There is also no single vision of what microcredentials are trying to achieve, or of their future trajectory. The future looks different from the perspective of governments, industries and workplaces, HEIs, learners and educators. Broadly speaking, there are four main visions for the future: expanding learning opportunities, recognising learning, strengthening employment-related learning, and making money. These are not mutually exclusive but are combined in a variety of ways.

Vision: expanding learning opportunities

The vision of expanding learning opportunities has been associated with microcredentials since the term was first introduced. Community college staff interviewed by Howley (2010) were responding to an awareness that learners studying with the intention of moving into paid employment did not want to sign up for two-year degree programmes but were looking for diplomas or certificates that would take only a year or a semester of study.

Ten years later, a report on a European approach to microcredentials set out how this could be achieved not just in one college but across a continent.

> Short-term learning opportunities leading to microcredentials can help to substantially widen learning and skills development opportunities, and further shape the lifelong learning dimension in higher education. A European approach to micro-credentials will allow higher education institutions to offer such courses on a larger scale and in a comparable manner throughout Europe, ensuring agreed quality standards, and facilitating their recognition and portability across the EU. (European Commission 2020: 4)

This vision of expanding learning opportunities is shared around the world. In a series of provocations published in the *Journal of Teaching and Learning for Graduate Employability*, authors in Malaysia outlined possibilities for a more flexible system, enabling increasing numbers of individuals from around the world to access education (Ahmat et al. 2021). In Australia, Healy (2021) emphasises that microcredentials should be designed and delivered in a lifelong learning ecosystem of educational, employment and social support systems, while Kift notes that, '[a]t their best, shorter, stackable (micro)credentials should allow for flexibility and learning pathways for those who do not necessarily want or need an expensive and [inflexible] formal qualification' (Kift 2021: iii).

The vision of expanding learning opportunities encompasses some of the challenges faced by traditional forms of education, such as certifying competencies, developing employability, and widening access to higher education (Martinez-Marroquin & Male 2021). Microcredentials, particularly stackable microcredentials, could enable learners to personalise accredited learning pathways to a greater extent than was previously possible, building their skills and competencies by collecting evidence of learning in flexible ways, at their own pace, and according to their own priorities (Morrin, Jones & Salem 2021). Crow (2016) identifies ways in which learning could be opened up with the introduction of courses that would be more accessible, more affordable, shorter, personalised, and available on demand.

Vision: recognising learning

One of the challenges associated with current university education is that it only accredits some forms of learning. Microcredentials have been proposed as a way:

> to allow learners to receive formal recognition of their new knowledge and skills. Through the use of authenticated badges, learners can accumulate digital evidence of their knowledge, skills, and abilities and may receive transferable academic credit through a network of partner colleges. (Davis 2012: 90)

A report from Trinity University Texas goes into more detail:

> Online tracking of student accomplishments makes it possible to document student learning at multiple milestones. Rather than focusing on a course grade, a diploma or transcript, microcredentials are awarded for learning achievements. (Browne et al. 2012: 6)

Microcredentials make it possible to 'recognize a variety of skills, knowledge and experiences, both inside and outside of traditional educational settings' (Clements, West & Hunsaker 2020: 154). They have the potential to be 'a form of credentials which represent competencies, skills, and learning outcomes derived from assessment-based, non-degree activities and specify a location for evidence of the content of the earned achievement' (Ehlers 2018: 2). They can also be used to demonstrate that individuals are engaged and productive members of a community (Fedock et al. 2016).

This vision is associated with a focus on ways in which learning can be recognised – through certificates, digital badges, professional or academic credit. 'Microcredential' refers not only to the learning experience but also to the qualification awarded (Lantero, Finocchietti & Petrucci 2021). It is important not only that learning takes place but also that it is understood by wider society to have taken place.

Learners in European universities report that lack of awareness and appreciation of microcredentials, especially from industry, 'significantly decreases the value of micro-credentials to them' (Kukkonen 2021: i). A survey of 201 Canadian/employers in 2020/21 found that only 10% had a good understanding of the term, while 59% were not familiar with it at all (Pichette et al. 2021). It is therefore not surprising that a 2020 consultation in Australia reported strong support for a recommendation that 'the approach to micro-credentials should focus on development, recognition and certification of micro-credentials' (Government of South Australia 2020: 4).

Vision: strengthening employment-related learning

It is possible to expand learning opportunities and recognise a wide variety of learning without specifying a study focus. Following a desk research study, MICROBOL, a European project concerned with microcredentials and their links to existing frameworks, stated that '[a] micro-credential is designed to provide the learner with specific knowledge, skills or competences that respond to societal, personal, cultural or labour market needs' (MICROBOL 2020: 7). However, this definition is wider than many others. There is a widespread view that not only should these courses be short; they should also be focused on preparation for, or advancement within, employment.

In terms of professional development, microcredentials are seen to provide opportunities 'to engage in rigorous, self-paced, job-embedded professional learning' (Acree 2016: 1), to strengthen professional learning at scale (Brown 2019), and to transform professional development (Berry, Airhart & Byrd 2016). They are also viewed as a potential solution to the rapid upskilling required in society (Oliver 2019) and as a way of developing the work-based learning of employees to support both reskilling and upskilling (Nic Giolla Mhichíl et al. 2020).

Even when microcredentials are placed in a wider context of learning and development, as they were by MICROBOL, the link with employment is present. 'The micro-credentialing movement offers great promise in helping to redesign and even reimagine more future-fit and complementary credential frameworks to enhance employability, continuous professional development and the goal of a thriving learning society' (Brown and Nic Giolla Mhichíl 2021: 1).

However, despite the implication in many reports and papers that workers and potential workers are searching for new forms of accreditation, there is little evidence that the impetus for the introduction of microcredentials has come from the workforce. This is a top-down, rather than a bottom-up, initiative that is considered important:

> because of the disruption in labour markets being caused by automation and digitalisation, which has been

intensified by the economic impact of Covid-19, the labour market is rapidly changing, and governments believe that the labour force needs massive re-training in order to adapt. Microcredentials, being employer-focused and relatively short (and hence low-cost), offer potential benefits in this restructuring of the labour force. (Bates 2021)

Vision: making money

Government- and industry-led initiatives are often associated with income opportunities and so it is not surprising that some providers have moved into this market with an eye on the opportunities it provides for them rather than for learners. In 2021, a market intelligence platform predicted 'Online Degree and Micro-Credential Market to reach $117B by 2025' (HolonIQ 2021), an indication of how attractive this development could be for investors. At the start of 2022, education group Pearson agreed to buy the certification company Credly in a deal that valued it at 200 million dollars. At the time, Pearson's chief executive officer stated that verified credentials were increasing in importance, making individuals either better employees or more employable (Holton 2022).

Microcredentials can be seen as

> an outgrowth of the neoliberal learning economy. In this economy, education resembles a commodity, a product, or service marketed and sold like any other commodity … Educational institutions adapt to competitive market pressures by behaving like profit-seeking firms, not only conceiving education as a commodity but also treating students and their employers as paying clients. (Ralston 2021: 85)

Wheelahan and Moodie argue that 'micro-credentials are gig credentials for the gig economy … an income stream for universities, including the most elite universities' (2021b: 1), while Golden and her colleagues (2021) note that short learning programmes such as microcredentials provide HEIs with a source of revenue that is less regulated by governments than much of their other income.

From this perspective, microcredentials can be seen as an example of the 'Silicon Valley narrative', which declares that the current educational system is broken and requires transformation along the lines of hi-tech companies (Weller (2015) explores and critiques this view). However, as Brown and Nic Giolla Mhichíl (2021) point out, microcredentials are developed in many contexts with a variety of objectives and cannot be treated as a uniform entity. Some people see them as an important new revenue stream; some have other visions, and simply want these new courses to cover their costs.

Large-scale visions

Perhaps the most influential visions are those that will shape large-scale, national or transnational initiatives, some of which were introduced in earlier chapters.

One of the largest – extending far beyond microcredentials – consists of the 17 Sustainable Development Goals (SDGs) created by the United Nations in 2015. The fourth of these is quality education: 'Ensure inclusive and equitable quality education and promote lifelong learning opportunities for all' (United Nations 2015). One suggestion here is that, because microcredentials offer new routes to lifelong learning, they can support citizens to be more active, and help to achieve development goals by reducing gender and other inequalities and supporting education for all (Brown, McGreal & Peters 2023). Another idea is that microcredentials could enhance sustainable practice by structured development of the workforce (Curnow & Mori 2021). Gwin and Foggin suggest that:

> Encouraging learners to progress through a series of small, culturally-relevant educational packages that address personal educational goals, and 'badging' their successes in a way that motivates them and validates their achievements, could greatly enhance the overall level of attainment of development goals (Gwin & Foggin 2020: 3).

These possibilities may prove to be true but, at this stage, they remain speculative and there is no clear route from microcredential implementation to achieving any of the goals.

However, although the route to the SDGs remains unclear, national and continent-wide frameworks do indicate how microcredentials can be implemented to achieve a vision. The Netherlands began a microcredentials pilot involving 32 HEIs in October 2021. This unites three visions for microcredentials.

> Our aim with the pilot is for educational institutions' continuing professional development (CPD) offer to have a clear and recognised value in the system … give lifelong learning in the Netherlands a significant boost … support individuals and society in flexible (lifelong) professional development. (Acceleration Plan 2022)

Europe set out its approach to microcredentials at the end of 2020 (European Commission 2020). The foreword to this document sets this work firmly in the context of the European Pillar of Social Rights, particularly 'the right to quality and inclusive education, training and life-long learning in order to maintain and acquire skills that enable them to participate fully in society and manage successfully transitions in the labour market' (European Commission 2017: 11). Overall, this European approach sets its sights on two visions: expanding learning opportunities and strengthening employment-related learning. This link is also apparent in Australia's National Microcredentials Framework (Microcredentials Working Group 2021), which aims not only to enhance lifelong learning but also to relate microcredential knowledge and skills to industry needs.

In New Zealand and parts of Canada, the vision is of employment-related learning. New Zealand is making microcredentials a key part of its qualification strategy, replacing training schemes across the country with microcredentials. In each case, there must be 'strong evidence of need from employers, industry and/or community' (NZQA 2022). In Canada, the Ontario government committed almost $60 million to a microcredential strategy that focused on employment-related upskilling (Pichette et al. 2021). Although a report related to this initiative referred to lifelong learning, one of its main conclusions was that 'institutions and governments should focus their microcredential strategies on upskilling adult learners with specific training needs, whose prior learning and experience has already provided a strong foundation of knowledge and transferable skills' (Pichette et al. 2021: 2).

Achieving the vision(s)

Overall, around the world microcredentials are part of a move to expand learning opportunities, with a focus on strengthening employment-related learning. Part of this strategy, though usually not central to it, is a move to accredit learning that previously went unrecognised. Underpinning this vision may be an intention to make money but this is seldom stated explicitly, whereas the value of microcredentials to learners and to society as a whole is frequently identified as a benefit.

In terms of an overall vision, this could be phrased as:

In 10 years, microcredentials will have increased access to learning opportunities, particularly opportunities to gain credit for workplace-related skills.

An examination of the educational complex of which microcredentials are a part makes it possible to see how attainable this vision is.

Achieving the vision: national and international contexts

The first elements of the educational complex that need to be taken into consideration are the broad contextual elements that affect these courses. These include policy context, the wider environment, funding opportunities and possibilities for revenue generation (Scanlon et al. 2013). In terms of policy, there is good support for microcredentials initiatives, with frameworks already developed to guide policy refinement in a host of countries. However, those frameworks indicate some of the complexities of the issue. The eight-line definition of microcredentials produced by Europe's MICROBOL project in 2020 refers to:

- the context of the European Higher Education Area (EHEA),
- alignment with the Lisbon Recognition Convention (law relating to the recognition of qualifications in Europe),
- the need for explicitly defined learning outcomes at levels in line with qualifications frameworks in the European Higher Education Area and National Qualification frameworks (QF-EHEA/NQF),

- an indication of workload in terms of the European Credit Transfer and Accumulation System (ECTS), and
- quality assurance in line with the Standards and Guidelines for Quality Assurance in the European Higher Education Area (ESG). (MICROBOL 2020)

Worldwide, work is needed not only to align microcredentials with multiple existing frameworks but also to align them across countries and continents. There is a danger that different standards will be developed in parallel, as is already happening, leading to unnecessary confusion.

The complexity increases when the wider environment of microcredentials is taken into account because that environment includes not only government policies but also the standards associated with different industries, professions and providers. A particular area of tension is associated with quality assurance standards. Good-quality online courses are expensive to develop, so HEIs need to be able to present each course as many times as possible in order to recoup costs. At the same time, they must be able to demonstrate that the quality of the course is consistent across time, and in line with the standards of other parts of the curriculum. Fast-changing industries, such as information technology (IT), are less interested in consistency over time and more concerned with courses being up to date. A need for just-in-time training is not easily met by a course that must go through rigorous quality assurance processes to demonstrate it meets local and national standards.

Although there is a lot of work to be done in this area, there is also the political will to achieve it, as evidenced by government initiatives supporting quality assurance and standards agencies to incorporate microcredentials within their work (see, for example,

QAA 2022). At the same time, platforms are developing pathways to study that do not necessarily lead to academic credit but do lead to industry-relevant certification. For example, Coursera offers professional certificates in areas such as IT support and data analysis that are accredited by Google. FutureLearn offers ExpertTracks, which lead to a digital certificate, and microcredentials leading to professional qualifications such as PRINCE2 project management certification.

These different alliances provide various routes to accreditation and multiple ways of linking education with the job market. They are also being used to explore a variety of business models. Commercial companies and venture capitalists are unlikely to invest in or develop microcredentials if they see no return on their investment. Non-profits, including universities, will expect to be able to break even or, at least, to balance any financial loss against a gain in other areas. Partnerships with large companies are likely to attract learners willing to pay for qualifications that help them to get a job in the sector, and may also bring in revenue from companies interested in outsourcing their staff training. At the same time, learners need to be confident that the qualification in which they are investing time and money is recognised by potential employers and will continue to be recognised. A university degree maintains its currency for a lifetime – will the same be true of microcredentials?

There are currently multiple ways in which professional and academic accreditation are linked. Only some of these are described as microcredentials, but many exist within the same space and the differences are unlikely to be clear to potential learners. It is in this hinterland that a struggle between competing visions is playing out – on the one hand the visions of commercial companies that see lucrative opportunities in providing training, and on the other hand those of not-for-profit organisations more interested in ways access to training can be extended. Central to this struggle is the issue of which accreditation learners value and who controls access to that accreditation.

Achieving the vision: learners

One conclusion of a review of the microcredential literature is that, '[d]espite the name, micro-credentials are no micro task for students to complete' (Nguyen et al. 2023: 1547). Oxley and van Rooyen (2021) consider microcredentials from the perspective of learners, writing 'as students enrolled in double undergraduate degrees across two institutions'. Considering the approach to microcredentials at both those institutions, they conclude that 'neither approach addresses how gaps in undergraduate skillsets translate to employment outcomes' (p. 45). They propose an approach that includes the use of microcredentials to reward and incentivise university students as they develop employment-related skills.

As yet, there has been little investigation of the learner experience on microcredentials other than evaluations and market research that are not widely disseminated outside the institutions that produced them. The small-scale studies (Kazin & Clerkin 2018; Yilik 2021) that have been published focus on the experience of undergraduates, who are not typical microcredential learners in that they are already enrolled on a course of study at university level.

An internal report on microcredentials produced by The Open University (Papathoma & Ferguson 2020) drew on interviews with 27 learners from 10 countries. It found that microcredentials were appreciated because they provide short, focused training to cover skills gaps, enabling learners to explore areas relevant to progression in a new or current career. However, some learners found the courses demanding in terms of the study skills they required. A subsequent internal report in the same series (Chandler 2023) drew on interviews with 42 learners. It found that more than a third (36%) had selected their microcredential to help with their current work, and another 29% had done so because government funding to help people develop their employment skills was available. Six of those interviewed had changed jobs since studying the course, and only one of these said studying the course had not been a factor in securing their new post.

The price of microcredentials was identified as a barrier for some learners (Papathoma & Ferguson 2020). Those interviewed from India, Nigeria and Saudi Arabia found these courses an expensive way of gaining the certificates they wanted. Interviews with enrolment advisers drew attention to the number of learners from developing countries asking whether fee reductions, paying by instalments, or scholarships would be possible because otherwise the microcredentials would not be affordable. This is a significant challenge when working towards a vision of increased access to learning opportunities. If these courses are only accessible to those from wealthy economies, then they could increase the size of the digital divide rather than helping to reduce it.

More broadly, this opens up other problems related to inclusion and accessibility. Universities typically have some degree of support available for learners with disabilities. In many countries, this is a legal requirement. There is substantially less support available on a MOOC platform, where many courses or elements of courses are available free of charge, which means there is relatively little resource available for learner support. As many microcredentials are based on these platforms, this raises challenges for potential learners who have disabilities. Iniesto's (2020) accessibility audit of MOOC platforms concluded that 'MOOC development processes need to be updated to produce more accessible MOOCs from the early design stages, with an important change in focus from legislation to actually meeting learners' needs' (p. 211). This is particularly challenging for educational institutions offering microcredentials because learners are not based on the same campus or even in the same country but are distributed around the world.

Achieving the vision: educators

To address these issues requires work from the educator teams who produce and present microcredentials. They face multiple other challenges. Microcredentials need to:

- be aligned with multiple existing frameworks as well as across countries and continents;
- strike a balance between requirements for high-quality just-in-time training and the time required to carry out quality assurance processes;
- offer value to learners, institutions and employers;
- ensure that learners are equipped with the study skills that will enable them to complete the course successfully;
- take into account the needs of those who are least likely to have access to high-quality education – otherwise they run the risk of widening the digital divide.

These courses must be produced in a landscape that is changing rapidly and where there are few experts to advise on the best ways forward. One way of doing this is to locate a wider support network: current examples include Microcredentials Sans Frontières (www.microcredentialssf.org), the Microcredential Observatory run by Dublin City University (www.dcu.ie/nidl/micro-credential-observatory), and the FutureLearn Academic Network for those hosting microcredentials on the FutureLearn platform. Smaller-scale initiatives have also been set up at some institutions, such as the microcredentials community of practice at Trinity College Dublin (twitter.com/tcdmicrocreds).

Some academics are well used to collaborating with industry or with professional organisations so they can align their courses with extra accreditation, arrange for students to gain workplace experience, or integrate academic study with professional development. Others will be moving out of their comfort zone when developing microcredentials that require them to 'co-design with industry partners, drawing on contemporary real-world practice and know-how or incorporating professional associations' accreditation standards' (Rossiter & Tynan 2019: 6). They may need support both in setting up these collaborations and in establishing shared ways of working that enable them to succeed.

A point of conflict could be the pedagogic approach. One view of microcredentials is that larger qualifications can be disaggregated into components and unproblematically reassembled, the sum is the total of the parts, and the outcomes of learning are assumed to be observable, unproblematic and transferable (Wheelahan & Moodie 2021a). This view is more likely to be held by people who do not work in an educational setting. As Chapter 2 showed, larger qualifications require progression – courses aimed at final-year undergraduates are more complex and more specialised than those developed for first-years. In addition, the soft skills and study skills that can be developed over a year or more of study cannot all be broken into parts and studied in any order. This means there are misconceptions about learning and teaching in the context of microcredentials that need to be addressed when hybrid educational/professional teams are working on course development.

In addition, there are extra challenges to be addressed in terms of expectations. Learners 'highly value the ability to personalise the experience by creating individualised learning sequences based on their pre-existing knowledge or skills, diagnostics or formative assessments' (Rossiter & Tynan 2019: 7). Personalising courses is always desirable but is particularly difficult to achieve in settings where costs are being kept low, meaning little individualised support is available and the majority of formative feedback is necessarily automated or provided by peers. This places a demand on technical support teams to help find ways of supporting individual learners as much as possible without overloading educators.

Achieving the vision: technical work

At the most basic level, microcredentials require a great deal of technical work. This may simply involve setting up a new type of course on a familiar platform. However, it is more likely to require a range of systems that need to be connected in new ways. The technical team needs to take into account the entire user journey from enquiry through registration, study and assessment to award. This is likely to include interaction with the following systems.

Search engines to find a relevant microcredential. Internal search engines need to be primed to find these new courses; choice of title and metadata are low-cost ways of raising a course's profile on external search engines, while more elaborate forms of search engine optimisation (SEO) can be carried out to raise awareness more widely.

Registration system(s). If the microcredential is not hosted on the main platform of the university or educational provider, two or more registration systems will need to be linked. If the learner is already registered on one or more of these systems, there needs to be some process for connecting accounts. This is problematic, as learners may not remember their previous sign-in details, and information such as name and contact details may have changed.

Payment and finance systems. Payment for a microcredential must be linked to both payment and accounting systems, with a system in place to process any refunds. In some cases, bulk payment will need to be enabled so that multiple registrations can be paid by an employer or another funding organisation. If the price varies by region, or if there are discounts available for some groups, these variations need to be built into the systems and updated as necessary.

Communication systems. Newly registered learners need information about their course and the support available, as well as about their registration and future options. Too little contact will leave them confused; too many emails about trivial details can result in all communications being ignored – another source of confusion.

Course systems. These include materials on the learning management system (LMS); communication with educators and with others studying at the same time; contact with educators; access to library materials, technical support, and any external materials associated with the course. If microcredential learners are paying lower prices than full-time students, they may have only limited access to these systems. In such cases, the differences need to be agreed and clearly defined.

Assessment system. A secure method of submitting assessment is essential on courses taken for credit. At one or more points, the identity of the learner will need to be verified – a difficult task when students are based in a variety of countries. Work to be assessed must be transferred to markers and to those responsible for validating the result.

Plagiarism check and/or proctoring. Most awarding bodies will require some system in place to provide assurance that the work submitted is the work of the learner registered for the qualification.

Achievement. Marks, results and feedback on work must be communicated to learners and results recorded securely in case they need to be evidenced in future or counted towards a stackable qualification. If this is the last element in a stackable qualification, the award of the microcredential should trigger award of the qualification.

Certification. Successful completion should trigger release of a badge, certificate or way of accessing these. Rossiter and Tynan (2019) draw attention to the importance of using metadata to describe and define the microcredential, stressing that adherence to metadata standards underpins the degree to which microcredentials are accepted because those standards ensure an accurate representation of each microcredential, including how it was earned, who issued it and how its holder's identify was verified.

Follow-up. Completion (or dropout) may trigger a variety of other systems, including evaluation surveys, marketing information about related courses, and invitations to join professional bodies or alumni groups.

Data journey. Each of these different systems will collect data about learners. Some of this data, such as search engine analytics or payment data, may be collected outside the educational institution and then transferred to it. Some, such as registration details and results, may be collected within the institution and then passed outside it – for example, to the platform hosting the microcredential. Some data will be collected within one system and passed to others; some is highly personal and should not be shared at all. In each case, secure methods of data storage and transfer must be in place.

Moving forward

Overall, creating a thriving microcredentials infrastructure is hard. It is not the same as introducing a new course or subject – the existing system is structured to make that possible. It is a more profound change, which requires buy-in at every level, as well as recognition of the need for change in every area of the existing ecology of practices. A Delphi study carried out to explore how micro-credentials might shape higher education in the coming decade found that, 'in order for the wider-scale influence of micro-credentials to be felt, there is a need for considerable international and national strategy development and implementation to overcome a variety of policy- and technology-related barriers that HEIs cannot influence or tackle on their own' (Pirkkalainen et al. 2023: 40).

Nevertheless, the vision of increasing access to learning opportunities, including opportunities to gain credit for workplace-related skills, is a positive one, well worth the effort. More than a quarter of a century ago, prominent educationalist Sir John Daniel observed that 'a sizeable new university would now be needed every week merely to sustain current participation rates in higher education' (Daniel 1996: 4). Despite the high number of new universities opening in countries such as China and India, the percentage of the world's population successfully completing a college degree remains around 7% (100 People 2016). There is also a great disparity from country to country, with the average individual in

Belgium, Greece, New Zealand and Australia expecting to receive 20 or more years of schooling, while individuals in 18 countries in Africa and Asia will receive on average less than 10 years (CIA 2022). There is an enormous educational gap to be filled and microcredentials present one way of achieving this.

Despite the challenges, new developments offer different ways of supporting microcredential learners. MOOCS are already making use of emergent learning technologies. These include:

> learning analytics to improve feedback, adaptive learning that offers personalised pathways, social network analysis tools that highlight connections, discourse analytics that support automated assessment, semantic web technologies that provide customised support, virtual problem-based learning that allows learners to develop their skills within immersive environments. (Ferguson, Sharples & Beale 2015: 8)

At the same time, new pedagogies are being trialled and developed. The following examples, which are particularly relevant to microcredentials, are drawn from the Innovating Pedagogy reports published annually by The Open University since 2012.

Action learning

Action learning is a team-based approach used to address both real and immediate problems (Ferguson et al. 2019). It is particularly relevant to microcredentials because it was developed for workplace learning. Action learning is used both to improve existing skills and to solve problems that are significant to those taking part. Learners work in small groups with a trained facilitator. Each group contains a diverse set of people who have different interests and experiences. Each learner introduces a problem or issue of concern. Groups meet regularly and share different perspectives, enabling them to find and apply solutions. They are supported to do this by being prompted to ask questions, share experiences and reflect on their actions. The approach is particularly well suited to microcredentials studied by cohorts from the same company or based in the same location.

Artificial intelligence in education

Artificial intelligence (AI) describes computer systems that interact with people and the world in ways that imitate human capabilities and behaviours (Kukulska-Hulme et al. 2020). Learning systems that make use of AI are increasingly deployed in educational settings around the world, as well as in corporate training. In addition to the generative AI tools such as ChatGPT that began to grab the headlines in late 2022, student-facing applications of AI include intelligent tutoring systems, dialogue-based tutoring systems, exploratory learning environments, automatic writing evaluation, and conversational agents.

Computational thinking

Computational thinking is a powerful approach to thinking and problem-solving (Sharples et al. 2015). The approach involves breaking large problems down into smaller ones (decomposition), recognising how these relate to problems solved in the past (pattern recognition), setting aside unimportant details (abstraction), identifying and developing steps necessary to reach a solution (algorithms) and refining these steps (debugging).

These computational thinking skills can be valuable in many aspects of life, not only while studying a microcredential but also in the workplace. The aim is to teach learners to break problems down and then structure them so they can be solved. This is a skill that can be applied across disciplines – it is as relevant when studying mathematics and science as it is while studying art. This is an approach that microcredential learners can add to their set of study skills, enabling them to master an art of thinking that will enable them to tackle complex challenges in the workplace and beyond.

Evidence-based teaching

Evidence-based teaching (Kukulska-Hulme et al. 2021) uses research evidence to inform decisions about the best pedagogical approach to apply. Decisions might relate to the most appropriate teaching strategy for a specific topic, capturing learners' progress over time, or assessing the effectiveness of teaching. Evidence-based teaching can support educators to identify and apply best teaching practices, debunk harmful myths about teaching and improve current teaching and learning.

Evidence-based teaching examines research findings to determine whether a given approach has proven benefits, or to identify the conditions under which an approach will work. For example, robust evidence supports the provision of good-quality feedback and the development of skills that can help students understand how they learn. Several HEIs carry out studies that examine in a systematic manner which techniques are beneficial, how different approaches are perceived by learners, and what their impact may be on what is learned.

Online laboratories

In scientific disciplines, laboratories are important resources that enable students to apply their knowledge and develop their skills. However, there are times when it is not possible or not appropriate to use a physical laboratory; this may be when studying a microcredential at a distance or when learners need to engage with dangerous activities. In these cases, online laboratories provide a viable alternative (Kukulska-Hulme et al. 2020).

An online laboratory is an interactive environment where simulated experiments can be created and conducted. In some cases, these labs are accessed through the web; in others they may be a program running on a computer. The aim is that learners will experience the procedures involved in carrying out a science experiment (including the consequences of any mistakes) and will get the results of those experiments. Learners are also able to interact with real scientific equipment at a distance through 'remote labs'. Although the sights and smells of experiments are missing from the experience, online labs are increasingly used in HE science and engineering courses. They offer flexible access, a reduction in costs, and instant feedback. They also enable learners to work with materials that would not be available to them in physical labs because they are too rare, dangerous or costly for most universities to source.

Virtual studios

Just as the laboratory is an important learning environment for science disciplines, the studio is the primary learning environment for many creative disciplines, including design and architecture. It is typically a hub of activity, a base for experiential and constructive ways of learning where tutors observe, comment and critique and students learn through doing (Ferguson et al. 2019). Virtual studios make use of the sharing experiences available on social media platforms but focus on learning activities associated with artefacts, including models, images and videos.

Virtual studios are not simply an online version of physical studios. They have their own educational value and offer new possibilities. Like physical studios, they enable exchange of ideas and rapid feedback from both tutors and other learners. They also provide tools for recording, reflecting and archiving, enabling groups to work together even when they are far apart and not necessarily able to access the virtual studio at the same time as each other. A major benefit is scale – virtual studios can link hundreds, or even thousands, of students, enabling them to develop networks of support and learning. A globally distributed design, specification and fabrication studio is no longer an impossibility; it is a probable future for both design practice and education.

Conclusion

Microcredentials hold out the possibility of extending access to education, particularly at tertiary level and in career-relevant subjects. However, the development of a new type of course on a worldwide scale is a major endeavour, requiring input at all levels from groups including learners, educators, managers and technical staff. At present, the field is confused – the term 'microcredential' means different things in different regions, in different institutions, and even in very similar settings. There are substantial challenges to be overcome in order for these courses to be recognised and valued worldwide.

One evident gap at present is a learner-centred perspective. Governments see microcredentials as a route to upskilling their workforce, companies view them as a route to enhancing recruitment and training, and universities are exploring them as a way of expanding their offering. Learners are relatively silent – relatively few researchers and report authors have sought learner views on what is on offer and how it relates to the types of education they are looking for. In addition, the usual ways in which student voice is heard – through student unions, student associations, alumni groups, face-to-face meetings and so on – are much more limited on courses that last only weeks or months than they would be on a degree course, apprenticeship programme or extended training programme. At the time of writing, there is little evidence that learners believe microcredentials are increasing access to learning opportunities, particularly opportunities to gain credit for workplace-related skills – and even less evidence that this is a vision that is important to learners. Amplifying and paying attention to their voices will be an important aspect of developing successful microcredentials programmes around the world that are really valued by learners.

At the same time, staff buy-in is crucial. Many educational initiatives show early promise, supported by the enthusiasm of staff to try something new and to explore new ways of teaching and learning. However, once the initial excitement has passed, the addition to already heavy workloads often becomes unsustainable and the innovation is set aside or replaced by something new. In the case of microcredentials, new ways of working are required, as are changes across the institution. The change required is not simply a matter of writing a few new courses or slimming down existing material – without support from other teams, educators will be overloaded. The vision for microcredentials needs to be one that teams across the institution are interested in achieving, as well as one that they view as having value for learners.

However, this is not just work for one institution. For a new type of qualification to be introduced successfully, it must extend nationally or internationally. Microcredentials need to have a value that is as well understood and recognisable as that of other qualifications. Degrees, apprenticeships, school-leaver qualifications and professional and technical certificates have different names in different countries, but the relevant local versions of these are well understood, and these qualifications can often be transferred internationally with relative ease. This is not yet the case with microcredentials but it should be in the future as work at both national and international levels is creating the frameworks that can support this endeavour, while work at the institutional level continues exploring what is possible.

As this book has shown, developments in both technology and pedagogy can be used strategically to produce a new type of course that is not simply a cut-down version of a full credential, but an entity in its own right. Microcredentials are still a work in progress but they offer exciting possibilities for the future. If they are to achieve the vision of increasing access to learning opportunities – particularly opportunities to gain credit for workplace-related skills – then the experience of the educators and researchers on whose work this book is based will be an essential resource.

References

100 People. (2016). *100 People: A world portrait. A global education toolbox*. Available at https://www.100people.org/statistics-details

Acceleration Plan. (2022). *Microcredentials pilot*. Acceleration Plan: Educational Innovation with ICT. Available at https://www.versnellingsplan.nl/en/Kennisbank/pilot-microcredentials

Acree, L. (2016). *Seven lessons learned from implementing microcredentials*. Raleigh, NC: Friday Institute for Educational Innovation at the NC State University College of Education. Available at https://www.nysed.gov/sites/default/files/principal-project-phase-2-seven-lessons-about-implementing-microcredentials-lauren-acree.pdf

Ahmat, N. H. C. A., Bashir, M. A. A., Razali, A. R. and Kasolang, S. (2021). Micro-credentials in higher education institutions: Challenges and opportunities. *Asian Journal of University Education*, 17(3): 281–290.

Bates, T. (2021). *Understanding microcredentials: A report from HEQCO* (31 May). Online learning and distance education resources. Available at https://www.tonybates.ca/2021/05/31/understanding-microcredentials-a-report-from-heqco

Berry, B., Airhart, K. M. and Byrd., P. A. (2016). Microcredentials: Teacher learning transformed. *Phi Delta Kappan*, 98(3): 34–40.

Brown, D. (2019). *Research and educator micro-credentials*. Available at https://digitalpromise.org/wp-content/uploads/2019/02/researchandeducatormicrocredentials-v1r2.pdf

Brown, M., McGreal, R. and Peters, M. (2023). A strategic institutional response to micro-credentials: Key questions for educational leaders. *Journal of Interactive Media in Education*, 2023(1).

Brown, M. and Nic Giolla Mhichíl, M. (2021). *Micro-credentials untethered: A wolf in sheep's clothing?* Dublin City University. Available at https://irelandseducationyearbook.ie/downloads/IEYB2021/YB2021-Higher-Education-08.pdf

Browne, J., Chapman, A., Chapman, R., Connin, S. and de los Santos, A. (2012). *Technology strategic plan narrative*. Available at https://digitalcommons.trinity.edu/cgi/viewcontent.cgi?article=1000&context=univreports

Chandler, K. (2023). Microcredentials evaluation phase 3 final report (internal report). Milton Keynes: Open University.

CIA. (2022). *The world factbook*. Available at https://www.cia.gov/the-world-factbook/field/school-life-expectancy-primary-to-tertiary-education

Clements, K., West, R. E. and Hunsaker, E. (2020). Getting started with open badges and open microcredentials. *The International Review of Research in Open and Distributed Learning*, 21(1): 154–172.

Crow, T. (2016). *Micro-credentials for impact: Holding professional learning to high standards*. Digital Promise. Available at https://learningforward.org/report/micro-credentials-impact-holding-professional-learning-high-standards

Curnow, D. and Mori, K. (2021). *Micro-credentials as an enabler of sustainability* (24 November). Available at https://www.qaa.ac.uk/news-events/blog/micro-credentials-as-an-enabler-of-sustainability

Daniel, J. (1996). *Mega-universities and knowledge media: Technology strategies for higher education*. Kogan Page.
Davis, P. (2012). Establishing a US national FOSS4G academy. In: Open Source Geospatial Research & Education Symposium (OGRS), Yverdon-les-Bains, Switzerland, 24–26 October 2012.
Ehlers. U.-D, (2018). High creduation – degree or education? The rise of micro-credentials and its consequences for the university of the future. In: EDEN, Genoa, Italy, 17–20 June 2018.
European Commission. (2017). *European pillar of social rights*. Available at https://ec.europa.eu/info/strategy/priorities-2019-2024/economy-works-people/jobs-growth-and-investment/european-pillar-social-rights_en
European Commission. (2020). *A European approach to microcredentials – Output of the Micro-credentials Higher Education Consultation Group – final report*. Available at https://education.ec.europa.eu/sites/default/files/document-library-docs/european-approach-micro-credentials-higher-education-consultation-group-output-final-report.pdf
Fedock, B., Kebritchi, M., Sanders, R. and Holland, A. (2016). Digital badges and micro-credentials: Digital age classroom practices, design strategies, and issues. In: Ifenthaler, D. *Foundation of digital badges and micro-credentials: Demonstrating and recognizing knowledge and competencies*. Springer International.
Ferguson, R., Coughlan, T., Egelandsdal, K., Gaved, M., Herodotou, C., Hillaire, G., Jones, D., Jowers, I., Kukulska-Hulme, A., McAndrew, P., Misiejuk, K., Ness, I. J., Rienties, B., Scanlon, E., Sharples, M., Wasson, B., Weller, M. and Whitelock., D. (2019). *Innovating pedagogy 2019: Open University innovation report 7*. Available at http://www.open.ac.uk/blogs/innovating
Ferguson, R., Sharples, M. and Beale, R. (2015). MOOCs 2030: A future for massive online learning. In: Bonk, C. J., Lee, M. M., Reeves, T. C. and Reynolds, T. H. *MOOCs and open education around the world*. Routledge.
Golden, G., Kato, S. and Weko, T. (2021). *Micro-credential innovations in higher education: Who, what and why?* OECD. Available at https://www.oecd-ilibrary.org/education/micro-credential-innovations-in-higher-education_f14ef041-en

Government of South Australia. (2020). *Micro-credentials in South Australia. Consultation outcomes Report*. Available at https://www.voced.edu.au/content/ngv%3A89032

Gwin, R. and Foggin, M. (2020). *Badging for sustainable development: Applying edtech micro-credentials for advancing SDGs amongst mountain and pastoralist societies*. Available at https://www.preprints.org/manuscript/202003.0402/v1

Healy, M. (2021). Microcredential learners need quality careers and employability support. *Journal of Teaching and Learning for Graduate Employability*, 12(1): 21–23.

Holon IQ. (2021). *Online degree and micro-credential market to reach $117B by 2025*. Available at https://www.holoniq.com/notes/global-online-degree-and-micro-credential-market-to-reach-117b-by-2025

Holton, K. (2022). *Pearson buys certification group Credly in deal valued at $200m* (31 January). Available at https://www.reuters.com/business/exclusive-pearson-buys-certification-group-credly-deal-valued-200m-2022-01-31

Howley, C. (2010). Serving displaced workers: A rural community college initiative. In: 102 Annual Meeting of the National Rural Education Convention and Research Symposium, Branson, Missouri, 15–17 October.

Iniesto, F. (2020). *An investigation into the accessibility of massive open online courses (MOOCs)*. Thesis (PhD). The Open University. Available at https://oro.open.ac.uk/70010

Kazin, C. and Clerkin, K. (2018). *The potential and limitations of microcredentials*. Available at https://docplayer.net/102365139-The-potential-and-limitations-of-microcredentials.html

Kift, S. (2021). Future work and learning in a disrupted world: 'The best chance for all'. *Journal of Teaching and Learning for Graduate Employability*, 12(1): i–v.

Kukkonen, A. (2021). *The value of microcredentials for higher education students*. Thesis (master's). Tampere University, Tampere.

Kukulska-Hulme, A., Beirne, E., Conole, G., Costello, E., Coughlan, T., Ferguson, R., FitzGerald, E., Gaved, M., Herodotou, C., Holmes, W., Mac Lochlainn, C., Nic Giolla Mhichíl, M.,

Rienties, B., Sargent, J., Scanlon, E., Sharples, M. and Whitelock, D. (2020). *Innovating pedagogy 2020: Open University innovation report 8*. Available at http://www.open.ac.uk/blogs/innovating

Kukulska-Hulme, A., Bossu, C., Coughlan, T., Ferguson, R., FitzGerald, E., Gaved, M., Herodotou, C., Rienties, B., Sargent, J., Scanlon, E., Tang, J., Wang, Q., Whitelock, D. and Zhang, S. (2021). *Innovating pedagogy 2021: Open University innovation report 9*. Available at http://www.open.ac.uk/blogs/innovating

Lantero, L., Finocchietti, C. and Petrucci, E. (2021). *Micro-credentials and Bologna key commitments: State of play in the European Higher Education Area*. MICROBOL. Available at https://www.enqa.eu/wp-content/uploads/Microbol_State-of-play-of-MCs-in-the-EHEA_19.02.2021.pdf

Martinez-Marroquin, E. and Male, S. (2021). Micro-credentials for recognition of workplace learning. *Journal of Teaching and Learning for Graduate Employability*, 12(1): 52–57.

MICROBOL. (2020). *Micro-credentials linked to the Bologna key commitments: Desk research report*. MICROBOL. Available at https://eua.eu/downloads/publications/microbol%20desk%20research%20report.pdf

Microcredentials Working Group. (2021). *National microcredentials framework*. Australian Government Department of Education, Skills and Employment. Available at https://www.education.gov.au/higher-education-publications/resources/national-microcredentials-framework

Morrin, M., Jones, M. and Salem, L. (2021). *The pathway to lifelong education: Reforming the UK's skills system*. London: ResPublica. Available at https://www.lifelongeducation.uk/research-1/the-pathway-to-lifelong-education%3A-reforming-the-uk%27s-skills-system

Nguyen, T. N. H., Spittle, M., Watt, A. and Van Dyke, N. (2023). A systematic literature review of micro-credentials in higher education: A non-zero-sum game. *Higher Education Research & Development*, 42(6): 1527–1548.

Nic Giolla Mhichíl, M., Brown, M., Beirne, E. and MacLochlainn, C. (2020). *A micro-credential roadmap: Currency, cohesion and *consistency*. Dublin City University. Available at https://www.skillnetireland.ie/wp-content/uploads/2021/03/A-Micro-Credential-Roadmap-Currency-Cohesion-and-Consistency.pdf

NZQA. (2022). *Micro-credentials*. Available at https://www.nzqa.govt.nz/providers-partners/approval-accreditation-and-registration/micro-credentials/#heading2-0

Oliver, B. (2019). *Making micro-credentials work for learners, employers and providers*. Melbourne: Deakin University. Available at https://dteach.deakin.edu.au/wp-content/uploads/sites/103/2019/08/Making-micro-credentials-work-Oliver-Deakin-2019-full-report.pdf

Oxley, C. and van Rooyen, T. (2021). Making micro-credentials work: A student perspective. *Journal of Teaching and Learning for Graduate Employability*, 12(1): 44–47.

Papathoma, T. and Ferguson, R. (2020). *Evaluation of Open University microcredentials: Final report of phase one* (internal report). Milton Keynes: The Open University.

Pichette, J., Brumwell, S., Rizk, J. and Han, S. (2021). *Making sense of microcredentials*. Toronto: Higher Education Quality Council of Ontario. Available at https://heqco.ca/pub/making-sense-of-microcredentials

Pirkkalainen, H., Sood, I., Padron Napoles, C., Kukkonen, A. and Camilleri, A. (2023). How might micro-credentials influence institutions and empower learners in higher education? *Educational Research*, 65(1): 40–63.

QAA. (2022). *Characteristics statement: Micro-credentials*. Gloucester: The Quality Assurance Agency for Higher Education. Available at https://www.qaa.ac.uk/docs/qaa/quality-code/micro-credentials-characteristics-statement.pdf?sfvrsn=32bda081_4

Ralston, S. J. (2021). Higher education's microcredentialing craze: A postdigital-Deweyan critique. *Postdigital Science and Education*, 3(1): 83–101.

Rossiter, D. and Tynan, B. (2019). *Designing and implementing micro-credentials: A guide for practitioners*. Commonwealth of Learning. Available at https://oasis.col.org/items/e2d0be25-cbbb-441f-b431-42f74f715532

Scanlon, E., Sharples, M., Fenton-O'Creevy, M., Fleck, J., Cooban, C., Ferguson, R., Cross, S. and Waterhouse, P. (2013). *Beyond prototypes: Enabling innovation in technology-enhanced learning*. Available at https://oro.open.ac.uk/41119

Sharples, M., Adams, A., Alozie, N., Ferguson, R., FitzGerald, E., Gaved, M., McAndrew, P., Means, B., Remold, J., Rienties, B., Roschelle, J., Vogt, K., Whitelock, D. and Tarnall, L. (2015). *Innovating pedagogy 2015: Open University innovation report 4*. Available at http://www.open.ac.uk/blogs/innovating

United Nations. (2015). *The 17 goals*. Available at https://sdgs.un.org/goals

Weller, M. (2015). MOOCs and the Silicon Valley narrative. *Journal of Interactive Media in Education*, 2015(1): 1–7.

Wheelahan, L. and Moodie, G. (2021a). Analysing micro-credentials in higher education: A Bernsteinian analysis. *Journal of Curriculum Studies*, 53(2): 212–228.

Wheelahan, L. and Moodie, G. (2021b). Gig qualifications for the gig economy: Micro-credentials and the 'hungry mile'. *Higher Education*, 83: 1279–1295.

Yilik, M. A. (2021). Micro-credentials, higher education and career development: perspectives of university students. *Higher Education Governance and Policy*, 2(2): 126–139.

Index

A

academic credit   6, 58, 72, 208, 209–211
  see also credit transfer; stackability of microcredentials
accessibility   23–24, 38–40, 204–207, 277
  see also inclusivity
accreditation   207–211, 275
achievement record   282
action learning   284
activity types   129–130
administrative processes   61–63, 153–154, 280–282
agile approach to production   115–118, 228
Amherst College   164
artificial intelligence (AI) tools   195–196, 285
assessment   173–211
accreditation   207–211, 275
administrative considerations   62, 154, 281
alternatives to exams   40, 193–194, 204–206, 207
artificial intelligence (AI) tools   195–196
competency-based   28, 178–179
ecological (authentic)   194
exam proctoring (invigilation)   191–194, 282
feedback   200–203
group   196–199
as learning   130, 176
for learning   175, 200–203
of learning (summative assessment)   177, 200

learning outcome alignment   178, 199
multiple-choice questions (MCQs)   182–189
need for   174–175
online exams   189–194, 206–207
renewable   194
technical system   281
technology-enabled   179–194, 206–207
test anxiety   203–207
audio clips, time taken to listen   135
Australia   65, 99–104, 163–164, 221, 272
authentic (ecological) assessments   194
automated feedback   200–203
autonomy of learners   164–165

B

badges, digital   7–9, 62, 91, 98–99, 209, 282
belonging, learners' sense of   42, 157–158
Brigham Young University   97–99
business models   275

C

Canada   63–64, 84, 92, 221, 225, 229, 272
capabilities model of wellbeing   149–150
careers advice   73
case studies of microcredential development   92–106
case-based learning   28–29
certification   154, 275, 282
  see also digital badges
cheating, prevention of   191–194, 208, 282
choice (learner autonomy)   164–165
Christensen, Clayton M   67
Cognitive Class platform   8
Common Microcredential Framework   5
communication systems   281
communications lead (staff role)   60
competency frameworks   178–179
competency-based learning   27–28, 95–97, 178–179
computational thinking skills   285
computer-aided assessment   179–194, 206–207
confidence of learners   153–154, 156, 159
consistency, course   128, 133, 274
conversational learning   30–32
copyright issues   131, 132
costs   24, 57–58, 72, 208, 210, 277–278

course content   43, 77, 92, 122, 130–135
course design *see* designing microcredentials; learning design
course planning *see* planning a microcredentials programme
course production   113–118
course systems   281
Coursera platform   22, 67, 68, 275
Creative Commons licences   132
credit transfer   44, 63, 87, 289
  see also stackability of microcredentials
curriculum infusion   162–164

D

data storage and transfer   282
democratisation of knowledge   42–43
designing microcredentials *see* case studies of microcredential development; learning design
digital badges   7–9, 62, 91, 98–99, 209, 282
digital development editors   114
Digital Promise platform   95–97
digital wellbeing   166–168
disabilities, learners with   24, 38–40, 144, 190, 193, 206, 207, 277
  see also inclusivity
discussion spaces   160–163, 167, 249
disruptive innovation   67–68
distance education   22, 75–77
  see also online working
diversity *see* disabilities, learners with; educational equity; inclusivity; international participation; multicultural participation
dropout follow-up   282

E

e-assessment   179–194, 206–207
ecological (authentic) assessments   194
educational equity   246–248, 270–271
  see also disabilities, learners with; inclusivity; international participation; multicultural participation
educators, roles of
future of microcredentials   278–280

learners' mental health and
    wellbeing 144–145,
    148, 155, 156, 158, 159,
    160–163
microcredentials
    context 54, 74–77
    see also learning design;
    production methods
EduOpen platform 208
edX platform 22, 67, 68, 70
employers
    accreditation by 44
    partnerships with 65–66,
        85–86, 279
    requirements of 10–11,
        85–86, 130
employment-related
    learning 20–21,
    26–32, 267–268
enquiry process 153, 241, 280
equity, educational 246–248,
    270–271
    see also disabilities, learners
        with; inclusivity;
        international
        participation;
        multicultural
        participation
ethical evaluation 248–249
Europe and European Union
    competency
        frameworks 178
    credit transfer and
        stackability 44, 63
    defining microcredentials
        4–6, 267, 273–274

European Credit Transfer
    and Accumulation
    System (ECTS) 5,
    63–64, 222, 274
identity (ID)
    verification 208
MICROBOL project 4, 44,
    63, 267, 273–274
Micro-credentials
    Higher Education
    Consultation
    Group 53, 221–223
MOOCKnowledge
    Project 251
on partnerships 65
quality assurance
    standards 219–221,
    221–223, 227, 228–229
vision for
    microcredentials 271
evaluation 229–255
    criteria for 128, 240
    defining 229–231, 234
    dissemination of
        findings 254–255
    ethical 248–249
    focus of (initial
        planning) 234–236
    logic models 236–240
    models of 250–251
    of online teaching 121,
        231–232, 235–236
    process of (examples) 97,
        99, 106
    questions, indicators and
        standards 240–246

stakeholder involvement 77, 246–248
theory of change (ToC)-based 251–253
types of 232–234
units of analysis 234–236
value of 58, 234
evidence-based teaching 286
exam proctoring (invigilation) 191–194, 282
examples (case studies) of microcredential development 92–106
exams, online 189–194, 206–207

F

feedback 36, 200–203
finance systems 281
finances 24, 57–58, 72, 208, 210–211, 277
follow-up systems 282
FUN platform 208
future of microcredentials *see* visions of the future
FutureLearn platform 22, 30, 69, 112, 208, 275, 279

G

Georgetown University 164
goal-setting (study skill) 33
graduates, employers' requirements 10–11
group assessment 196–199

I

IBM 8
identity
ID verification 191–194, 208, 281
sense of, and wellbeing 154–156
inclusivity 38–43, 123–127, 277
see also accessibility
income opportunities 269–270
indicators, evaluation 242–244
induction process 32–34
industry *see* employers
inquiry-based instruction 90–91
International Council for Open and Distance Education (ICDE) 244–246
international participation 23, 29, 40, 57–58, 193, 207, 277
see also multicultural participation
international recognition 43–45, 289
international standards 218–225, 273–274
internet connection and reliability 34, 153, 167, 190

invigilation (proctoring), exam 191–194, 282
IT support 70–71, 280

J

job-related learning 20–21, 26–32, 267–268
see also employers

K

kanban boards 117–118
W K Kellogg Foundation 230, 235, 237
Kirkpatrick evaluation model 250–251
knowledge, democratisation of 42–43

L

laboratories, online 286–287
learner/educator ratio 24
learner-centred perspective 88–92, 105, 276–277, 288
learners
  administrative processes, concerns over 153–154
  assessment for learning 175
  autonomy of 164–165
  benefits of microcredentials 88–92, 276
  caring responsibilities 21, 190, 193
  contribution to course content 43, 77, 92, 122
  contribution to course evaluation 77, 232, 246–248, 276–277
  diversity and individuality 41–43, 123–127, 155–156, 246–248
  group working 196–199
  interaction with peers 23, 78
  mental health see mental health of learners
  motivation and confidence 153–154, 156, 158–159, 200, 202–203
  numbers of 24, 30
  online learning skills 22
  role of 77–78
  in scenario-based design 122–127
  self-assessment 176, 199
  self-regulation skills 34–38, 41, 42, 152, 155–156
  student personas 123–127
  student status 72, 132
  study skills 32–34, 152
  support for 34, 37, 70–74, 144–145, 277, 280
  work commitments 21, 190
  workload required of 133–135

learning design   118–137
   activity types   129–130
   course content, rights and
      workload   130–135
   learning outcomes   127–128
   origins of   119–122
   scenarios   122–127
   student personas   123–127
   the writers' room   135–137
   see also case studies of
      microcredential
      development
learning designers   114
learning methods *see*
      pedagogies; pedagogy,
      factors influencing
learning opportunities,
      expansion of   264–265
learning outcomes   127–128,
      178, 199
learning to learn   34–38
learning, recognition of
      266–267
library access   71–72, 72,
      103–104, 132, 281
Lisbon Recognition
      Convention   44, 273
logic models for
      evaluation   236–240

M

Malaysia   63, 93–94
MARA Technological
   University
   (UiTM)   93–94

markers and marking   207, 217
marketing of microcredentials
      68–70, 179, 280
massive open online courses
      see MOOC platforms
mental health of
   learners   141–169
   belonging, sense of,
      and   157–158
   Covid-19 pandemic
      145–146
   curriculum infusion
      162–164
   digital wellbeing   166–168
   discussion spaces and
      160–163, 167
   education-related barriers
      and enablers   150–154
   educators' role   144–145,
      148, 155, 156, 158, 159,
      160–163
   global context   142–143
   identity and   154–156
   introduction   143–145
   learner autonomy and
      164–165
   models of   147–150
   motivation and   158–159
   test anxiety   203–207
   wellbeing and   146–147
metadata standards   282
MICROBOL project   4, 44,
      63, 267, 273–274
Micro-credential Learner Value
   Framework   89–90

Micro-credential Users' Guide, The (MicroHE Consortium)   87–88
microcredential, definition of term   3–11
MiríadaX platform   208
MOOC (massive open online course) platforms
  accessibility issues   277
  accreditation opportunities   174
  digital badge pioneers   8–9
  Digital Promise case study   95–97
  ID checks survey   208
  liaison with   22, 24, 66–68, 87
  scaling learning, methods of   30
  variety of microcredential offerings   69
  see also Coursera platform; FutureLearn platform; OpenLearn platform
MOOCKnowledge Project   251
Moran, Matthew   113–114, 135
motivation of learners   153–154, 158–159, 200, 202–203
Mozilla Foundation   8
multicultural participation   23, 40, 155–156, 157–162, 193
  see also international participation
multiple-choice questions (MCQs)   130, 182–189, 201, 202, 204–205

N

national frameworks and standards   86–88, 226, 289
Netherlands   223–225, 271
New Zealand   6, 66, 272
note-taking (study skill)   34
numbers of learners   24, 30

O

Oliver, Beverley   84–85, 89–90, 102
online laboratories   286–287
online studios   287
online study
  activity types   129–130
  automated feedback   200–203
  evaluation of   121, 231–232, 235–236
  exam proctoring (invigilation)   191–194, 282
  IT support   70–71, 280
  learning design and   121–122
  mental health and   166–168
  pedagogical considerations   21–23, 29, 105

self-regulation skills   34–38, 41, 42, 152, 155–156
study skills   32–34, 152
technology-enabled assessment   179–194, 206–207
workload of learners   133–135
OnTask feedback tool   201
Open Badges standard   8
Open Educational Resources (OER)   132
Open Research Online (ORO)   254
Open University, The (OU)
  course design and production   112–118, 119–120, 124–125, 129–130, 131
  course stackability   45, 210
  discussion guidelines   161–163
  learner perspectives   276–277
  logic model example   238–242
  microcredentials experience   2
OpenLearn platform   9, 24, 112

P

partnerships, education and industry   65–66, 85–86, 279
pastoral support   71, 144–145
payment systems   281
pedagogies
  action learning   284
  artificial intelligence (AI) applications   285
  case-based learning   28–29
  competency-based learning   27–28, 95–97, 178–179
  computational thinking   285
  conversational learning   30–32
  evidence-based teaching   286
  inquiry-based instruction   90–91
  online laboratories   286–287
  virtual studios   287
pedagogy, factors influencing   19–46
  accessibility   23–24, 38–40
  employment focus   20–21, 26–32
  inclusivity   38–43
  online working   21–23, 29, 105
  stackability   25, 43–46, 279
  summary of challenges   25–26
peer evaluation   199
Perryman, Leigh-Anne   161–163, 238–240, 251, 252–253

personas (in learning design)   123–127
plagiarism   154, 192, 195, 206, 282
planning a microcredentials programme   83–106
  examples (case studies)   92–104
  integration within larger frameworks   86–88, 255
  learners' perspectives   88–92, 105, 276–277, 288
  summary of stages   104–106
  types and purpose of microcredentials   84–86
platforms *see* MOOC platforms
policies and regulations   59–60, 196
policymaking, external   65
pricing   24, 57–58, 72, 208, 210–211, 277
proctoring, exam   191–194, 282
production methods   113–118
professional development   20–21, 26–32, 268
project team roles   53–54, 55–58
publishing evaluation findings   254–255
purpose of microcredentials   84–86

Q

qualifications frameworks   45, 87, 222
quality assurance
  assessment requirements for   207–208
  contexts   227–229
  course changes and   133, 274
  international standards   218–225, 227, 228–229
  metrics for quality assessment   217–218
  national standards (UK)   226
  student status and   72
quality enhancement   58, 228
Queensland University of Technology (QUT)   100–102

R

reading speed   134
recognition of learning   266–267
recognition of microcredentials   43–45, 86–88, 282, 289
registration   61–62, 153, 281
regulations *see* policies and regulations
renewable assessments   194
reports (evaluation findings)   254–255
rights issues   131, 132

Royal Melbourne Institute of Technology (RMIT)   102–104

S

scaling learning   30
scenario-based design   122–127
science laboratories, online   286–287
scrum (agile process framework)   116–117
search engine optimisation (SEO)   179, 254, 280
self-assessment   176, 199
self-regulation skills   34–38, 41, 42, 152, 155–156
Shadbolt Review   10–11
SMART objectives   128
sponsors   55
stackability of microcredentials   25, 43–46, 63–65, 209–211, 279, 282
staff buy-in   289
staff roles   iv–24, 51, 54
  educators *see* educators, roles of
  financial lead   57–58
  internal alignment   54, 59–63
  outward-facing   54, 63–70
  project sponsor   55
  project team   53–54, 55–58
  support   54, 70–74

standards
  evaluation   244–246
  metadata   282
  qualifications frameworks   45, 87, 222
  quality assurance   218–226
students *see* learners
studios, virtual   287
study hours   133–135
study skills   32–34, 152
study space   34, 167, 190, 192
support
  for educators   279
  for learners   34, 37, 70–74, 144–145, 277, 280
  from stakeholders   105, 289
Sustainable Development Goals (SDGs)   270–271

T

tax issues   57–58
teaching methods *see* pedagogies; pedagogy, factors influencing
team-working skills   29, 197, 199
technical support   70–71, 280
technical systems   280–282
technology-enabled assessment   179–194, 206–207
test anxiety   203–207
theory of change (ToC)-based evaluation   251–253
time requirements

course production 113–115
workload of learners 133–135
time-management (study skill) 33
transactional distance 22
transfer of credit 44, 63, 87, 289
  see also stackability of microcredentials
types of microcredential 84–86

U

Udacity platform 22, 68
UK, quality assurance standards 226
United Nations Sustainable Development Goals (SDGs) 270–271
Universal Design for Learning (UDL) 38–40, 42, 152, 165, 204–207
University of the West of England 164
USA, examples of microcredential development 95–99

V

VAT (value-added tax) 58
videos
  production process 56
  time taken to watch 135
virtual laboratories 286–287
virtual studios 287
Virtual University for Small States of the Commonwealth (VUSSC) 121
visions of the future 263–272
  achieving the visions 272–282

W

W K Kellogg Foundation 230, 235–236, 237
Wakeham Review 10–11
wellbeing 146–147
  see also mental health of learners
workload of learners 133–135
workplace-related learning 20–21, 26–32, 267–268
  see also employers
workspace (study space) 34, 167, 190, 192
writers' room, the 135–137

www.ingramcontent.com/pod-product-compliance
Lightning Source LLC
Chambersburg PA
CBHW041731300426
44115CB00022B/2975